THE CHANNEL FOUR BOOK OF
RACING

SEAN MAGEE
Introduction by Brough Scott

HAMLYN

CONTE

First edition p
by Sidgwick &

This edition, c
by Hamlyn, ar
Michelin Hou
and Auckland,
in association

Copyright © 1

The author ha

A CIP catalog
is available fro

ISBN 0 600 58

All rights rese
stored in a ret
electronic, me
without the p

Designed by
Printed in Gr

Half-title: Lochson
in the 1994 Prix d
Title spread: Merry
1995 Tote Chelten

Horses

THE THOROUGHBRED

'You can put your investment into many things. But how many things are as beautiful as a horse?'

SHEIKH MOHAMMED

GOOD COMPANIONS

Racehorses can be nervous creatures, and many find the constant companionship of another animal soothing. The most obvious companion, when turned out in a field, is another horse or a donkey, but some horses have had more unusual friends. That great French mare Allez France was accompanied by a sheep, as has been the case with the brilliant chaser Remittance Man (whose chum is called Nobby). Gilbert the Goat is a key member of trainer Dr Jon Scargill's staff at Newmarket, keeping stable star Our Rita in the frame of mind which won her the 1994 Lincoln Handicap. Foinavon, 1967 Grand National winner, also teamed up with a goat. Sunnyhill, a gigantic Irish chaser of the later 1950s, had a goose for a pal, while 1929 Grand National winner Gregalach was almost inseparable from a rough-haired terrier.

Crudwell was the last horse to win fifty races in Britain – seven on the Flat, four over hurdles and thirty-nine steeplechases, including the Welsh Grand National (ridden by Dick Francis) in 1956. His first victory was over twelve furlongs at Leicester in March 1950, his fiftieth at Wincanton on 15 September 1960 when, ridden by Michael Scudamore (father of Peter), he won the Somerset Chase at the age of fourteen. He did not race again.

Previous spread: Thoroughbred foals at the National Stud in Newmarket.

A glorious compound of power and elegance, of strength and beauty, of stamina and speed, the English Thoroughbred racehorse is a highly specialized animal whose evolution has been skilfully contrived by breeders over the three hundred years since the importation of Arabian stallions at the end of the seventeenth century. Its influence has been huge: all the major racing nations of the world (and most of the minor) have imported English Thoroughbreds and based their own breeds of racehorse on the English model.

All modern Thoroughbreds trace their ancestry in the male line to just three founding stallions brought to England from the Near East.

The Byerley Turk, foaled around 1680, had seen action at the Battle of the Boyne before being sent to stud in County Durham: among his distinguished descendants in more recent times is The Tetrarch, 'The Spotted Wonder', who was unbeaten in seven races in 1913 and was probably one of the fastest horses of all time, and – much more recently – Derby winners such as Blakeney and Dr Devious.

The Godolphin Arabian, foaled in 1724 and (according to some accounts) discovered in Paris pulling a water cart, is the direct ancestor of 1964 Derby winner Santa Claus.

But the most influential of the three was the Darley Arabian, foaled in 1700 and sent to England as a four-year-old. He is the progenitor of the vast majority of modern Thoroughbreds, and many of the most powerful bloodlines of the twentieth century are offshoots of his, notably that of Northern Dancer, sire of Nijinsky, The Minstrel and El Gran Senor.

Apparently none of the three founding sires ever raced, but it was not long before their influence on the racing scene became very marked. The Darley Arabian's son Flying Childers, foaled in 1714, is held to be the first truly great English racehorse despite running in only two races, and Flying Childers's full brother Bartlett's Childers was the great-grandsire of the legendary Eclipse.

Eclipse, foaled in 1764, was bred by the Duke of Cumberland, and sold on the Duke's death in 1765 to William Wildman, a Smithfield meat salesman, for 75 guineas. Wildman allowed Eclipse plenty of time to mature and did not put the horse into serious training until he was five years old. In April 1769 he held a secret trial on Banstead Downs, near Epsom, which touts tried to witness. According to a contemporary report, the touts arrived late: 'But they found an old woman who gave them all the information they wanted. On inquiring whether she had seen a race, she replied she could not tell whether it was a race or not, but she had just seen a horse with a white leg running away at a monstrous rate, and another horse a great way behind, trying to run after him; but she was sure he never would catch the white-legged horse if he ran to the world's end.' Eclipse – the 'horse with a white leg' – first ran in public the following month, in a race of four-mile heats at Epsom. Favourite at 4–1 on following rumours of the trial, he won the first heat with ease, at which point an Irish gambler named Dennis O'Kelly bet that he could predict the placings of the runners in the next heat in their correct finishing order. When challenged to do so he pronounced the phrase which was to become part of racing language: 'Eclipse first, the rest nowhere.' His prediction – that all the other runners would be 'distanced' by Eclipse (that is, finish over 240 yards behind him) proved triumphantly correct, and O'Kelly went on to purchase a half share in the horse for 650 guineas, and later the other half for 1,100 guineas. In eighteen races Eclipse was never headed, let alone beaten, and never whipped or spurred. Retiring to stud in 1771, he sired three of the first five Derby winners, and his skeleton is now in the National Horseracing Museum in Newmarket.

Two other famous horses of the Eclipse era ensured the perpetuation of the lines of the Byerley Turk and the Godolphin Arabian. Herod, a great-

great-grandson of the Byerley Turk, was bred like Eclipse by William, Duke of Cumberland, and foaled in 1758. After a fine racing career his achievements at stud included siring the winners of 1,042 races, among them three of the first five runnings of the Oaks, but as a racehorse he had been prone to break blood vessels, and is thought to be the source of this tendency in many modern Thoroughbreds. Matchem (born 1748) combined in his pedigree strains from both the Godolphin Arabian and the Byerley Turk, and was one of the few racehorses in history to have been much more successful as a stallion than as a racer: blessed with exceptional longevity and virility, he covered a mare at the extreme age of thirty-three (and got her in foal) a few days before his death. The Eclipse, Herod and Matchem lines are the only direct sire lines which have lasted to modern times, but mention should also be made of two other famous eighteenth-century racehorses. Highflyer, a son of Herod enjoying almost equal proportions of the blood of the three founding sires, was never beaten in races and proved a highly successful stallion. And Gimcrack, the tiny grey commemorated in the famous two-year-old race at the York August meeting, has the distinction of being the first English horse to make a raid on France, winning a match by covering twenty-two and a half miles in one hour in 1766. Ironically, on the two occasions when he raced at York, he was beaten.

The late eighteenth century was also a time of great change in the pattern of racing in England, with the exceptionally long races (usually around four miles) run in heats gradually giving way to different sorts of race and rendering obsolete the practice of waiting until horses reached the age of four or five before starting their racing careers. Two-year-old races were instituted late in the century; the introduction of handicaps, aiming to level out the chances of the field, made horse racing a more entertaining betting medium; and, most significantly, what became the Classic races were first staged – the St Leger in 1776, the Oaks in 1779 and the Derby in 1780, with

The pulsating finish of the 1995 Madagans 2000 Guineas at Newmarket. Pennekamp (Thierry Jarnet, near side) resists the renewed challenge of Celtic Swing (Kevin Darley).

Not all familiar racehorses are Thoroughbreds, at least over jumps. The Fellow, winner of the King George VI Chase in 1991 and 1992 and the Cheltenham Gold Cup in 1994, is a French Saddlebred (*selle français*) – a purpose-bred strain evolved from selective breeding with non-Thoroughbreds, though the breed remains predominantly Thoroughbred.

the Guineas races following early in the next century (see pages 73–8).

As these developments became established in the nineteenth century, racehorses were bred to run faster and mature earlier, and they were bigger. The Darley Arabian had stood 15 hands, and Eclipse was considered tall at 15 hands 3 inches. By the middle of the nineteenth century the average Thoroughbred was about six inches taller than his forebear of a century and a half earlier, and decades of selective and judicious breeding in conditions of better feeding and care had brought about major improvements in speed and scope, if not in constitution. Now the major aim was precocity, a trend which continued well into the twentieth century, as the status of staying races continued to decline and breeders concentrated on producing animals capable of winning over five and six furlongs as two-year-olds, even though the accepted ideal of the English Thoroughbred was the horse capable of staying one and a half miles as a three-year-old – the conditions of the Derby.

The imposition of the Pattern (see page 71) has encouraged a move away from extreme precocity: there is no Group 1 race for two-year-olds in Britain before autumn, and it is very significant that many of the top Classic horses of recent years have not been raced at all at the highest level as juveniles: Nashwan ran in two fairly minor races as a two-year-old (the first in August), as did Dancing Brave; and Commander In Chief, winner of the 1993 Derby, did not race at all as a juvenile.

FAVOURITES

Everyone with the slightest interest in racing has favourite horses, and the criteria for attracting such affection vary: it may be that the horse did you a particularly good turn at 'double carpet', or it may be an old campaigner whose continued participation year after year brought continuity to the experience of following the sport; or a horse who was simply so good that its every appearance was a great racing occasion, or a horse who triggers special memories – the grounds are numerous, but to take a horse to your heart is one of the best experiences of racing. The following field of memorable racehorses covers the whole span of the sport, and each has a particular place in the affections of one of the Channel Four Racing team.

ARKLE

'We shall not look upon his like again' – the phrase could have been coined for Arkle. The bare facts of his career – winner of twenty-two of his twenty-six steeplechases, including the Cheltenham Gold Cup in 1964, 1965 and 1966, the Hennessy Gold Cup in 1964 and 1965, the Whitbread Gold Cup and King George VI Chase in 1965, the Irish National in 1964 – tell only part of the story. For Arkle was a freak – a horse so transcendentally good that the rules of handicapping in Ireland had to be changed to allow for his superiority, with one set of weights to include 'Himself' (as he was widely known in his home country), another framed without him.

Humbly bred in County Dublin, Arkle was bought by Anne, Duchess of Westminster at public auction as a three-year-old and went into training with the great Tom Dreaper. He was beaten in his first two outings before scoring at 20–1 in a novice hurdle at Navan in January 1962. As Dreaper came down off the stands after Arkle's surprise victory, he uttered to his wife Betty one of the great racing understatements: 'I think we've got something there!'

After winning three more times over hurdles Arkle was sent across to Cheltenham for a winning debut over fences, and went through the 1962–63 season unbeaten.

He was clearly an exceptional young horse, but so was Mill House – Irish-bred but trained in Lambourn by Fulke Walwyn – who had won the 1963

COLOUR

A Thoroughbred horse's colour is registered at birth, though colouring can occasionally change with age. The basic colours are:

Bay *All shades of brown, with the 'points' (muzzle, mane, tail and extremities of the legs) black.*

Brown *Distinctly brown all over.*

Black *Distinctly black all over.*

Chestnut *A range of shades from a light golden colour to a dark 'liver' chestnut.*

Grey *A range from pure white to dark grey. Grey horses tend to get whiter as they get older. (About 3 per cent of racehorses are greys.)*

Roan *A combination of red, white and yellow or black, white and yellow hairs which gives a washy appearance. The colour is unusual in racehorses, but not unknown: Roan Rocket won the Sussex Stakes in 1964.*

Colour is sometimes held to be an indication of a horse's temperament. A 'flashy' chestnut (in particular a filly) is often thought to be unreliable, and there is a theory – which discards horses such as The Minstrel – that you cannot trust a chestnut with four white legs.

Cheltenham Gold Cup at the tender age of six, and the rivalry between these two great horses made the mid-1960s a golden age of British steeple-chasing.

They clashed first in the 1963 Hennessy Gold Cup at Newbury, when Arkle lost his chance through a slip after the final ditch and Mill House powered home to an easy victory. This set the scene for the famous Cheltenham Gold Cup in March 1964, perhaps the most keenly anticipated horse race since the war. Mill House was favourite at 13–8 on, with Arkle 7–4, and the only other runners King's Nephew and Pas Seul 20–1 and 50–1 respectively. The big two had the race to themselves on the second circuit before Arkle – ridden as in all his chases by Pat Taaffe – took the lead on the run to the last and charged up the hill to win by five lengths.

When the two met again in the Hennessy Gold Cup in November 1964 it was no contest, Mill House crumpling to finish fourth as Arkle swept imperially to victory. A week later Arkle put up one of his greatest performances when humping 12 stone 10 pounds in the Massey-Ferguson Gold Cup at Cheltenham and narrowly failing to concede lumps of weight to Flying Wild and Buona Notte. He then won the Leopardstown Chase in Ireland, a second Cheltenham Gold Cup from Mill House, and the Whitbread under 12 stone 7 pounds.

November 1965 saw perhaps his greatest race of all, the Gallaher Gold Cup at Sandown Park, when he displayed stunning acceleration on the final turn to surge past Mill House – the fifth and last occasion they met – to whom he was conceding 16 pounds, in a time which beat the course record by 17 seconds! Mill House was eventually passed for second place by Rondetto.

Arkle then won the Hennessy, the King George, the Leopardstown Chase and a third Gold Cup, and looked invincible. He had amassed a huge popular following, drew vast crowds every time he raced, was deluged with fan mail (some addressed to 'Arkle, Ireland') and even had a song recorded about him by Dominic Behan.

His 1966–67 season proved horribly short. First time out he was beaten half a length by Stalbridge Colonist, to whom he was conceding 35 pounds, in the Hennessy. He then won the SGB Chase at Ascot and went to Kempton for what seemed like a formality in the King George. He started

I never had the privilege of commentating on one of his races, but I witnessed most of his outings in England and watched the rest on the box. He was a true colossus. There'll never be another like him.

RALEIGH GILBERT

Arkle in full flight – with Pat Taaffe up, leading Mill House (David Nicholson) in the Gallaher Gold Cup at Sandown Park in November 1965.

All children have heroes and Rondetto was mine. A tough, bloody-minded sort of handicap chaser, he was chronically unlucky in National after National before finally getting round to finish third, aged thirteen, to Highland Wedding. I don't mind admitting that one thirteen-year-old watched another through tears of pride that day as his hero finally conquered Aintree.

ALASTAIR DOWN

If authorial prerogative will allow me to sneak in a favourite of my own, it has to be Credo's Daughter.

SEAN MAGEE

outgunned by another Irish import – a huge horse named Mill House, as a four-year-old one year Rondetto's junior.

Winning hurdles was one thing, but Rondetto's real forte was chasing, and he became a familiar sight in most of the big staying chases. Six times he ran in the Grand National, his best placing coming in 1969 when he finished third, beaten thirteen lengths, behind Highland Wedding: that was the only occasion he completed the National course (though like so many others he suffered at the twenty-third fence in 1967), and he was the last thirteen-year-old to finish in the first three.

Rondetto was second to Arkle, beating Mill House, in the famous Gallaher Gold Cup at Sandown Park in November 1965 (see page 15) and third in the Scottish Grand National in 1968. But his greatest moment, and the highlight of his twenty-one victories in Britain, was the 1967 Hennessy Gold Cup at Newbury, when after improving his position gradually through the second circuit he led after the last, and was all out to beat Stalbridge Colonist – who had beaten Arkle in the race the previous year – by a head.

He finally retired after running fourth in a chase at Stratford in May 1970 at the grand old age of fourteen.

CREDO'S DAUGHTER

As the star turn of a small stable and a regular and willing contestant in the major handicap chases of the 1970s, Credo's Daughter epitomized much that is so appealing about steeplechasing.

She won four Flat races and one hurdle in Ireland before moving to England in 1971 – initially to Auriol Sinclair, and then to the Sussex yard of Syd Woodman, from where she raced in the colours of actor James Bolam, winning eight steeplechases. In all she ran in fifty-six races, winning thirteen.

In the mid-1970s Credo's Daughter established herself as a standing dish in the big handicaps, an exceptionally game and tough mare who was always there or thereabouts, never discouraged by not getting her handsome head in front where it mattered. She was fourth to The Dikler in the 1974 Whitbread, but the purple patch of her career came in its final phase, the autumn of 1975. Within the space of just seven weeks she was runner-up to Clear Cut in the Mackeson Gold Cup at Cheltenham, dead-heated for fourth behind April Seventh in the Hennessy at Newbury, back at Cheltenham to come second to Easby Abbey in the Massey-Ferguson Gold

Credo's Daughter (Charlie Goldsworthy) leaving the paddock at Newbury before the 1975 Hennessy Gold Cup.

Cup, and fourth to What A Buck in the SGB Chase at Ascot. She then signed off her racing career in the best possible style when running on gamely to beat Pengrail (ridden by John Francome) in the aptly named Ladbroke Finale Chase at Kempton Park – a farewell appropriately greeted by the *Sporting Life* with the headline: 'She's a Bride At Last!'

Ever the bridesmaid, never – well, only occasionally – the bride may have been a crisp summing up of Credo's Daughter's racing career, but she had made herself immensely popular with her honesty and consistency at the highest level, and as a broodmare left the bridesmaid tag behind with a vengeance, producing several winners – notably the top-class hurdler and chaser King Credo, winner of the 1992 Imperial Cup and 1993 Tote Gold Trophy.

Credo's Daughter – in the words of her owner James Bolam 'Such a game mare, so honest, so genuine' – was put down in July 1991 at the age of twenty-five.

MIESQUE

Of all the great fillies and mares to have run on the Flat in the last decade, perhaps only the globe-trotting Triptych came close to Miesque in achievement and durability. Owned by Stavros Niarchos and trained by François Boutin, Miesque ran sixteen times over the three seasons from 1986 to 1988, winning twelve races and only once coming worse than second. By any standards, Miesque was one of the modern greats.

As a two-year-old in 1986, she won three out of four and was clearly a filly of immense promise, which she confirmed through a brilliant three-year-old career.

She started 15–8 favourite in a field of fourteen for the General Accident One Thousand Guineas at Newmarket and, once extracted from an awkward-looking pocket by jockey Freddie Head, burst to the front with a spectacular turn of foot to beat Milligram and Interval. Just over two weeks later she started at 5–1 on for the French equivalent, the Dubai Poule d'Essai des Pouliches at Longchamp, and won easily from Sakura Reiko. She was the first to complete the Guineas double since Imprudence in 1947.

Both these Classics were over one mile, but when stepped up in distance for the extended ten furlongs of the Prix de Diane Hermes – the French Oaks – she understandably found a top-of-her-form Indian Skimmer (see page 18) on her preferred soft going a tough nut to crack, and went down by four lengths. Returned to a mile, Miesque regained the winning thread with superb displays in the Prix Jacques Le Marois at Deauville and the Prix du Moulin at Longchamp before going down to Milligram in the Queen Elizabeth II Stakes at Ascot. At Hollywood Park for the Breeders' Cup Mile she showed magnificent speed from the home turn to storm home by three and a half lengths from Show Dancer, with Sonic Lady third.

Miesque remained in training as a four-year-old. After scraping home by a short neck in the Prix d'Ispahan at Longchamp, she faced a strong field for her second Prix Jacques Le Marois, including top milers Warning and Soviet Star, and became the first to win this important French mile race twice when beating Warning by a length. Soviet Star, fourth in that race, reversed the form in the Prix du Moulin, but Miesque then went to Churchill Downs, Kentucky, to end her career in scintillating style by taking her second Breeders' Cup Mile, unleashing her usual burst of speed in the home straight and surging home to win by four lengths from top American miler Steinlen, with the likes of One Thousand Guineas heroine Ravinella, Arlington Million winner Mill Native and Warning down the field. She was the first horse to win two Breeders' Cup races.

As a broodmare Miesque's achievements have already started to match her racing record. Her first foal was the brilliant miler Kingmambo and her second East Of The Moon – both winners of Classics in France.

It seemed appropriate for me to choose a filly and they don't come better than Miesque. Throughout her career she epitomized all you could ask for in a racehorse – tough, genuine, consistent, versatile and, over a mile, brilliant. Ten Group or Grade One wins including two Breeders' Cups. And she has gone on to be a great broodmare, passing on her ability to her progeny with two Guineas winners from her first two foals in Kingmambo and East Of The Moon. A true champion.

LESLEY GRAHAM

Miesque has a good blow after winning the General Accident One Thousand Guineas at Newmarket in 1987.

BREEDING

Bloodstock breeding at the highest level may seem to be virtually monopolized by a few very rich men – the Maktoum family, Robert Sangster, Khalid Abdullah, the Aga Khan – but in reality it is much more than the exclusive domain of the super-affluent. Desert Orchid may be a far cry from a Maktoum blue-blood in terms of pedigree, but no one could doubt the greatness of the horse home-bred by James Burridge from a mare whose dam he had purchased for 175 guineas.

All sorts of theories have been tried out in the quest for the perfect racehorse, the crudest being the notion of mating the best with the best to produce the best. It is not that simple, of course, as the late John Hislop has written: 'All that the breeder can do is to try to arrange matters so that there is a reasonable chance of the right genetic shakeup emerging, and hope for the best.' That unassuming comment, though, belies the amount of thought and study that can go into choosing the right match, especially when the coffers are not bottomless. Hislop himself had acquired, for 400 guineas, a broodmare who traced back to the immortal Pretty Polly, winner of three Classics in 1904. From this mare he bred La Paiva, sending her to the unfashionable stallion Queen's Hussar. One of Queen's Hussar's attractions was that he was cheap, his covering fee at the time being £250; but he was also very well bred and had a particularly fine conformation. His offspring showed a preference for firm going, a trait balanced by the family of La Paiva, for the stock of her sire, Prince Chevalier, act well on soft going. Many other signs suggested that a mating between Queen's Hussar and La Paiva would produce a very good horse, and it did. He was called Brigadier Gerard.

The aim in breeding is to produce a balance of both temperamental and physical attributes that will provide the ideal combination of speed, stamina, toughness, conformation and courage which is the perfect racehorse. Many breeders seek this through inbreeding (that is, choosing a mating in which a particular horse or a particular family of horses appears on both sides of the pedigree) in order to strengthen some chosen feature.

The opposite of inbreeding is outcrossing, where the parents do not have ancestors in common in their recent pedigree: the stallion and the mare may each be closely inbred, but they are unrelated to each other. Queen's Hussar was inbred 3 x 3 to Fair Trial: that is, the famous stallion Fair Trial appears twice in the third generation of Queen's Hussar's pedigree, being both the grandsire of his sire and the grandsire of his dam. Her Majesty the Queen's mare Highlight was inbred to the legendary stallion and 1933 Derby winner Hyperion, who was Highlight's great-grandsire on the sire's side and grandsire on the dam's side. Thus Queen's Hussar and Highlight had no close common ancestors, but each had strong inbreeding in its pedigree. The Queen sent Highlight to Queen's Hussar, and the product was Highclere, who won the One Thousand Guineas and the Prix de Diane and foaled Height of Fashion, dam of Unfuwain and Nashwan.

Breeding on an international scale is an immensely complex business, but the fundamental cycle of the breeding year in Britain is fairly straightforward. On the day after St Valentine's Day begins the unromantically named 'covering season', which lasts until 15 July. The owner of the mare will have decided, usually after much research, advice and pondering, which stallion he wishes to mate her with. The stallion will normally be standing at a stud, and the mare is sent there during the covering season. If she is carrying a foal conceived the previous year she will arrive shortly before that foal is due, and after the foal is born will await the next covering. She will come into season ('on heat') about eight to ten days after foaling, and thereafter at three-weekly intervals.

If the mare appears to be in season she will then be subjected to the attentions of a 'teaser', a stallion kept by the stud simply for the purpose of

---

There is no good reason why a fit and willing horse should not combine stallion duties with racing. Environment Friend, winner of the Eclipse Stakes in 1991, went to stud the following year but continued to race during 1993, 1994 and 1995. Nor is there any good reason why a mare should not race during the early stages of pregnancy. Indian Queen won the 1991 Ascot Gold Cup at 25–1 when in foal to Night Shift.

As the covering season in the southern hemisphere is much later than that in the northern, some stallions of a particularly durable constitution perform in both. For example, the late Ahonoora sired 1992 Derby winner Dr Devious at the Coolmore Stud in County Tipperary and also stood at Coolmore's outpost in Australia – where he was put down after an accident in 1989.

Stallions take a stroll in the autumn sunshine at the National Stud, Newmarket. Leading the field is 1991 Prix de l'Arc de Triomphe winner Suave Dancer.

RETIREMENT AND DEATH

Only a very small proportion of racehorses retire to stud after their racing days are over. For the rest there are few alternative careers. The 1983 Grand National winner Corbiere had an honourable go at show jumping, and 1990 Grand National winner Mr Frisk turned his hand to eventing – as did 1973 Cheltenham Gold Cup winner The Dikler who, remarkably for such a large and headstrong racehorse, proved a dab hand at the dressage stage. It is not unknown (though somewhat rare) for an ex-racehorse to find employment as a polo pony.

The Thoroughbred is a highly strung and highly specialized animal and few make suitable riding-school hacks, though it is common for ex-chasers to enjoy a stint following hounds in their twilight years. Grand Canyon, a marvellous chaser in the mid-Seventies and dual winner of the Colonial Cup in South Carolina, joined the Household Cavalry.

Others find a retirement job as a trainer's hack. Devon Loch, whose sensational slide on the run-in of the 1956 Grand National is described on page 96, became hack to Noel Murless, Tingle Creek to Tom Jones, Comedy Of Errors to Mercy Rimell; Special Cargo, the Queen Mother's chaser who won the famous 1984 Whitbread Gold Cup (see pages 173–5), was tried out as Julie Cecil's hack but soon disgraced himself by setting off up the gallops with the two-year-olds – not the idea at all – and was promptly dispatched to a more placid retirement at Sandringham.

Red Rum, a celebrity on the racetrack, became a bigger celebrity off it, his services much in demand for personal appearances opening supermarkets and betting shops, and a similar devotion to public service has kept Desert Orchid busy.

Some ex-racehorses – including familiar National Hunt names Casamayor, Gainsay and South Parade – have found a new career as police horses.

Those who are able to reproduce the species do not always get the opportunity to do so in the sylvan glades of Newmarket, Kildare or Kentucky. Scottish Rifle, winner of the Eclipse Stakes in 1973, became champion sire in Czechoslovakia, and the brilliant two-year-old Provideo took up stud duties in Tasmania.

Many racehorses end their days quietly at grass, but some have more dramatic ends. Whatever happened to Shergar after he was kidnapped from the Ballymany Stud in County Kildare on the night of 8 February 1983, he is generally assumed to have been killed by his abductors, though his body was never recovered.

Less sensational but no less distressing are the deaths in action, for it is a sad fact that the sport of racing is dangerous and stressful for its participants and will always claim its equine victims. The death of any horse during or as a direct result of a race is always a matter for deep regret and often the stimulus to change the conditions under which that race is run (as when the configuration of Becher's Brook on the Grand National course was amended after the deaths of two horses, Brown Trix and Seeandem, in the 1989 running). Inevitably it is the famous horses whose loss is most keenly felt, and it is painful to recall some of the notable chasers and hurdlers of recent times who have lost their lives on the racetrack, among them Alverton, Brownes Gazette, Celtic Ryde, Dawn Run, Ekbalco, Forgive N' Forget, Golden Cygnet, Killiney, Lanzarote, Noddy's Ryde, Ten Plus, Royal Gait, Pegwell Bay, Cahervillahow, Thetford Forest, Rushing Wild and Baydon Star. (Other famous horses, such as Bula and Mighty Mogul, have had to be put down due to serious injuries sustained on the track.) But it is not only in National Hunt racing that deaths in action occur: two horses – Dovekie and Serenader –

were put down after accidents on successive days of the Royal Ascot meeting in 1990, and the Breeders' Cup, world showpiece of Flat racing, has seen several fatal accidents in running, notably the deaths of the great American filly Go For Wand in the Distaff at Belmont Park in 1990 and of Richard Hannon's July Cup winner Mr Brooks, ridden by Lester Piggott, in the Sprint at Gulfstream Park in 1992. Death marred two of the big Flat races in 1995: Daffaq was put down after sustaining irreparable injuries in the Vodafone Derby at Epsom Downs in June, and later the same month The Little Thief had to be destroyed after breaking down in the Gold Cup at Ascot.

Spanish Steps, winner of the Hennessy Gold Cup in 1969 and many other big chases, in retirement at Edgcote, near Banbury in Oxfordshire. He was thirty-one years old when photographed in 1994.

AILMENTS AND INJURIES...

The racehorse is a strong and powerful creature, but its life subjects it to a great deal of stress and strain – imagine the pressure put on the forelegs of a steeplechaser as it lands over a jump at 30 miles per hour. Horses are susceptible to all sorts of disease and injury; the following are some of the problems that crop up most often in racing stables.

THE VIRUS

'The virus' is common racing parlance for a variety of respiratory conditions. Virus infections can spread rapidly in stable yards and on racecourses, and often the first sign of the presence of the virus is a lacklustre performance on course. Equine flu is a severe viral respiratory infection: its major symptom is a dry cough – hence the horror of coughing in a racing stable – accompanied by high temperature and a nasal discharge. It usually takes a horse two to three weeks to recover, after which it will need a period of convalescence.

SOFT PALATE DISEASE

When a horse has a soft palate complaint it 'swallows its tongue', usually when under pressure at the climax of a race: the horse gurgles and suddenly slows right up, then gets its breath back. What has

happened is that the junction between the larynx and the soft palate has become unsealed, causing the passage of air to be obstructed. Once the horse can swallow and reseal the junction, it recovers.

WHISTLING AND ROARING

These are noises caused by paralysis of the vocal cords in the larynx. When the horse breathes in, they flap around in the airway, making noises and causing an obstruction to the incoming air. The vocal cords and ventricles can be removed surgically – by an operation known as hobdaying, after its originator Sir Frederick Hobday, former Principal of the Royal College of Veterinary Surgeons – to improve the airflow through the larynx. A metal tube can be inserted below the larynx in the trachea to allow the air to bypass the obstruction; this is known as 'tubing', and is visible by a small hole under the horse's neck. Party Politics, who has suffered various wind infirmities over the years, is a prominent example of a tubed horse; he had also undergone a 'tie-back' operation, in which the paralysed muscle in the larynx is substituted with elastic material which keeps the larynx open permanently.

TENDON STRAIN

Tendons attach muscles to bones. In the foreleg, the muscles are all above the knee and the tendons attach them to the pastern and pedal bones, above and in the hoof. Tendons are obviously subjected to great strain when a horse is galloping, and are placed under particular stress by jumping. Uneven going, tired muscles and jolts to the leg all increase the likelihood of tendon strain, which in severe cases causes the tendons to tear and elongate or give way completely – commonly known as 'breaking down'.

A common method of treating tendon strain until recently was 'firing'. After the area is locally anaesthetized, red hot irons are applied to the skin around the damaged tendon, on the principle that the scar tissue that will form is stronger than the damaged tissue. In bar or line firing the iron is drawn across the skin in lines about an inch apart; in pin firing the iron is inserted through the skin to the tissue or to the tendon; acid firing involves the application of concentrated sulphuric acid to the skin. Unpleasant as such treatments sound, they are held by many to be very effective; but veterinary opinion is nowadays against firing, and the Royal College of Veterinary

---

On New Year's Day 1992 Salsabil, winner of the One Thousand Guineas, Oaks and Irish Derby in 1990, gave birth to a filly foal by Nashwan. Had the foal been born one day earlier she would formally have become a yearling on her second day alive – and thus, a little less developed than her fellow yearlings, despite her exquisite breeding not much of a racing proposition. The foal, named Firdous, never saw a racecourse, but her full sister Bint Salsabil revived memories of her illustrious parents as a two-year-old in 1995.

The **Juddmonte Farms** banner covers the bloodstock operation of Khalid Abdullah, whose Banstead Manor Stud near Newmarket is the home of stallions Rainbow Quest, Zafonic and Generous.

The **Royal Studs** in Sandringham – owned by the Crown – have a long and distinguished history, and a prosperous present through the labours of top stallion Shirley Heights .

The **Coolmore Stud**, near Fethard in County Tipperary, Ireland, is the largest stallion station in Europe, with some fifteen stallions serving mares there and at related studs. Star turn is the great Sadler's Wells (sire of such horses as Old Vic, Salsabil, In The Wings, Barathea, Opera House, Intrepidity, King's Theatre and Moonshell), supported by the likes of Caerleon, Royal Academy, Last Tycoon, Be My Guest and more recent arrivals such as Bigstone and Grand Lodge. Part-owners of Coolmore are Vincent O'Brien and Robert Sangster, who have built the place up into the only European stud to rival the great farms of Kentucky – such as **Claiborne**, where such legends as Nijinksy, Sir Ivor and Secretariat went after their racing days were done. Other famous Kentucky studs whose names you may hear in connection with top European horses on the Flat include **Spendthrift**, **Gainesway** and **Three Chimneys**.

...AILMENTS AND INJURIES

Surgeons tried unsuccessfully to outlaw the practice in 1991. A new method of treating damaged forelegs is the implantation of carbon fibres to strengthen the tendons: the Queen Mother's chaser Special Cargo underwent such treatment and after an absence of two years advertised its benefits through the revival of his racing career in the spring of 1984, culminating in his memorable victory in the Whitbread Gold Cup (see pages 173–5).

SPLINTS

Splint bones are small bones between the knee and the fetlock, and a 'splint' is the common name for a bony enlargement of one of these, caused by a kick or by stress on the bones and ligaments.

SORE SHINS

Common among young racehorses, inflammation of the shins results from the stress placed on the legs by fast work or racing on hard ground.

FRACTURES OF THE KNEE

A horse's knee joint consists of ten bones, and repeated stress on the front aspect of these bones can result in 'chip' or 'slab' fractures. These usually occur in young horses at the end of a race, when the muscles are fatigued, making the knees less stable. The chips can be surgically removed and the larger slabs screwed back into place. The horse must then be rested. Premature resumption of work will cause the condition to deteriorate.

OVERREACHING

An overreach is a cut on the back of a front foot just above the heel, caused by the front of the hind shoe striking the front heel, often when the horse is stretching towards the end of a race.

BREAKING BLOOD VESSELS

To see a horse pull up with blood coming out of its nostrils is a distressing sight. This indicates a haemorrhage in the lungs caused by strenuous exertion, and can be treated by drugs and by a period of rest which can take from a few days to several months. The horse will be 'scoped' – subjected to endoscopic examination of its airways – and while the condition will not necessarily recur each time the horse races, a tendency to break blood vessels is worrying in any horse. Master Oats, winner of the 1995 Tote Cheltenham Gold Cup, is a recent example of a horse whose tendency to break blood vessels has been successfully suppressed.

CAST IN BOX

A horse is said to have been 'cast in its box' if it lies down in its box in such a way that it is trapped – often against a wall or under the manger – and cannot get up without assistance. The experience will probably leave it stiff and distressed.

COLIC

Colic is severe pain in the abdomen of the horse, caused by a variety of conditions such as lack of blood supply to the intestines (due to parasitic worm larvae around the blood vessels), impacted foodstuffs or displacements of the bowel. It is usually treated with pain-killing drugs and bowel lubricants, but displacements may call for surgery – as in the case of Arazi after his first season as a stallion.

LAMINITIS

Laminitis is an inflammation of the laminae, the tissue connecting the pedal bone to the wall of the hoof. This causes great pain as the hoof cannot expand to accommodate the swelling associated with the inflammation. It can be caused by overfeeding or severe infections, and is treated with pain-killers and reduced feeding of high-energy food.

Nashwan at the Nunnery Stud in Norfolk.

A HORSE BY ANY OTHER NAME...

A horse at birth is a **foal**, a **colt** if male and a **filly** if female. Its father is its **sire** and its mother its **dam**. (A horse is 'by' its sire and 'out of' its dam.) The foal will stand for the first time normally within an hour of being born and will suck from its dam within two hours; it has a close bond with its dam but shows increasing independence before being weaned at about five months old. The official birthday of every racehorse in the Northern Hemisphere is 1 January, and at the start of the year after its birth the foal becomes a **yearling**. At the age of five a colt becomes a **horse**, and a filly a **mare**.

Another horse sharing the same dam is its **half-brother** (or **half-sister**). Another horse sharing the same sire and dam is its **full brother** (or **full sister**). Another horse sharing the same sire but not the same dam is *not* described as its half-brother (or half-sister). Twins are rare, for while as many as 30 per cent of conceptions result in twins, in most cases one of the eggs is 'popped' by a vet to ensure that only one foal is born: twin foals would probably be too weak, though there are instances of successful racing twins.

A **gelding** is a horse that has been castrated ('cut'). The operation usually takes place in the autumn of the horse's second year; although it can be done later it is unwise to delay too long. The operation is performed under local anaesthetic and is quite painless. It comes as a surprise to some non-racing people to learn that the likes of Arkle, Red Rum and Desert Orchid cannot procreate, but had they not been gelded they would not have achieved what they did in steeplechasing. Although the common explanation for gelding a potential chaser – that only an exceptionally well adjusted 'full' horse would willingly launch itself over four and a half feet of packed birch – is plausible enough, there is more to it than that, for the ungelded horse is likely to have his mind on other things as he matures and will find it difficult to stand up to the wintry rigours of the jumping game.

An ungelded horse is an **entire**, and there have been few chasing entires of note – Fortina won the Cheltenham Gold Cup in 1947, and the last entire to win the Grand National was Battleship in 1938. Hurdlers tend to be younger than chasers and the obstacles they face are easier to negotiate; consequently several horses have enjoyed notable hurdling careers without being gelded: Monksfield, for instance, won two Champion Hurdles before starting a stud career tragically abbreviated by his death in 1989, and the 1995 Champion Hurdle was won by the entire Alderbrook. Of course, geldings do not run only under National Hunt Rules, and though they may not compete in the Classics (on the argument that it would do no good for the breed were a Classic race to be won by a horse which could not pass on his excellence), most of the big Flat races are now open to them, and old geldings such as Teleprompter, Bedtime and Chaplins Club had a hold on the affections of the racing public which few here-today-gone-tomorrow Classic winners could match. Arcadian Heights became the first gelding to win a Group One race on the Flat in Great Britain when taking the Ascot Gold Cup in 1994.

A **rig** is a horse imperfectly gelded, or in whom only one testicle has descended: not surprisingly, such horses are often rather difficult. Selkirk, a very good miler who won the Queen Elizabeth II Stakes at Ascot in 1991, was a rig, and his form improved markedly once the offending gland had been removed. In the Queen Elizabeth II Stakes he beat the filly Kooyonga, whose trainer Michael Kauntze had an apt comment about the winner in the following Monday's *Racing Post*: 'If I'd been running around all my life with an inflamed testicle and it was suddenly sorted out, I'm sure I'd run faster.'

An entire at stud is a **stallion**, and a mare used for breeding is a **broodmare**.

Celtic Swing, whose dam is Celtic Ring, is named after a Van Morrison song . . . Rubstic, winner of the 1979 Grand National, was named after the Swedish version of the Brillo Pad . . . Tough sprinter Amron owes his name to that of owner Roy Peebles's wife, Norma . . . 'Bint' – as in Bint Salsabil – is Arabic for 'daughter of', and Lammtarra is Arabic for 'invisible' . . . Josh Gifford-trained 'iggins in 1995 became the first horse whose name begins with an apostrophe to be entered in a race in Britain.

Arcadian Heights (Michael Hills) becoming the first gelding ever to win a Group One race in Britain when landing the Ascot Gold Cup in June 1994.

NAMES

Until 1946 a horse could run unnamed (it would be identified by the name of its dam); today the naming of racehorses is controlled by Weatherbys, and names are restricted in length to eighteen characters (including spaces), a rule which causes weird conflations like Thethingaboutitis or Blessingindisguise. But you do not have to own a horse to register a name: you may secure the name against having the horse to go with it some time in the future.

No longer can a horse's name consist solely of initial letters (such as 1956 Grand National winner ESB), though these can be spelled out phonetically (for instance, Cee-Jay-Ay). The list of *Registered Names* contains nearly a quarter of a million protected names which cannot be used: they include those of any racehorse up to ten years after its death, broodmares up to fifteen years after death and stallions up to twenty-five years after death or being taken out of stud, and in perpetuity the names of all Classic winners and the winners of the Ascot Gold Cup, King George VI and Queen Elizabeth Diamond Stakes and Grand National.

Royal Mail won the 1937 and another Royal Mail won the Whitbread Gold Cup in 1980, but the Whitbread winner had '(NZ)' after his name to indicate that he was bred in New Zealand; a horse bred outside the British Isles carries a suffix to its name to indicate its country of foaling (not conception). This can cause all sorts of confusion when two horses with the same name but different suffixes are in training at the same time. Winged Victory (IRE), trained by Ian Balding, and Winged Victory (USA), trained by John Gosden, both four-year-olds, ran in successive races at Newbury on 25 May 1994. Both finished second. And a few weeks later, in the Hemsby Stakes at Yarmouth on 30 June 1994, three-year-olds named Averti (IRE), trained by Willie Muir, and Averti (USA), trained by Henry Cecil, ran in the same race: the Irish one was fifth, the American one sixth.

The names of particularly celebrated horses not covered by the general regulations (such as Arkle) are protected by dispensation of the *International List of Protected Names*. None the less, familiar names do recur, and in the last few years horses called Crisp, Dunkirk, Predominate and Lanzarote have revived memories of the much greater animals which bore those names in the past – and enraged purists who consider the use of such distinguished names an affront to the memory of great horses.

Weatherbys, who receive about 10,000 applications for registration of new names every year, can always turn down a proposed name on the grounds of good taste – though the naming of the globe-trotting Snurge should not have got past anyone with access to a copy of Eric Partridge's *Dictionary of Slang and Unconventional English*. And it is possible for Weatherbys to be overruled. A two-year-old filly called Wear The Fox Hat, whose name had been allowed through, was entered in a race at Folkestone in March 1995, but the Jockey Club Stewards, no less, spotted a possible problem and insisted that the horse be renamed. She was – as Nameless.

A horse's name is often a creative compound of the names of its sire and dam (thus Milly Ha Ha by Dancing Brave out of Mill On The Floss), but an increasing number of companies are advertising themselves through the names of horses they own or sponsor, including such notable performers as 1994 Two Thousand Guineas winner Mister Baileys, owned by Baileys Horse Feeds. This commercialization of names has not pleased everyone, not least those punters who have had to stand in betting shops cheering home Geary's Cold Rolled, Sunday Sport Star or CD Super Targeting.

Sometimes an apparently mysterious name has an explanation in a personal association of the owner. 'Snurge' was owner Martyn Arbib's nickname at school, and a school-days code explains the name of Kybo, a fine hurdler and chaser owned by Isidore Kerman. When Kerman was away at boarding school his mother would send him letters which ended with the exhortation KYBO – 'Keep Your Bowels Open'.

The great Amrullah, losing-most horse in the history of British horse racing, pictured at Sandown Park (with Gary Moore up) in March 1992 en route to his seventy-third consecutive defeat. In all Amrullah ran – and failed to come first – in seventy-four races. His first outing was in a two-year-old maiden event at Newmarket on 1 October 1982, when he was unplaced behind no less a horse than Tolomeo, and his last appearance came in a novices' chase at Fontwell Park in March 1992. In between he often acquitted himself respectably in top-class company and won over £26,000 in place money; but he simply would not win, and towards the end of his historic career seemed to have little mind to: Timeform afforded him the dreaded 'double squiggle' – the indication of complete unreliability – over both hurdles and fences, and snootily labelled him 'thoroughly irresolute'.

Courses

'An American friend who was over here to see Epsom, Ascot, Goodwood, Newmarket and other places of historical interest,' wrote the former jockey Jack Leach in his *Sods I Have Cut on the Turf*, 'remarked to me once that it was curious that they did not have a band playing some appropriate tune during the parade for the Derby. He said, "As far as I can make out, Epsom has everything; all the fun of the fair, gypsies, tipsters, millions of people, everything, but no band." I pointed out the Salvation Army Band which was playing some mournful dirge and had banners displaying "Prepare to meet thy God," but that was not quite what he meant.'

That was some decades ago; were Leach's American friend to return today he would almost certainly find music – a steel band or a jazz band at Sandown Park or Goodwood, a military band at Ascot. Were he to attend one of the immensely popular summer evening meetings on Newmarket's July Course, he might find himself bopping the night away to Edwin Starr or The Hollies.

British racecourses have woken up to the fact that they are in the business of entertaining the public, and the gradual modernizing of buildings is being accompanied by a modernizing of attitudes. Courses are promoting themselves more actively and ensuring that what they have on offer is more in keeping with the modern family day out – even if the notion of bouncy castles and creche facilities is not entirely to the liking of the more old-fashioned racegoer.

There are fifty-nine racecourses in Great Britain, offering over a thousand fixtures annually – 1,029 days at the races in 1994. Of these fifty-nine (sixty if you count Newmarket's two courses – the Rowley Mile and the July Course – separately), sixteen staged flat racing only in 1995, twenty-four jumping only, and the remaining nineteen put on both. Three tracks – Lingfield Park, Southwell and Wolverhampton – have all-weather tracks (see page 43).

From Perth in the north to Newton Abbot in the south, from Yarmouth in the east to Bangor-on-Dee in the west, the diversity of terrain they offer to horse and jockey and the range of facilities they provide for the spectator form one of the abiding attractions of the British racing scene.

On Newmarket's Rowley Mile course a ten-furlong race is straight but undulating; a horse running over the same distance at Chester negotiates an almost constant left-hand turn over ground which is dead flat. At Ascot and Newmarket spectators are ferried up and down by escalators in the grandstand; at Bangor-on-Dee there is no stand at all.

Since the end of the Second World War many courses have closed, most recently Teesside Park (formerly Stockton), which held its last meeting in 1981, Lanark in 1977 and Wye in 1974. Alexandra Park was the only racecourse in London when it shut in 1970 at the end of a particularly grim decade which had seen the loss of such venues as Buckfastleigh (1960), Hurst Park (1962), Manchester and Woore (both 1963), Lewes and Lincoln (both 1964) and Birmingham, Bogside and Rothbury (all 1965). Gatwick, where the Grand National was run during the First World War, staged its last official meeting in 1940.

Nowadays the number of meetings required to sustain the programme of fixtures in Britain and generate a high level of betting turnover demands the regular use of a large number of courses, for grass needs time to recover from racing (unlike America's dirt tracks, where the sport can take place over a single circuit for weeks on end). With all-weather tracks now established in Britain, the nature of the sport is bound to change in some ways at the margins; but the wonderful variety in British racecourses remains.

This variety manifests itself both in the more obvious aspects of a course, such as turf, layout, size, shape or landscape, and in the less tangible but no less marked matters of atmosphere and style, contrasts which come across even on television. At Sandown Park, where the horses emerge out of the parade ring on to the Rhododendron Walk and return along it and then through the crowd to the unsaddling enclosure, the proximity of the

---

THE GOING

The 'going' is the condition of the ground, a crucial factor in any horse race.

The Clerk of the Course announces the probable state of the going for a meeting some time in advance to advise trainers about the likely conditions, and will announce alterations at intervals thereafter until on the day of the meeting he (or she) declares the official state (which can alter during the course of an afternoon's racing, say in the case of torrential rain). The seven official states of the going in Britain for turf races are:

hard;
firm;
good to firm;
good;
good to soft;
soft;
heavy.

The official states of the going for all-weather races are:

fast;
standard;
slow.

Previous spread: Epsom.

spectators to the action heightens the excitement for both racegoers and television viewers, whereas the vast open spaces of Newmarket can provide a less hectic atmosphere: many Newmarket racegoers find the time spent waiting in the stands as the runners for the Cesarewitch in mid-October make their way to the two-and-a-quarter-mile start the best opportunity all year for quiet contemplation or for the first draft of the Christmas card list.

The difference between Newmarket and Sandown Park reflects an important moment in the history of racecourses. Newmarket racing grew out of a Royal enthusiasm for coursing and hunting on the heath in the early seventeenth century; at other places race meetings evolved as part of civic celebrations such as festivals and fairs, or as the town became popular for other reasons – Epsom, for instance, established itself as a spa town in the seventeenth century on account of the medicinal properties of its waters (Pepys recorded in 1667 that 'I did drink four pints and had some very good stools by it'), and horse racing became an established part of its social fabric. Races which had developed in this way were usually held on common land.

But Sandown Park was the first of the 'park' courses – that is, the first course to charge admission to all who wanted to watch the racing. Until Sandown opened in 1875, money was charged at courses only for entrance into the stands and enclosures; access to the rest of the course was open and free to all. The Sandown experiment of enclosing the whole course with a fence was a great success, and soon led to the founding of other courses close to London, such as Kempton Park, Hurst Park and Newbury, which held its first meeting in 1905.

The variety extends further, to ownership – Ascot is owned by the Crown, while Epsom, Kempton Park and Sandown Park form United Racecourses Ltd, now owned by Racecourse Holdings Trust, which is in turn owned by the Jockey Club, while some courses are limited companies in their own right – and finance, which may come from money taken at the gate, grants and subsidies from the Betting Levy Board, sale of hospitality facilities, television rights, rights to Satellite Information Services (SIS) to beam pictures into betting shops, and so on; and through putting the racecourse to alternative uses when racing is not taking place.

On 4 July 1981 Paul Cook rode a winner on each of three different courses: Princes Gate in the 2:15 at Sandown Park, Ramannolie in the 5:00 at Bath and Pavilion in the 7:50 at Nottingham. The feat was emulated by Gary Carter on 14 June 1991 with Luvly Jubly in the 1:30 at Southwell, Romany Rye in the 4.40 at York and Able Susan in the 8.15 at Doncaster.

Cheltenham: the field for the 1992 Sun Alliance Chase approaches the packed stands.

FENCES AND HURDLES

Steeplechase fences (except water jumps) must not be lower than 4 feet 6 inches in height. Plain fences are usually constructed of birch packed together and held in place by a wooden frame on the ground; on the take-off side an apron of gorse is sloped to the fence to encourage horses to jump, and painted rails along the ground provide a 'ground line' by which the horse will judge when to take off. An open ditch incorporates a ditch protected by a low rail on the take-off side, forcing the horse to make a bigger jump than it would at a plain fence. In the first two miles of a race there must be at least twelve fences and in each succeeding mile at least six. For each mile there must be at least one open ditch. (The fences on the Grand National course at Aintree are of an unorthodox build – thorn dressed with gorse, fir and spruce.)

Hurdles are constructed like sheep hurdles, with gorse and birch woven into a wooden frame which is driven into the ground: they give if clouted. They must not measure less than 3 feet 6 inches from the top bar to the bottom bar. In the first two miles of a hurdle race there must be at least eight flights of hurdles, with an additional flight for every completed quarter mile beyond that.

During the 1993–94 season experiments were undertaken using an alternative form of hurdle, constructed from plastic birch like a small steeplechase fence. These were generally well received by jockeys and trainers, but for the majority of hurdle races the traditional sheep-hurdle construction is likely to remain.

Hurdles may be lower and less substantial than steeplechase fences, but speed, accuracy and fluency at the obstacles are vital to a top-class hurdler: at the last flight of the Smurfit Champion Hurdle at Cheltenham in March 1995 runner-up Large Action (Jamie Osborne) shows the way to winner Alderbrook (Norman Williamson), with fifth-placed Mysilv (Graham Bradley, no. 14) on the far side.

Sandown Park has been a leader in this last respect, with its golf course and driving range and artificial ski slope, and other courses have joined the search for ways to use their grounds on the very many days each year when there is no racing. Several now have caravan parks and golf courses, and many offer the use of their buildings for non-racing activities such as conferences, exhibitions and banquets.

The urge to mix banquet and sport on race-days themselves is increasingly evident in the entertainment and hospitality facilities which courses offer. Most new racecourse grandstands are designed with an eye to the need for corporate hospitality, which during the 1980s and 1990s became an increasingly important source of revenue for racecourses.

Horses have simpler tastes and no need of banqueting facilities, but many display a distinct predilection for a certain sort of racecourse, or indeed for one specific course, and the 'horses for courses' theory is one which the punter ignores at his peril, particularly at tracks with unusual terrain, such as the switchbacks of Epsom and Brighton or the tight bends of Plumpton and Fontwell. Horses have general preferences – despite his memorable win in the 1989 Tote Cheltenham Gold Cup, Desert Orchid

THE STEWARDS

Time was when Stewards were not necessarily the models of probity that they are today. The tale is told of the callow young Steward in the 1920s who, with an older and more experienced colleague, witnessed a piece of patent non-trying in a race. 'Did you see that?', he asked his senior. 'Yes, I saw it.' 'What are you going to do?' 'Do?' replied the old Steward: '*Do?* Back it next time out, of course!'

It is the duty of the course Stewards at any race meeting to see that the Jockey Club's Rules of Racing are adhered to. Appointments are made by the racecourse and approved by the Stewards of the Jockey Club, and there must be at least four Stewards for every meeting. A Stewards' Secretary (the Stipendiary Steward or 'Stipe') provides the Stewards with advice relating to the conduct of the meeting and to the Rules.

The responsibilities and powers of the Stewards (who are unpaid for their duties), as laid down in the Rules, are wide-ranging. They include the power to abandon the meeting or to abandon certain races within the meeting (usually on account of the weather), and control over all the stands and enclosures; they can 'enquire into, regulate, control, take cognisance of, and adjudicate upon, the conduct of all officials, and of all owners, nominators, trainers, riders, grooms, persons attendant upon horses, and of all persons frequenting the Stands or other places used for the purpose of the Meeting' (Rule 14(viii)).

The Stewards' most public function is to identify and rule upon possible breaches of the Rules during the race itself. To this end they are assisted by the technology of the outside broadcast unit (see page 41) and by having some of their number stationed in a raised position looking straight down the course, from which vantage point it will be possible to see interference, misuse of the whip and so on. They will be on the look-out for horses apparently not being asked to run on their merits, for extraordinary changes in form (which might suggest that a horse's ability has deliberately been concealed) and for other signs that any race might not be truly run and fairly contested. They can instigate investigations of their own (a Stewards' Enquiry) or respond to an objection from a jockey or, more unusually, an official – for example, the Clerk of the Scales (see page 170), who has to object if a rider does not weigh in at the correct weight. They can impose a hefty fine and, in the case of riding offences, suspend a jockey from competing for up to fourteen days.

If the Stewards of the meeting require a possible breach of the Rules to be investigated at a higher level (or want to suspend a rider for more than fourteen days) they report the matter to the Stewards of the Jockey Club in London, popularly known as 'referring the case to Portman Square'.

was widely held to be better on a right-hand circuit than left-handed – and preferences for certain sorts of track. The latter usually relate to physique or action: an exceptionally long-striding horse such as Nashwan would be seen to best effect at a 'galloping' course (that is, a course without tight bends to slow him down) like Newmarket, where he won the General Accident Two Thousand Guineas in 1989, while a more compactly built animal will be at an advantage on a sharp track: the wiry little chaser Gambling Prince, for example, won seven times around the tight bends of Stratford. Rapid Lad won twelve races at Beverley (the last in 1990) and had a race on the course named after him, while during its comparatively short lifespan all-weather racing has already thrown up plenty of specialists: Tempering, for example, has won no fewer than twenty races at Southwell up to the end of June 1995. At the more idiosyncratic courses an older horse who has won there already is always worthy of consideration. 'Horses for courses' can be a useful maxim, but nevertheless a good horse should be able to act anywhere.

And a good racegoer should be able to act anywhere, from the atmospheric but less than ideally angled grandstand at Kelso which was built in 1822 to the modern comforts of York.

Spectator numbers have remained fairly constant in recent years, registering a slight increase in 1994 over 1993: total attendance at the 1,029 fixtures in 1994 was 4,412,935, an average of 4,289 per fixture.

The Derby is no longer the best-attended race of the year in Britain, that honour now going to the Ascot Gold Cup: a crowd of 74,424 watched Double Trigger's 1995 victory, while the official attendance at Epsom Downs for the 1995 Vodafone Derby won by Lammtara was 54,266, of whom 23,497 paid to go into the enclosures (the remainder watching proceedings from the Downs).

A crowd of 57,804 (a course record) piled into Cheltenham for the 1995

The first evening meeting in Great Britain was held at Hamilton Park on 18 July 1947.

THE CLERK OF THE COURSE AND RACECOURSE MANAGER

The **Clerk of the Course** bears sole responsibility to the Stewards for the general arrangements of a race meeting. The role has an importance far beyond that of oiling the wheels: Clerks such as the late John Hughes, of Liverpool and Chepstow, and Bill McHarg, of Ayr and other Scottish courses, exerted a tremendous influence on the very nature and quality of the sport at their courses.

The formal duties of a Clerk of the Course are: to conduct the racing at meetings authorized by the Jockey Club, including responsibility for the condition of course and fences, for the correct measurement of distances and for adequate marking of the course; to provide a parade ring and ensure that all horses are paraded therein having been saddled in the appointed place; to see that each horse carries a clean number-cloth; and to make sure that horses owned by disqualified persons are not started for any race. In practice, of course, the duties are much wider. The Clerk will declare the condition of the going, and will be responsible for making any changes to that description. He (or she) will arrange for the compilation and printing of the racecard. He will negotiate with sponsors about particular races or meetings, and with the Jockey Club about the programme of racing on his course, which will be formulated on his initiative in accordance with regulations laid down by the Jockey Club.

The less official duties of Clerk of the Course are shared at some of the bigger courses by a **Racecourse Manager**, who will be concerned with such matters as marketing the course and its major meetings, seeking new sponsors and keeping existing ones happy, and developing the non-racing activities of the venue. Every course also needs ground staff to maintain the track and buildings, and, on race-days, an army of casual workers in the shape of gatemen, catering staff, car park attendants, and so on.

Tote Gold Cup won by Master Oats, and there were 58,159 at Aintree to see Royal Athlete storm home in the Martell Grand National.

But although thousands may flock to a great event, for large numbers of racegoers the variety in British courses is the spice of the sport, and a quiet day at Ludlow can dispense joys which those squeezing into their morning suits and cramming into the Royal Enclosure for the Ascot Gold Cup can only envy.

TECHNICALITIES

Technology is of vital importance to modern racing. Not only do the millions of pounds involved in the betting and breeding sides of the Turf demand that results are as fair and as unequivocal as possible, but the lure of racing as a spectator sport necessitates the use of the best available technology for enhancing the enjoyment of those who follow it – both on the track and off.

The technological support for a race meeting is provided by RaceTech (the new name of Racecourse Technical Services), a subsidiary of the British Horseracing Board, which provides the starting stalls and the teams which man them, the photo-finish equipment, the outside broadcast unit which films each race, official electrical timing facilities, the racecourse public address and race commentary system (first used on a British racecourse at Goodwood in 1952) and the radio links whereby officials on the course can communicate with one another.

STARTING STALLS

Starting stalls were first used to start a race in Britain in the Chesterfield Stakes at Newmarket on 8 July 1965 (they had been in use in France since 1962). Experiments continued throughout the 1966 season and in 1967 they were first used in the Classics. Today they are used for all races on the Flat, unless special reasons (such as location, high wind or very heavy going) make them impractical or unsafe. Starting stalls are mobile, and are moved from meeting to meeting, towed by Land Rover, from the depot in Newmarket. RaceTech (whose main base is in South London) maintains over twenty sets of ten-bay stalls and can cover up to six race meetings per day: the number of sets of stalls needed for a course varies depending on how many horses can

A **furlong** is one-eighth of a mile (220 yards).
'The distance' is 240 yards from the winning post.

Starting stalls in perfect working order at Kempton Park for the 'Crinkley Bottom' Handicap in April 1993.

be accommodated in line across the track. At each meeting there is a team of nine professional horse handlers, under the direction of a leader, whose role is to load the horses into the stalls as efficiently and speedily as possible. This can be a hazardous occupation, and injuries to handlers from kicks or from being pushed against the stalls are not uncommon.

The stalls are so designed that the horse is led in by the handler, who then gets out by ducking under the front gate. It is dangerous for the jockey to let the horse get its head down to that gap under the gate as it may try to wriggle out. Within the stall there is a small shelf on each side on which a jockey whose mount is loaded early may rest his feet in order to take the weight off the horse's back while the other runners are being loaded.

ELECTRICAL TIMING

Electrical timing on all major courses is controlled by RaceTech and involves the breaking of an electrical circuit when the Starter presses the button which opens the front gates of the stalls: that instant is the start of the race. The timing is plotted on the photo-finish strip so that an accurate time can be read off for each horse finishing.

THE OUTSIDE BROADCAST UNIT

RaceTech provides complete video coverage of each race for post-race scrutiny by the Stewards (and, where appropriate, by television viewers: the head-on pictures which you will often see immediately after a race are usually taken from the official camera patrol). Nowadays cameras pick up every part of the race, and can illuminate an incident by supplying pictures taken from different angles: much of the most telling evidence in the controversial disqualification of Royal Gait from the 1988 Ascot Gold Cup, when jockey Cash Asmussen was judged to have ridden recklessly in bumping El Conquistador just after the turn into the straight, came from a camera behind the runners – the 'remote' camera. The cameras are directed from a scanner van in much the same way as television coverage is controlled.

Video coverage was a major innovation in racing: by scrutinizing every moment of a race it reduces the possibility of foul riding and non-trying, and by providing head-on pictures of the finish it ensures that a horse not keeping a straight course will be spotted (this can be very difficult to notice from the stands). Those who backed Brook in the Queen Anne Stakes at Ascot in 1974 had special reason to be grateful for the presence of the film patrol: he finished fourth behind Confusion, Gloss and Royal Prerogative, but those of his backers who tore up their tickets should have heeded the advice never to do this before 'weighed in' is declared, for the camera patrol revealed that the first three home had all been engaged in a sustained bout of scrimmaging. All three were disqualified and the race was awarded to the fourth past the post: Brook.

THE PHOTO FINISH

The photo-finish camera was introduced to British racecourses at Epsom on 22 April 1947. The first Classic to be decided by photo finish was the 1949 Two Thousand Guineas, which Nimbus won by a short head from Abernant; and Nimbus was again the victor later that year in the first Derby to be decided by photo.

On the racecourse, the photo-finish camera is usually situated directly above the Judge's box. Normally two cameras are used, one to cover the whole width of the track and the other to concentrate on that part of the track by the winning post furthest away from the stands in order to make the maximum use of the strip of mirror (six inches wide and six feet tall) which is attached to the far winning post and which enables the Judge to see what is happening from the far side if the finish is so close that the view from the stands side does not give him enough information.

The camera has a vertical adjustable slit aperture the size of which varies according to the light (the most common setting is 0.008 inches): whatever passes through this aperture when the camera is operating is recorded on a strip of moving film, so that a photo-finish picture is essentially one of time rather than of area. The camera operator adjusts the speed of the film moving

The Stanley Wootton Handicap at Epsom on 7 June 1990 provided an early opportunity for the then novel colour photo-finish equipment to show its worth. Lyndseylee (no. 4) dead-heats with Maison Des Fruits (no. 15), with Lake Mistassiu (no. 3) third and Night at Sea (no. 1) fourth. The distances were: dead heat, head, head, neck, short head, half a length, three quarters of a length.

through the camera according to the speed at which the runners are likely to pass the post: thus a horse which comes through much more slowly than anticipated will appear elongated on the photo-finish strip. The camera is left running until the last horse crosses the finishing line, and the Judge will name the distances between horses from the evidence of the photo-finish strip.

A 'spinner' attached to the base of the far winning post names the course and date and records this information constantly on to the strip. (Since early 1990 photo-finish equipment on most British racecourses has facilitated the production of a colour negative, which allows for greater accuracy than the old black-and-white method.)

As soon as the last runner has passed the post the film is developed (this takes less than a minute) and the image is transmitted to the Judge by means of a negative video converter. He can then study the picture on his colour television monitor and has the facility to enlarge the picture by up to six times if necessary.

If the Judge cannot place the leading horses without recourse to the camera he announces 'photograph' (which he should do when the distance in question seems to be less than half a length) and consults the evidence on the monitor.

If the finish is so close that the judge cannot pronounce on that evidence, he will ask for a print, from which it is easier to distinguish small distances. Identical prints may then be produced for public display: the white line superimposed on the print displayed is produced by stretching a length of cat gut across the paper carrier in which it is made.

At Goodwood in May 1995 another major advance in racecourse technology was unveiled in the shape of Hawkeye, a computer-based photo-finish camera which can determine the result of tight finishes much more quickly than the conventional film method: Hawkeye can enable the judge to give his or her verdict within about thirty seconds of the horses passing the post. RaceTech's aim is to have Hawkeye in general use, replacing the old film method, by the end of 1996.

ALL-WEATHER RACING

'I used to get sand kicked in my face as a kid, and now I'm getting paid for it,' said jockey Richard Fox at Lingfield Park on 30 October 1989. It was a historic date in the history of British racing, for that Lingfield meeting heralded a revolution in the sport with the advent of all-weather racing. Britain's second all-weather track, at Southwell, held the first hurdles meeting two days later on 1 November. A third all-weather track came into being when Wolverhampton staged its first fixture on the artificial surface on 27 December 1993, and brought British racing into a new era with two races under floodlights the same afternoon.

Lingfield's all-weather course is made of Equitrack and Southwell's and Wolverhampton's of Fibresand: in both compounds the actual racing surface consists of specially graded sand, stabilized with synthetic fibres. Their installation followed many years of concern about the number of racing fixtures lost to the weather, brought to a head after the sacrifice of seventy-two days in January and February 1985. The Jockey Club investigated the

Racing under floodlights at Wolverhampton.

For handicapping purposes, horses which race on the Flat on all-weather surfaces are given a Jockey Club rating separate from their turf rating.

feasibility and desirability of all-weather racing, and in November 1985 approved the go-ahead 'to minimise the effect on racing and betting of adverse weather conditions during the winter months'.

Several courses investigated the possibility of staging such racing, and eventually the pioneering role went to Lingfield and Southwell.

It was Niklas Angel, a three-year-old colt trained by Conrad Allen and ridden by Richard Quinn, who went into the history books as the first winner of an all-weather race in Britain, and the first impressions of the opening meetings were favourable. However, teething troubles followed: weak markets brought criticism that they could be easily manipulated by the big bookmaking firms; some fixtures, ironically, were lost to the weather (fog and, on one occasion, snow which blocked the approach roads to Lingfield so that the course, all-weather or not, was unreachable); and the plastic hurdles first used for all-weather jumping claimed an early casualty when a horse named Bahu Pahat had to be put down at Lingfield after injuring her fetlock.

All-weather jumping was never popular with jockeys, who claimed that the lack of 'give' in the surface made some falls much more serious – for horse and jockey – than they would have been on turf. During the early part of 1994 a succession of equine deaths on all-weather tracks gave rise to serious concern, and when War Beat died after falling at the final flight at Lingfield on 24 February, he was the twelfth fatality on the all-weather jumping circuits since 5 January. The British Horseracing Board (by then the governing body of racing) decided that enough was enough, and all-weather jumping was suspended pending an enquiry and consultation.

One lasting – and controversial – effect of the advent of all-weather racing is that it has changed the formal shape of the Flat season, which tradition-ally began with the opening fixture at Doncaster in late March and ran through to Doncaster again – or, in recent years, Folkestone – on some gloomy afternoon in the middle of November. Since 1990 the Flat season has officially begun on 1 January and ended on 31 December, thus removing any formal distinction between all-weather racing and turf; and later, after some resistance, it was agreed that the same period would be used to decide seasonal championships. Frankie Dettori took spectacular advantage of the change in 1994, kick-starting his season with a winner in the first race at Lingfield's all-weather fixture on 1 January and storming through the early weeks of the year to such effect that by the time the turf season started and his main championship rivals returned to the saddle, he had built up an unassailable 51-winner lead. By the end of racing on 31 December 1994 he was champion jockey with 233 winners, 54 of which had been on all-weather tracks. Jason Weaver, second in the championship with 200 winners, had topped the all-weather table with 57 winners.

All-weather racing has had its critics, and there are legitimate worries about how it has affected other areas of the sport: it is said, for instance, that it has caused a decline in the number of jumpers, as some owners have kept their horses on the Flat through the winter rather than sending them hurdling.

No one would pretend that an afternoon watching low-grade all-weather sport at Southwell has the glamour of Royal Ascot or the charm of Kelso. But for a great number of horses, owners, trainers and jockeys at the humbler end of the racing spectrum it has provided a host of fresh opportunities when there would otherwise be none, and it has kept the sport in general going – and punters punting – during bouts of bad weather.

But all-weather action is not only for the humbler end of racing society. On 3 March 1995 a horse named Warluskee, trained by Mark Johnston and ridden by Willie Ryan, gave Sheikh Mohammed his first winner on an all-weather track in Britain.

Like it or not, all-weather racing is here to stay.

RACECOURSES OF THE BRITISH ISLES

Flat

National Hunt

Flat and National Hunt

A/W: all-weather track

RACECOURSES OF GREAT BRITAIN

This section gives brief characteristics of all the courses in Britain. For a description of the major meetings of the racing year, see pages 87–9.

AINTREE

National Hunt

Home of the Grand National, Aintree has two left-handed courses. The National course itself is two and a quarter miles round and its sixteen fir fences – including household names such as Becher's Brook, Valentine's and the Chair – pose a unique challenge to a steeplechaser, while the more orthodox Mildmay course is twelve furlongs round and very fast. Facilities have been greatly improved in recent years, and the revival of the November meeting, featuring the Becher Chase, has proved a great success.

Major races: Grand National, Aintree Hurdle, John Hughes Chase, Martell Cup, Fox Hunters' Chase, Becher Chase

ASCOT

Flat and National Hunt

A right-handed course of about fourteen furlongs round, with a steady uphill rise from Swinley Bottom, Ascot is one of the finest courses in the country under both codes. The standard of racing here is invariably tip-top, with the Royal Meeting in June dominating the calendar and the King George VI and Queen Elizabeth Diamond Stakes in July and the Festival of British Racing in September, featuring the Queen Elizabeth II Stakes, providing sport of the highest class. The jumping course – the turf for which came from the defunct circuit at nearby Hurst Park, which closed in 1962 – is inside the Flat track, and was the scene of Arkle's last victory, in the SGB Chase in December 1966.

Major races: *Flat* – King George VI and Queen Elizabeth Diamond Stakes, Gold Cup, St James's Palace Stakes, Coronation Stakes, Royal Hunt Cup, Wokingham Stakes, King's Stand Stakes, Queen Elizabeth II Stakes, Fillies' Mile, Royal Lodge Stakes, Victoria Cup; *Jumps* – Victor Chandler Chase, Long Walk Hurdle, Betterware Cup

Aintree: The Fellow (Adam Kondrat) and subsequent winner Miinnehoma (Richard Dunwoody) take the fourteenth fence in the 1994 Martell Grand National.

AYR

Flat and National Hunt

The premier racecourse in Scotland and home of two of the great events of the racing year in the Scottish National and the Ayr Gold Cup, Ayr is a left-handed track just over one and a half miles round, its long straights, easy bends and gentle undulations making it ideal for long-striding horses with plenty of stamina. It was to Ayr that the 1989 St Leger was transferred after the cancellation of the race at Doncaster following subsidence on the course – the only time an English Classic has been run outside England.

Major races: *Flat* – Ayr Gold Cup, Scottish Classic; *Jumps* – Scottish National, Scottish Champion Hurdle

BANGOR-ON-DEE

National Hunt

Approximately one and a half miles round, left-handed, triangular and mostly flat, Bangor-on-Dee is suited to the nimble sort of horse rather than the relentless galloper. It is famous for (a) being near Wrexham and not at the Bangor in North Wales, though some horsebox drivers still forget this, and (b) not having a grandstand. It does not need one, having a perfectly good hill facing the finishing straight, and the facilities and a strong local following always ensure a good atmosphere.

BATH

Flat

A left-handed track of just over one and a half miles round with a gradual uphill finish, Bath suits the galloping type of horse and provides a very fair test. There is a slight left-hand turn in the straight about a furlong from the winning post which can cause bunching in a tight finish.

BEVERLEY

Flat

Beverley is a right-handed track with gentle undulations, about thirteen furlongs round. The straight five-furlong course rises from start to finish and provides a demanding test, especially in soft going.

BRIGHTON

Flat

Brighton's track is similar to Epsom – left-handed, twelve furlongs in length and suited to horses well able to cope with bends and undulations – and used to be a favoured place for trying out Derby hopes: Cacoethes, third to Nashwan at Epsom in 1989, started his three-year-old career here. As at Epsom, the straight falls steeply downhill, before rising a furlong out.

Brighton.

CARLISLE

Flat and National Hunt

The right-handed circuit of twelve and a half furlongs at Carlisle is very testing and undulates throughout, culminating in a stiff climb towards the finish. The ideal Carlisle horse has a lengthy stride and plenty of stamina. With a strong local following, Carlisle is a highly enjoyable course to visit.

CARTMEL

National Hunt

Cartmel, in the Lake District, is an immensely popular course, partly on account of the rarity value of racing there (five days a year is the standard) but principally because of the charm of its location. An intimate track set in Cumbrian parkland, it has a left-handed circuit of little over a mile, with a run-in from the last fence of half a mile – the longest in the country.

CATTERICK BRIDGE

Flat and National Hunt

Just under eleven furlongs round, the left-handed Catterick Bridge (near Richmond in Yorkshire) is a fast and sharp track on which front-runners often excel.

CHELTENHAM

National Hunt

Cheltenham is Britain's premier National Hunt track, located in spectacular Cotswold surroundings and famed for its National Hunt Festival (see page 87), now the jewel in the crown of Channel Four's jumps coverage. There are three left-handed courses at Prestbury Park: the Old Course, the New Course (similar to the Old but using separate ground for most of the circuit, and mainly distinguishable from the Old by having two fences from the home turn rather than one), and the Park Course, which does not require the runners to go to the top of the very demanding hill at the far end of the track. Cheltenham places a great premium on stamina as well as jumping ability, and the steep uphill climb to the winning post after the final obstacle has changed the complexion of many a race.

Major races: Gold Cup, Champion Hurdle, Queen Mother Champion Chase, Triumph Hurdle, Sun Alliance Chase, Mackeson Gold Cup, Tripleprint Gold Cup, Bula Hurdle

CHEPSTOW

Flat and National Hunt

Just on the Welsh side of the Severn Bridge and home of the Welsh National, Chepstow is one of the most scenic courses in Britain. A left-handed circuit of fifteen furlongs round, it is very undulating, with a long climb out of the final bend putting a great emphasis on stamina.

Major races (Jumps): Welsh National, Rehearsal Chase, Free Handicap Hurdle

CHESTER

Flat

Situated between the banks of the River Dee and the old Roman walls of the city, Chester is the tightest Flat track in the country, with a circuit of scarcely more than one mile and a run from the final bend of just over a furlong. Consequently it favours the handy, nimble sort of horse who can break quickly and has no difficulty holding a good position. The draw is a crucial factor here, especially in shorter races, where runners with an inside berth (low numbers) have a distinct advantage. Chester racecourse – popularly known as the Roodee – can claim to stage the oldest race meeting still run at its original location, and the silver bell first run for at the request of the mayor in 1540 was the earliest recorded regular prize in racing history.

Major races: Chester Vase, Chester Cup, Ormonde Stakes, Cheshire Oaks, Dee Stakes

Chester: the home turn.

DONCASTER

Flat and National Hunt

Horses were being raced at Doncaster – home of the St Leger – in the late sixteenth century, though today's course on Town Moor was not established until 1778. The present grandstand was opened in 1969, and the siting of the parade ring right in front of the stands is a very popular feature with racegoers. Doncaster is a pear-shaped left-handed circuit of nearly two miles round. Its wide track and easy turn into the four-and-a-half-furlong straight make it a very fair course, and the only significant undulation is the slight rise and fall towards the end of the back straight. The ideal Doncaster horse is the long-striding type with the stamina and character to last home up the straight.

Major races: *Flat* – St Leger, Lincoln Handicap, November Handicap, Racing Post Trophy, Doncaster Cup, Champagne Stakes, Portland Handicap; *Jumps* – Great Yorkshire Chase

EDINBURGH

Flat and National Hunt

A right-handed track about ten furlongs round, Edinburgh has sharp turns and tends to suit the handy type of horse. A particular feature of the course is that it is often raceable even if the weather nearby is adverse. From 1 January 1996 the course is to be known as Musselburgh.

EPSOM DOWNS

Flat

Home of the Derby and Oaks, Epsom is an extraordinary racetrack, as the route of those Classics testifies. The runners go uphill on leaving the stalls before negotiating a slight right-hand bend, then tack across to the opposite rail to commence the long but irregular downhill sweep towards Tattenham Corner. The straight – just under half a mile long – has a very marked camber from the stands side towards the Downs, and after running downhill for most of its length goes slightly uphill just before the winning post. The straight five-furlong course is exceptionally fast.

Major races: Derby, Oaks, Coronation Cup, Diomed Stakes, Moët and Chandon Silver Magnum

In the spring of 1995 the Queen's Stand at Epsom Downs racecourse was used by film-makers on the new James Bond movie *Goldeneye* for a location shoot – as a Russian airport!

EXETER

National Hunt

Exeter (renamed from Devon and Exeter in 1992) is a right-handed course, two miles round and fairly stiff, providing a good test of stamina. After the downhill stretch in the back straight (where the horses disappear from view for a while), the track rises steadily, then rises further up the straight to the finish.

Major race: Haldon Gold Cup

FAKENHAM

National Hunt

Fakenham – in Norfolk, twenty-five miles north-west of Norwich – is typical of the small jumping tracks, a friendly and attractive course where the racegoers can get very close to the action on this exceptionally tight circuit. It is left-handed, one mile round and square in shape – thus ideal for compact and handy types and a good place for the front-runner.

FOLKESTONE

Flat and National Hunt

The only racecourse in Kent, Folkestone is a right-handed circuit of just over ten furlongs round, with sharp bends and marked undulations, better suited to the nippy type of horse than the long-striding galloper.

FONTWELL PARK

National Hunt

A compact figure-of-eight, the chasing course at Fontwell (near Arundel in West Sussex) provides one of the best viewing tracks in the country, while the hurdle course is a left-handed oval of about one mile which runs outside the chase track. The ideal Fontwell horse is handy and adaptable.

GOODWOOD

Flat

Perhaps the most scenically situated racecourse in the country, Goodwood is set high on the Sussex downlands with panoramic views across to the English Channel. Longer races here involve both left-hand and right-hand bends, and the track is notable for marked undulations and sharp turns, with a sweeping downhill straight which puts a premium on balance. The standard of racing is high the year round, with the July Meeting one of the highlights of the racing year.

Major races: Sussex Stakes, Goodwood Cup, Stewards' Cup, Richmond Stakes, Nassau Stakes, Celebration Mile

HAMILTON PARK

Flat

Twelve miles south-west of Glasgow, Hamilton Park consists of a straight six furlongs with a pear-shaped loop attached, and runners over the longer distances race away from the stands round the left-hand loop before swinging right and straightening up for home with five furlongs to run. The course is extremely undulating, with a stiff uphill finish.

Hamilton Park: the parade ring.

HAYDOCK PARK

Flat and National Hunt

Usefully located between Liverpool and Manchester, Haydock Park is an extremely popular venue with northern racegoers. The circuit is a left-handed oval about fifteen furlongs round, a good galloping track which, except for a slight rise throughout the straight, is fairly flat. The fences are among the most testing in the country, and under both codes the standard of sport is high.

Major races: *Flat* – Sprint Cup, Lancashire Oaks; *Jumps* – Peter Marsh Chase, Greenalls Gold Cup, Swinton Hurdle

HEREFORD

National Hunt

A right-handed track square in shape and just over a mile round, Hereford is a good galloping circuit with easy bends and a steady fall to the home straight.

HEXHAM

National Hunt

Set 800 feet above sea level in unspoiled Northumberland countryside, Hexham is one of the most scenic tracks in the land. The left-handed circuit is twelve furlongs round, with a steep climb at the end of the back straight and up the home straight.

HUNTINGDON

National Hunt

Set in flat Fenland, Huntingdon provides a fast, right-handed galloping track eleven furlongs round. Oval in shape and with easy bends, the course is suited to horses with plenty of speed.

KELSO

National Hunt

In the heart of the Border Country, Kelso has an atmosphere all its own, with strong local support and plenty of good horses in action. The left-handed chase course goes further from the stands than the hurdle course, and features a demanding run-in from the last fence of a quarter of a mile. The hurdle course is tight – little over a mile round – and suits the nippy sort of animal.

KEMPTON PARK

Flat and National Hunt

Near Sunbury-on-Thames and a few miles from the M25, Kempton, opened in 1878, has made very significant improvements to its facilities in recent years, and attracts enthusiastic following for high-class sport, particularly over the jumps: the year's highlights are Boxing Day, with the King George VI Chase, and the February pre-Cheltenham meeting, featuring the Racing Post Chase. The Kempton track is a right-handed triangle, with a straight six furlongs cutting across the middle and a spur for ten-furlong races. It is quite flat and sharp, putting the emphasis for jumpers on speed rather than stamina.

Major races: *Flat* – Easter Stakes, Queen's Prize, Rosebery Handicap, September Stakes; *Jumps* – King George VI Chase, Christmas Hurdle, Racing Post Chase

LEICESTER

Flat and National Hunt

At just under fourteen furlongs round, Leicester is a right-handed oval-shaped track that provides a strong test of stamina. There is a straight mile which runs sharply downhill almost to halfway, from where it climbs steadily to the winning post. The round course undulates throughout before joining the straight four and a half furlongs from home.

LINGFIELD PARK

Flat (turf and all-weather) and National Hunt

The turf course at Lingfield Park (near East Grinstead in Surrey) is regarded as a very useful preparation for the Derby and Oaks at Epsom: horses run to the top of the hill, about six furlongs from home, then face a sharp left-handed descent into the straight course under half a mile from home. The ten-furlong all-weather track is inside the turf.

Major races (Flat): Derby Trial, Oaks Trial

LUDLOW

National Hunt

Ludlow's right-handed course is situated in superb Shropshire countryside and features an Edwardian grandstand, built in 1904. The circuit, about one and a half miles long, is mostly flat and makes its way through a golf course, the hurdle course running further away from the stands than the chase track.

Lingfield Park displaying the true nature of all-weather racing.

MARKET RASEN

National Hunt

Sixteen miles north-east of Lincoln, Market Rasen is an exceptionally well-run and well-supported small jumping track. With minor undulations and fairly tight right-handed bends, the course is quite sharp, ten furlongs round and oval in shape, thus favouring the handy type of horse rather than the long-striding galloper.

NEWBURY

Flat and National Hunt

Newbury is widely agreed to be one of the finest racecourses in Britain. Left-handed, the circuit is just under fifteen furlongs round, wide and mostly flat, with two long straights and an easy home bend, providing a perfect test for horses at all distances under both codes. It is a particularly good track for two-year-olds (Brigadier Gerard had his first and third races here), while some jump jockeys consider the fences here the stiffest in the country, outside the Grand National course.

Major races: *Flat* – Lockinge Stakes, Fred Darling Stakes, Greenham Stakes, Super Sprint, Hungerford Stakes, Geoffrey Freer Stakes, Mill Reef Stakes, St Simon Stakes; *Jumps* – Hennessy Gold Cup, Tote Gold Trophy, Mandarin Chase

Newbury: the Berkshire Stand.

NEWCASTLE

Flat and National Hunt

Although Newcastle's most famous race is still the Northumberland Plate, a two-mile handicap first run in 1833, the course nowadays attracts most attention for its National Hunt racing, notably the Eider Chase, a traditional trial for the Grand National, and the Fighting Fifth Hurdle. The Whitbread Gold Cup was run here in 1973 while Sandown Park was being rebuilt. A very fair test of horse and rider, Newcastle has a left-handed triangular circuit of a mile and three-quarters with no sharp turns or severe contours.

Major races: *Flat* – Northumberland Plate, Beeswing Stakes; *Jumps* – Eider Chase, Fighting Fifth Hurdle

NEWMARKET

Flat

There are two racecourses at Newmarket – 'Headquarters' to racing folk on account of its being the original home of the Jockey Club and the major training centre in the country – and they are completely separate, apart from sharing a portion of track in the early stages of long-distance races. The Rowley Mile, used in the spring and autumn and home of the One

Newmarket: the Rowley Mile.

Thousand and Two Thousand Guineas as well as many other big races, is quite straight for races up to ten furlongs. Longer races have a dog-leg right-hand turn into the straight eleven furlongs from home. The runners race downhill into the Dip about a furlong out, then uphill to the line. The July Course is similar in shape to the Rowley but has a straight of about one mile, with a fierce uphill finish which makes for wonderfully exciting racing. The principal requirement for the ideal Newmarket horse on either course is the ability to see out every inch of the trip.

Major races: *Rowley Mile* – One Thousand Guineas, Two Thousand Guineas, Champion Stakes, Dewhurst Stakes, Cheveley Park Stakes, Middle Park Stakes, Cesarewitch, Cambridgeshire, Nell Gwyn Stakes, Craven Stakes, Free Handicap, Jockey Club Cup, Sun Chariot Stakes, Challenge Stakes; *July Course* – July Cup, Princess of Wales's Stakes, July Stakes, Criterion Stakes, Bunbury Cup

NEWTON ABBOT

National Hunt
The course at Newton Abbot (in Devon) is a flat, sharp, left-handed circuit about one mile round, and the tightness of its bends makes it best suited to handy, well-made horses. With its concentration of meetings in the summer months, the track is especially popular with West Country holiday-makers.

NOTTINGHAM

Flat and National Hunt
Nottingham is a left-handed track of twelve furlongs round, completely flat, oval in shape with a straight six furlongs running off at a tangent. A good galloping track and widely acknowledged as a fair test under both codes, it is particularly popular with the top Flat trainers looking to give their two-year-olds a pleasurable introduction to racing.

Nottingham.

PERTH

National Hunt
Set in the beautiful Scone Park alongside the River Tay, Perth is the most northerly of Britain's racecourses. The right-handed circuit is flat, ten furlongs round and oval in shape, with two quite easy bends and two somewhat tighter, making it a course for the nippy rather than the galloping sort.

PLUMPTON

National Hunt

Plumpton (ten miles from Brighton) may not be the most scenic of the 'gaffs' – the small jumping tracks – but the sight of a field of two-mile novice chasers hurtling down the back straight is enough to make anyone grateful not to be a jump jockey, and the atmosphere here is local and friendly. A left-handed circuit of about nine furlongs, the track has tight bends and favours the quick-jumping, nifty sort of horse.

PONTEFRACT

Flat

At about two miles round, the oval-shaped Pontefract is the longest Flat circuit in Britain. The left-handed track undulates considerably throughout and culminates in a stiff uphill finish which puts great demands on stamina, though the home straight is only two furlongs long.

REDCAR

Flat

This left-handed track, much frequented by holidaymakers, is fourteen furlongs round and flat, providing a true test for long-striding horses. The straight mile joins the round course five furlongs from home.

RIPON

Flat

Ripon is a narrow, right-handed oval, thirteen furlongs round with a six-furlong straight course. It is nearly flat but there is a pronounced dip a furlong out.

SALISBURY

Flat

Salisbury has always been a popular course on which to educate two-year-olds (Mill Reef had his first race here in 1970), as the turf is generally good and the straight course rises all the way from the mile start. All races over more than a mile involve the loop, which the runners negotiate as a left-hand turn away from the stands before swinging right-handed towards the tight home bend. Salisbury's other recent claim to fame is that it was here in April 1979 that Steve Cauthen rode his first winner in Britain – Marquee Universal for Barry Hills.

SANDOWN PARK

Flat and National Hunt

Opened in 1875, Sandown Park, near Esher in Surrey, was the first of the 'park' courses where all racegoers had to pay to get in and where, according to one early patron, 'a man could take his ladies without any fear of their hearing coarse language or witnessing uncouth behaviour'. Nowadays it is for many people the perfect racecourse, with excellent facilities, a circuit seemingly custom-built for dramatic races, and sport of the highest class both on the Flat and over jumps – with the Eclipse Stakes and the Whitbread Gold Cup the highlights of the Sandown year under their respective codes. The right-handed track is oval in shape and about one mile five furlongs round, and the very testing five-furlong sprint course cuts through the main course and has its own winning post. The highest point of the main course is beyond the winning post, making the straight a gradual uphill climb. The chasing course is among the most exhilarating in the country, the

Salisbury.

three Railway Fences in quick succession before the turn towards the Pond Fence (three from home) forming an especially tricky sequence.

Major races: *Flat* – Eclipse Stakes, Classic Trial, Gordon Richards Stakes, Brigadier Gerard Stakes, Temple Stakes, Solario Stakes; *Jumps* – Whitbread Gold Cup, Anthony Mildmay, Peter Cazalet Memorial Chase, Agfa Diamond Chase, Grand Military Gold Cup, Imperial Cup

SEDGEFIELD

National Hunt
About ten furlongs round, Sedgefield (eleven miles south-east of Durham) is a left-handed track which undulates considerably, and the bends are tight. But long-distance races here provide a true test of stamina, and the steep rise inside the final furlong has often changed the complexion of a race.

SOUTHWELL

Flat (turf and all-weather) and National Hunt
Southwell (five miles west of Newark-on-Trent) is a left-handed oval circuit, with a run from the final bend of about three furlongs. The Flat courses – turf and Fibresand all-weather – include a straight five furlongs. Some people complain of lack of atmosphere, but the facilities for racegoers here are excellent.

STRATFORD-UPON-AVON

National Hunt
Sharp and left-handed, Stratford is a track where the 'horses for courses' theory is often the place to start when assessing a race. The mile-and-a-quarter circuit is flat and fast, with two plain fences in the finishing straight often making for exciting finishes to chases.

Major race: Horse and Hound Cup

TAUNTON

National Hunt
Set amid the rolling hills of Somerset, Taunton is a right-handed track, ten furlongs round and sharp but easy in nature, with well-cambered bends now reducing the effect of its tightness.

THIRSK

Flat
Thirsk is a left-handed circuit about ten furlongs in circumference, with easy bends and minor undulations. Although on the sharp side, the track provides a fair test for horses and is blessed with good drainage and turf.

TOWCESTER

National Hunt
Towcester – eight miles south-west of Northampton – is a very testing right-handed track, fourteen furlongs round. From the stands the course rises to the first bend and then descends steeply into the back straight, which is level. From the turn out of the back straight the ground rises steadily all the way to the finish, putting great demands on a horse's stamina. Spectators here enjoy a wonderful view of the racing, which accounts in large part for the track's lasting popularity.

Opera House (Mick Kinane, right) pipping Misil (Frankie Dettori) in the 1993 running of the Coral-Eclipse Stakes, Sandown Park's biggest Flat race of the year.

UTTOXETER

National Hunt

One of the most go-ahead courses in the country, Uttoxeter (in Staffordshire, not far from Stoke-on-Trent) has made huge strides in recent years in improving the quality both of its racing and of its facilities. A gently undulating circuit with easy bends (mostly left-handed, but with a right-handed kink in the back straight) and a flat run for home, Uttoxeter is popular with jump jockeys, who consider it among the fairest of the small tracks.

Major races: Midlands National, Staffordshire Hurdle

WARWICK

Flat and National Hunt

Races from five furlongs to a mile at Warwick are very sharp, largely on account of the left-handed bend into the two-and-a-half-furlong straight. The course sets a very fair test in longer Flat and jumps races: the left-hand circuit is fourteen furlongs round and mostly flat.

Major races (Jumps): Warwick National, Regency Hurdle

WETHERBY

National Hunt

Wetherby, twelve miles north-east of Leeds, is the only course in Yorkshire to stage National Hunt racing alone, and consistently provides top-class sport. The track is a left-handed oval twelve furlongs round, with easy bends and mostly flat, and suits the free-running, galloping type of horse.

Major races: Charlie Hall Pattern Chase, Castleford Chase, Rowland Meyrick Chase

WINCANTON

National Hunt

Wincanton – located in Somerset between Yeovil and Frome – is a galloping and very fair course, about eleven furlongs round, with easy right-hand bends, no trappy undulations and well-made fences, making it the ideal venue for 'trial' races on the run-up to Cheltenham.

Major races: Desert Orchid Pattern Chase, Kingwell Pattern Hurdle, Jim Ford Challenge Cup

Yarmouth.

WINDSOR

Flat and National Hunt

Situated alongside the Thames, Windsor is an easy track, twelve furlongs round and quite flat. It is also very sharp: being a figure-of-eight, it has the runners on the turn for much of the race. The National Hunt course runs on the outside of the first loop and the inside of the second. Particularly popular here are the evening meetings in the summer, when the ideal way of getting to the course is to board a river boat at the Eton/Windsor bridge. A new grandstand at the course was opened by the Queen Mother in June 1995.

Major races (Jumps): New Year's Day Hurdle, Fairlawne Chase

WOLVERHAMPTON

Flat (all-weather)

Wolverhampton's place in racing history was assured when on 27 December 1993 it became the first course in the country to stage racing under floodlights, on the new all-weather track built on a site adjacent to the old turf course; the first meeting solely under floodlights took place on the course a few days later on 7 January 1994. Wolverhampton's £15.7 million development included a brand new grandstand which incorporates a 370-seat restaurant from which patrons can watch the racing, in the manner of punters at a greyhound track. The new course is left-handed, approximately nine furlongs round, completely flat – and highly reminiscent of an American circuit.

WORCESTER

National Hunt

Situated near the centre of the city hard by the banks of the Severn (which makes it susceptible to flooding), Worcester is a level course made up of two long straights joined at each end by fairly easy left-hand bends – thus a good track for galloping types. The fences are not stiff, making this an excellent course for a novice chaser, and the course is highly popular with jockeys and with Midlands trainers.

YARMOUTH

Flat

Yarmouth is left-handed, nearly flat, oval in shape and very much suited to long-striding horses. The straight course caters for races up to a mile and often attracts well-bred two-year-olds from the top Newmarket trainers, who view Yarmouth as the ideal introduction for the young horse.

YORK

Flat

One of the great British racecourses, York is situated just outside the city centre on the vast common land called the Knavesmire, which was once the place for public executions; racing has been taking place on the site since 1731. Wide and flat, the track is as fair a test of the Thoroughbred racehorse as can be imagined, with easy left-hand bends encouraging the relentless galloper. Races over less than a mile start on spurs off the main course. The standard of racing here is always high, with the August Meeting – including the International Stakes, the Yorkshire Oaks and the Ebor Handicap – dominating. Some have called York 'the Ascot of the North'; Yorkshire folk tend to think of Ascot as the York of the South.

Major races: International Stakes, Nunthorpe Stakes, Yorkshire Oaks, Ebor Handicap, Gimcrack Stakes, Lowther Stakes, Dante Stakes, Musidora Stakes, Yorkshire Cup, Magnet Cup

On 1 August 1898 the sporting press carried a full programme of runners and riders for a meeting at Trodmore, and the following day printed the results. But no such course existed: the scheme was an ingenious fraud, the perpetrators of which were never found. Whoever they were, their ingenuity was not rewarded, for most bookmakers refused to pay out.

York.

The Shape of Racing

The racing business employs many thousands of people, both directly and, through the betting and bloodstock industries, indirectly, and each year the destiny of billions of pounds is determined by the results of races. So it is of crucial importance that the sport is properly controlled, regulated, administered and financed. These roles belong, respectively, to the British Horseracing Board, the Jockey Club, Weatherbys and the Horserace Betting Levy Board.

THE BRITISH HORSERACING BOARD

The British Horseracing Board – BHB – was launched as the governing authority of British racing in June 1993 with the following formal aims and objectives: 'The British Horseracing Board will strive to secure and maintain significant improvements to the finances of the spectator sport, entertainment industry and betting medium of Flat and Jump horseracing. It will aim to do this for the benefit of all those who invest and work in Racing and derive enjoyment from it, and in order to enhance British Racing's competitive position internationally.'

Broadly, the BHB has taken over the role of racing's governing body from the Jockey Club, and its jurisdiction covers such areas as the fixture list and race planning, funding, training and education, marketing and the promotion of racing to potential owners, sponsors and racegoers. The board has eleven directors – four appointed by the Jockey Club, three by the Industry Committee, and two each by the Racehorse Owners' Association and the Racecourse Association – and its standing committees are the Industry Committee, the Race Planning Committee, the Racing and Thoroughbred Breeding Training Board, the Racing Development Committee and the Finance Committee.

THE JOCKEY CLUB

The Jockey Club, which was the governing body of racing until the BHB was set up and which remains responsible for such matters as discipline, the Rules of Racing and the licensing of officials, dates back to the middle of the eighteenth century.

Racing was then in a parlous state. Rules were practically non-existent, corruption and doping were widespread and criminality was rife. The Jockey Club came into being in Newmarket in an attempt to bring some sort of order to the sport. Originally it was more concerned with arranging matches and settling bets, but in due course it began to publish rules (its first recognizable order was issued in 1758) and generally establish authority over the running of races at Newmarket. A tendency developed for other racecourses to refer their disputes to the Jockey Club, and its influence grew steadily over the next century until it became the ruling body of the sport.

Three figures dominated its early history:

Sir Charles Bunbury, who became Steward of the Jockey Club in 1768, was especially influential both in building up the authority of the Club and in improving the speed of the Thoroughbred by introducing shorter races for younger horses. During his regime the Classics were founded, and the first Derby was won by his own Diomed.

Lord George Bentinck was a zealous reformer in the early nineteenth century, at a time when the sport was still very ill-regulated. He outlawed

---

SUNDAY RACING

Following an extensive campaign and in the wake of liberalizing of the Sunday trading laws, the first official race meeting on a Sunday in Great Britain took place at Doncaster on 26 July 1992. No cash betting could be allowed, but the course produced a fun-packed family day at the races – preceded by a brief religious service – which was hailed as a great success. Cheltenham followed up with a Sunday meeting the following November, and in 1993 Lingfield Park staged a Sunday meeting with a Wild West theme.

A further change in the law permitted cash betting on Sunday, and twelve fixtures were planned on the Sabbath for 1995 – though the distinction of hosting the first race meeting with cash betting goes to the Garth and South Berks Hunt point-to-point at Tweseldown on 15 January.

The first Sunday race meeting under Rules with cash betting was at Newmarket on 7 May, when the Madagans One Thousand Guineas, won by Harayir, enjoyed the distinction of being the first ever Sunday Classic.

**Previous spread:
Epsom Downs, Derby Day 1994.**

the custom of the winner's owner giving a present to the Judge after a big race, and sought a more efficient way of starting races than the prevailing one whereby the Starter shouted 'Go!' as soon as the field had made a rough line: indeed, he can be credited with the organization of race meetings in roughly the form we know them. He achieved many great benefits for English racing, but never his own ambition of leading in a Derby winner. He sold his racing interests in 1846 to concentrate on politics, and in 1848 Surplice, one of the yearlings he had disposed of, triumphed at Epsom. Bentinck was desolated: Benjamin Disraeli, encountering him in the House of Commons Library the day after the Derby, described how Bentinck 'gave a sort of superb groan. "All my life I have been trying for this, and for what have I sacrificed it?" he murmured.'

Admiral John Henry Rous, best remembered for working out the first weight-for-age scales, was elected a Steward of the Jockey Club in 1838 and gained a huge reputation as a handicapper. He became public handicapper in 1855 and pursued his duties energetically, watching races from the top of the stand with a large telescope (he was, after all, an admiral) and rushing down after the race to see which horses were blowing most. At Newmarket he would watch from the Bushes, about two furlongs from the winning post, and was in the habit of roaring at non-trying jockeys as they came by. Probably the most influential of all Turf administrators, Rous was instrumental in the transformation of racing from the ill-structured days of the early nineteenth century towards the organized sport that we now enjoy.

Today the Jockey Club formulates, enforces and administers the Rules of Racing. It investigates possible breaches of those Rules and hands out punishment to offenders. It licenses jockeys and trainers and ensures that they behave within the Rules, both on the racecourse and at training establishments. The Rules are extensive, and in order to ensure that they are all adhered to the Club has its own security service. It appoints Stewards to control individual race meetings and see that the Rules are observed, and supplies racecourse officials such as Judges, Starters, Clerks of the Scales and Veterinary Officers.

The Jockey Club – whose main base is now in Portman Square in London, though it still maintains the Jockey Club Rooms in Newmarket High Street – was incorporated by Royal Charter in 1970; changes in its Charter can be authorized only by the Sovereign in Council. It consists of six Stewards (including the Senior Steward and the Deputy Senior Steward), who are elected from the members and who serve for a period of three years (four years for the Senior and Deputy Senior Stewards), and approximately 120 individual members (each elected by the existing members), in addition to many *ex officio* members such as the Stewards of overseas Jockey Clubs.

Until comparatively recently the Jockey Club was the epitome of the male bastion, but in 1966, after years of resistance, it agreed to grant training licences to women – the first being Florence Nagle, who had to go to the Court of Appeal in order to secure the right. Another breakthrough occurred in December 1977, when the Countess of Halifax, Mrs Priscilla Hastings and Mrs Helen Johnson Houghton became the first women to be elected to membership.

A tribute to the global influence of the Jockey Club is the number of foreign racing authorities which have taken its name: the Jockey Club de Buenos Aires, the Australian Jockey Club, the Jockey Club de Belgique, the Jockey Club Brasiliero, the Royal Jockey Club of Thailand, the Jockey Club de Uruguay . . .

THE NATIONAL HORSERACING MUSEUM

Opened by Her Majesty the Queen on 30 April 1983, the National Horseracing Museum is situated, appropriately enough, at the very heart of British racing, next to the Jockey Club Rooms in the High Street, Newmarket. Over 25,000 visitors a year come to the Museum, in whose five galleries is displayed a wonderful collection of works of art, documents and memorabilia illustrating the rich history of racing over three centuries. Here you can see the skeleton of Eclipse and the stuffed head of Persimmon (who won the 1896 Derby when owned by the Prince of Wales, later Edward VII), as well as offcuts from various other famous horses. There is a reconstruction of a weighing room from the time of Fred Archer, whips and saddles used in big races, and even the woollen headband worn by Lester Piggott while he was recuperating from his horrendous accident when dragged under the Epsom stalls by Winsor Boy in 1981. Superbly mounted displays of exhibits and photographs illustrate all aspects of the sport, historic and modern – the great owners, great jockeys and trainers, racecourses, betting, and the technical wonders of the modern Turf. But the sport has not become simply a 'museum piece': films of famous races are played continuously, conveying the immediacy and excitement of the race itself.

WEATHERBYS

Weatherbys is racing's civil service, implementing the rules and regulations and generally ensuring that the day-to-day running of the sport goes as smoothly as is feasible.

The company, which operates from the BHB premises in Portman Square and from Wellingborough in Northamptonshire, is a family firm working under contract to the BHB. Its history goes back over 200 years, to the time when one James Weatherby was appointed Keeper of the Match Book, Stakeholder and Secretary to the Jockey Club in 1771. Weatherby's nephew, also James, published in 1793 the first volume of the *General Stud Book*, the official genealogical record of the English Thoroughbred, which has been published by the company ever since.

Weatherbys also produces the weekly *Racing Calendar*, the official organ of horse racing, in which are listed all big-race entries and weights, accounts of Stewards' Enquiries and other official information relating to the organization of the sport. The company maintains detailed statistical records of many aspects of the sport.

Among the particular functions for which Weatherbys is responsible are:

ENTRIES

Big races apart, a horse is entered for a race five days before it takes place. Weights are allocated the following day, either according to the advertised conditions of the race or by the BHB handicapper, depending on the nature of the event. The horse may be pulled out ('scratched') at any time up to the day before the race, when, if it is to take part, it must be declared to run.

The entry for most big races closes many weeks in advance, and the potential field is thinned out through a series of forfeit stages, when each owner will incur a further fee if he does not take the horse out of the race. Classic races close long before the running: closing date for the 1995 Vodafone Derby was 8 December 1993 (first entry fee £250), when the horses which would eventually run were yearlings, with a provision for horses to be entered as three-year-olds at a second entry stage in March 1995 at an initial fee of £6,000. For many big races a late entry will be accepted on payment of a large supplementary entry fee: you could supplement your horse for the 1995 Vodafone Oaks at Epsom Downs on 9 June seven days before the race, for a payment of £15,000.

ACCOUNTS

Every registered owner must have an account with the Jockey Club, the stakeholder Pratt & Co. or Weatherbys: the great majority choose to have one with Weatherbys. From this will be deducted entry fees, and to it will be added prize money won, after mandatory deductions have been made including percentages for the jockey, trainer, and so on.

Jockeys and trainers may have their own accounts with Weatherbys, and for jockeys who do so riding fees will be transferred directly from the owner's to the rider's account. No prize money is released to owner, trainer or jockey until the winning horse's specimen (if one has been taken) has been cleared by the Horseracing Forensic Laboratory in Newmarket.

NAMES AND COLOURS

All racehorses' names and all owners' colours must be registered with Weatherbys (see pages 33 and 92–3).

THE HORSERACE BETTING LEVY BOARD

Founded in 1961 following the legalization of off-course betting, the Levy Board provides racing with its major source of finance by collecting part of the betting turnover from the bookmakers (including the Tote) and distributing it for the greater good of the sport. The first annual levy (1962–63) raised less than £1 million; the thirty-fourth, for 1995–96, was expected to yield around £56 million.

The original purpose of the Levy Board was that the proceeds it raised should be used for 'the improvement of breeds of horse, the advancement or encouragement of veterinary science or veterinary education, and the improvement of horse racing'. Today it is the last of these aims with which the Board is principally concerned – for, with off-course betting severely depleting racecourse attendances and therefore takings at the gate, courses are in great need of financial support.

The Levy Board helps on several fronts. It provides grants and interest-free loans to racecourses, not only for the building of new stands and facilities but also for infrastructural improvements such as watering systems and drainage; it puts a large amount towards prize money, supplementing the contributions of owners, courses and sponsors; and it gives financial support in less visible areas, for example in providing more sophisticated technical equipment and subsidizing Jockey Club Security Services and the Horseracing Forensic Laboratory, with its highly elaborate techniques for detecting doping. It also puts money into the breeding industry and veterinary science.

PRIZE MONEY

The prize money for a race consists of

- stakes put up by the owners of the entered horses, plus
- added money, from sources such as sponsors, the racecourse, and the Levy Board.

It is distributed to the connections of the placed horses according to regulations set down by the Jockey Club, the distribution varying according to the sort of race and the number of placed horses' connections to be rewarded. (In recent years prizes in some big races have gone to horses placed as far down as sixth, rather than just to the customary first four. Thus the owner of Monsieur Le Cure, sixth in the 1995 Cheltenham Gold Cup, pocketed £2,534.)

Around 60 per cent of the total prize money goes to the winner, the exact proportion depending on the nature of the race. Connections of each of the first four horses receive mandatory percentages (which are separate from any 'presents' which the owner may wish to give jockey or trainer), and the regulations also allow for percentages to industry training, to the Jockeys' Valets' Attendance Fund, and to the Jockeys' Association Pension Fund. (The percentage for a winning jump jockey is higher than that for a Flat jockey, but if an amateur jockey qualifies for a percentage that sum goes to the British Horseracing Board.)

The prize money for the winning owner is expressed in terms of 'Penalty Value', which is the amount to be used for calculations should that winning horse be subject to a penalty under the conditions of a future race (and is the amount used for calculating prize money won by trainers, and so on). Penalty Value is the profit made by the winner's connections – that is, their portion of the total prize money less the owner's original stake money.

As an example, we can look at the Tote Cheltenham Gold Cup run on 16 March 1995, which falls into the category of a race where 58 per cent of total prize money must go to the winner. Tote sponsorship had meant the addition of £185,000 to stakes of £250 to enter, £500 if the horse was kept in after the first forfeit stage, and a further £250 if entry was confirmed. The race attracted an original entry of thirty-five horses, twenty-nine of whom stayed in at the forfeit stage, with nineteen confirmed (though in the event seventeen were declared to run and fifteen actually faced the Starter). Thus it cost £1,000 to run your horse in the Gold Cup, and the total entry fees were:

35 at £250	£8,750
29 at £500	£14,500
19 at £250	£4,750
total fees	£28,000

So the total prize money for the Gold Cup was:

entry fees	£28,000
added money	£185,000
total	£213,000

The Penalty Value is calculated:

58% of total prize money	£123,540
less winner's entry fee	£1,000
Penalty Value	£122,540

The race was won by Master Oats, and the prize money due to his owner Paul Matthews was specified in the Rules of Racing to be 43.39 per cent of total stakes – £92,420.70.

A few seconds from netting his owner £92,420.70, Master Oats (Norman Williamson) takes the last fence in the 1995 Tote Cheltenham Gold Cup.

THE SHAPE OF THE RACING PROGRAMME

Underpinned as it is by the essential functions of control, administration and finance, horse racing is about races, and the shape of the competitive side of the sport is carefully designed and controlled. In Flat racing the key element of this structure is the Pattern (page 71), which includes the Classics (pages 73–8).

But it is not only the top races which are subjected to strict control by the BHB. Regulations constantly monitored by the Race Planning Committee govern all meetings and the conditions of individual races, not only to guarantee the sport's participants and followers a great variety of competition, but also to provide a wide array of tests for the Thoroughbred horse and thus keep the breed on its mettle. The capabilities of horses at particular stages of development are borne very much in mind in the race-planning process, both to avoid putting unnecessary demands on a horse too early in its career and to ensure that the tests provided for it are carefully structured.

Thus races for yearlings have been banned since 1859, while two-year-olds may not run at all before the turf season starts in March, over more than six furlongs before June or more than seven furlongs before August. (In common racing parlance, on the Flat a sprinter races at five or six furlongs, a miler at around a mile, a middle-distance horse at one and a quarter to one and a half miles, and a stayer at one and three quarter miles and over.) A horse may not run in a hurdle race until 1 July of the year in which it is three years old, or four years old for a steeplechase.

There are conditions, too, for individual race meetings. For instance, at least one half of the prize money for a Flat meeting (other than an all-weather fixture) should be apportioned to races of a mile or over for three-year-olds and over; there can be no more than one selling race per day of the meeting; no single day may include more than four handicaps. In National Hunt racing at least 55 per cent of the prize money per meeting should generally go to steeplechases, and each day's programme must contain at least two chases, one of which should be of three miles or upwards.

THE PRINCIPAL TYPES OF RACE

Within this controlled programme are run many different sorts of race. The main categories of race are given below.

Weight-for-age

According to the BHB, a weight-for-age race is any race which is not a handicap or a selling race; so the category includes a variety of races. The official weight-for-age scale lays down the differences in weights to be carried by horses of different ages in order to compensate for the immaturity (and relative weakness) of younger horses. These differences vary according to the time of the year and the distance of the race: in late March a four-year-old would have to carry thirteen pounds more than a three-year-old over five furlongs, and one stone three pounds more over one mile; in early October, by which time the rapidly maturing three-year-old will almost have caught up his elder in terms of development, the difference over five furlongs will be just one pound, over a mile four pounds.

An additional factor is that fillies and mares are officially deemed to be the weaker sex, and carry less weight than colts of the same age: a female Derby runner would carry five pounds less than a male runner.

A weight-for-age race is sometimes referred to as a 'conditions race', for the entrants must satisfy certain conditions relating to age, sex or previous

The conditions of the Wysall Stakes at Leicester in October 1992 specified a one-pound weight penalty for every £500 the horse being entered had won. Trainer Paul Cole entered Run Don't Fly, presumably forgetting that the horse had won a Group Two race in Italy in 1991, and when the weights were published Run Don't Fly was down to carry . . . 21 stone 3 pounds! John McCririck could not do the weight, and the horse – unsurprisingly – did not run.

The range of racing sponsorship displayed at Goodwood in May 1992.

SPONSORSHIP

Sponsorship is a vital part of modern racing. Though some may lament the distortion that the attentions of commercial sponsors have wrought in the traditional nomenclature of the racing year – that famous old race the Nunthorpe Stakes at York, for instance, became the William Hill Sprint Championship between 1976 and 1989 – few could dispute that sponsorship has done racing a massive amount of good, by putting a great deal of money into the sport (around £10 million per year into individual races at present) and by bringing to racecourses large numbers of people whose interest would otherwise not have been engaged.

The first commercially sponsored horse race in Britain was the Whitbread Gold Cup in 1957, won by Much Obliged; the John Smith's Magnet Cup at York, first run in 1960, is the longest running sponsored Flat race. Most of the major races under both codes are now sponsored, though races at Royal Ascot are kept free from commercial links, and the Classics have been sponsored only since 1984.

A glance down the fixture list shows that alcohol and bookmaking loom large in racing sponsorship, but many companies and causes which have little or no obvious connection with racing itself are finding sponsorship an effective fund-raising or advertising medium. Taking the meetings on Easter Monday 1995 as a random sample, we find the High Tensile Bolts Handicap at Warwick ('Fancy anything in the High Tensile Bolts?') and a wide array of other sponsored events, including: Addenbrooke's Dialysis Centre Novices' Chase (Huntingdon); Gardens Night Club Novices' Chase (Wincanton); McEwans Lager Top of the North Novices' Hurdle (Qualifier) (Carlisle); Westminster-Motor Taxi Insurance Rosebery Handicap (Kempton Park); Racing Welfare Charities Mastercard Novices' Hurdle (Market Rasen); Thurlestone Hotel Four-Year-Old Novices' Hurdle (Newton Abbot); and the Pritchard Holdings plc National Hunt Flat Race (Uttoxeter).

Many sponsors will now under-write a whole day's programme, or even a whole meeting – such as the Bonusprint support of the Christmas fixture at Kempton Park or the Madagans festival at Newmarket's Guineas meeting – rather than just a single race; most supplement the prize money with an award to the stable lad or lass looking after the horse judged to be the best turned out in the parade ring; and some are even putting money towards improvement of the courses.

Taking advantage of a loosening in the sport's regulations, a fresh sponsorship initiative now making its presence very visibly felt in racing is commercial backing for training yards. Early in 1995 trainers in the Lambourn area came to an arrangement with the photocopier company Danka whereby jockeys riding Lambourn-trained horses would – with a few exceptions – advertise Danka on their silks. David Nicholson's horses were to be sponsored by Whitson Bloodstock, Michael Bell's by Kleinwort Benson – and in no time at all jockeys became miniaturized advertising hoardings, much in the way that soccer players had years earlier.

performance (winners of Group One and Group Two races, for instance, may not run in some Group Three races). Sometimes the conditions are more unusual: the Washington Singer Stakes at Newbury is restricted to two-year-old colts and geldings whose sires won a race over one and a half miles or more, a fact which caused the disqualification of 1988 winner Prince Of Dance when it was realized that his sire Sadler's Wells had not met this requirement. Weights are stipulated in the race conditions, and may vary according to age, sex, and whether the horse has won certain sorts of race – in which case it will incur a 'penalty' of a certain number of pounds above the basic weight. (A conditions race cannot be a maiden race, nor can it be a seller or claimer.)

Handicap

A handicap is a race in which the weight each horse is to carry is individually allotted by the official handicapper, who adjusts the weights according to past performance – the goal being to give all horses in a race a theoretically equal chance of winning. The BHB handicappers maintain a list of official ratings for every horse (from 0 to 140 for the Flat, 0 to 175 for National Hunt), so that handicaps can be framed very speedily. The ratings are revised weekly, but if a horse wins a race after the weights for a future race have been allotted he may incur a penalty for that later race in order to take account of the improvement in performance not yet reflected in his official rating. Weights are allotted from the highest (which will be specified in the race conditions) down to the lowest in accordance with the handicapper's assessment of each horse's chance, the lowest-ranked horse being allotted a weight which reflects its perceived chance compared with the top-ranked (and top-weighted) horse, however low such a weight may be and even if it is below the lowest weight actually to be carried in the race. This is the 'long handicap'. Any horse whose weight is so low that it is below the minimum to be carried is said to be 'out of the handicap'. If at the five-day or overnight declaration stage the highest-weighted horse still left in the race has less than the originally stipulated top weight to be carried, that horse's weight is raised to the level of the original minimum top weight and all the other weights are raised by the same amount – so a horse originally

Sponsorship of jockeys: Jamie Osborne advertising reproduction equipment at Cheltenham, 1995.

The first big handicap of the 1994 season, the William Hill Lincoln, goes to 16–1 shot Our Rita (Darryll Holland).

THE SHAPE OF RACING

THE LONG HANDICAP IN ACTION

When the weights for the Stakis Casinos Scottish Grand National at Ayr, run on 22 April 1995, were published in March, the top weight on 12 stone 7 pounds was Master Oats. Bottom of the eighty entries was Crown Eyeglass on 5 stone 12 pounds in the long handicap – though the conditions of the race stipulated that the minimum weight actually to be carried was 10 stone. Martin Pipe's Chatam was allotted 10 stone 6 pounds, and Willsford, one of Jenny Pitman's six entries, 9 stone 11 pounds.

In the event Master Oats did not run in the race – nor did any of the top nine horses in the handicap. The race conditions stated that the highest weight to be carried was not less than 11 stone 7 pounds, so Chatam – who did run – became top weight on that mark, 15 pounds higher than his original allocation, and all the weights were likewise raised 15 pounds to preserve the differentials between the horses who would take part – except that those horses still weighted below 10 stone would none the less have to carry 10 stone – so that Crown Eyeglass would be on 10 stone, even though his long handicap mark once the weights had been raised was 6 stone 13 pounds – and thus he was at a 28-pound disadvantage with Meleagris, who with his original weight of 8 stone 12 pounds raised to 9 stone 13 pounds was only one pound 'wrong' when carrying 10 stone in the race, as opposed to Crown Eyeglass being 29 pounds out of the handicap.

The raising of the weights worked to the advantage of several horses, including Willsford, whose 9 stone 11 pounds was converted by 15 pounds to 10 stone 12 pounds – thus putting him in the handicap. He won by two lengths from Sweet Duke – who was originally on 10 stone and in the race carried 15 pounds more at 11 stone 1 pound – giving Willsford three pounds. Had Master Oats or Miinnehoma (11 stone 10 pounds in the original handicap) run, and the weights not been raised, both Sweet Duke and Willsford would have carried 10 stone, and the result could have been an even closer race. (Crown Eyeglass, since you ask, pulled up.) Simplicity itself!

out of the handicap may then be racing off a true weight in relation to the new top weight (see panel).

A **limited handicap** is one in which the range of weights which the horses will carry is kept narrow (probably one and a half stone). This encourages high-class horses to be entered, as they will not be asked to concede more than a comparatively small amount of weight to any other runner. Another kind of modified handicap stipulates that the abilities of the horses taking part shall all be within a set range: for example, a handicap designated '0–70' would be open only to horses rated no higher than 70 on the BHB scale, and thus would afford an opportunity for a lower-class horse to chalk up a win.

A **nursery** is a handicap for two-year-olds, and a **rated stakes** on the Flat is a valuable handicap with a maximum weight range of 17 pounds.

By their very nature handicaps cannot be expected to sort out the very best horses, as the purest races can only be run on level terms. But by the same token they are excellent betting races: the big handicaps always attract large fields and the very notion of handicapping makes for open betting. Traditionally the major handicaps of the Flat season are the Lincoln at Doncaster, the Royal Hunt Cup (Royal Ascot), Stewards' Cup (Goodwood), Ebor (York), Ayr Gold Cup, Cambridgeshire and Cesarewitch (both Newmarket) and November Handicap (Doncaster). Many of the landmarks of the jumping season are handicaps, including the Hennessy Gold Cup and Tote Gold Trophy (both Newbury), the Whitbread Gold Cup (Sandown Park) – and, of course, the Grand National at Aintree.

Maiden race

A maiden is a horse which has not won a race. Maiden races are for 'maidens at starting', which means that if a horse is entered for a maiden race but between then and the day of the race has a win, it cannot then take part in its 'maiden'.

A racehorse can earn a very reasonable living for its connections and still remain a maiden. Needle Gun, trained by Clive Brittain, had earned £257,717 in place money from thirteen outings without winning before finally landing a small race at Yarmouth in October 1994.

Selling race

A 'seller' is a race in which the winner is sold at auction (with a reserve laid down) directly after the race, and in which other runners may be 'claimed' (bought) for an amount previously advertised. The owner of the winner may buy back the horse (in which case it is said to be 'bought in'), but even in this case a percentage of the proceeds of the sale goes to the racecourse. Selling races are usually the lowliest form of British racing.

Auction race

This is an event for two-year-old maidens which were bought as yearlings at public auction. Weight allowances are given to horses bought for lower sums. (Races with auction conditions open to winners are officially in the 'conditions stakes' bracket.)

The official definition of a **median auction race** is 'a Flat race, for maiden horses, restricted to the progeny of stallions which established a median price for the sale of yearlings contemporary with the entrants in the race based on the sale price of one or more animals at the specified sale'. Races with median auction conditions which are open to winners are officially classified as conditions races.

Claiming race

In a claiming race any runner can be claimed after the race for an advertised sum, and if the owner of any runner wishes it to carry less than the maximum weight the price at which it may be claimed is accordingly reduced. Thus the conditions for a claiming race may stipulate that the top weight to be carried is 9 stone 9 pounds and the maximum claiming price is £12,000, with a one-pound weight allowance for each £1,000 taken off the claiming price. If you put a claiming price of £6,000 on your horse when entering it, it will carry 9 stone 3 pounds. Claims for any individual horse are made by ballot, where a maximum of one claim is allowed per prospective buyer. An owner can make a 'friendly claim' and attempt to claim his own horse back.

While most of the above sorts of race take place in National Hunt racing, and the very best jumping races are organized into a Pattern similar to that which applies on the Flat, there are others which are exclusive to jump racing:

Novices' race

A novice hurdle or novice steeplechase is a race for horses which have not won a hurdle race or a steeplechase respectively before 1 May of the previous season. (Novice events are by no means confined to young horses: Panegyrist only lost his novice tag when winning a steeplechase at Ayr in March 1989 at the ripe old age of fourteen, and the legendary Amrullah (see page 33), who never won in 24 outings over hurdles and 39 over fences, was still formally a novice when he was retired.)

Hunter-chase

This is a steeplechase for horses which have been regularly hunted during the current season, according to a Hunter's Certificate which must be endorsed by a Master of Foxhounds. Hunter-chases are popular targets for some top chasers in the twilight of their careers, but the regulations have been tightened to prevent these high-class horses cleaning up all the big prizes at the expense of more 'genuine' hunters.

In both Flat and National Hunt racing, the programme of races is divided into seven categories – from A down to G – depending on each event's status and nature and the prize money on offer (and H in jump racing for hunter-chases and NH flat races). Thus on the Newmarket card on 20 April 1995, the Group Three Craven Stakes (Penalty Value £21,754) was Class A, the Wisbech Handicap (£5,900) Class C, and the Granby Maiden Stakes (£5,390) Class D.

THE JUMPING PATTERN

A fresh Pattern was introduced to the National Hunt season in 1990 to give more of a structure to the jumping season and bring a stronger emphasis to the mid-term period around Christmas. The Pattern divided in 1994–95 into Grades One, Two and Three, and consisted of 105 top races. Grades One and Two consist of the big events in twelve different categories (according to the nature of the race and its distance), plus one bumper, and each category has two Grade One races: thus juvenile hurdlers have Grade One events in the Finale Hurdle at Chepstow in late December and the Daily Express Triumph Hurdle at Cheltenham in March; the twin peaks for two-mile hurdlers are the Christmas Hurdle at Kempton and the Champion Hurdle at Cheltenham; long-distance hurdlers have their Grade One events in the Long Walk Hurdle at Ascot in December and the Stayers' Hurdle at the Cheltenham Festival. Likewise, each category of steeplechasers has two big dates: the two-milers have the Tingle Creek at Sandown in December and the Queen Mother Champion Chase at Cheltenham in March; the three-mile novices the Feltham Chase at Kempton on Boxing Day and the Sun Alliance at Cheltenham; and the three-mile chasers the traditional twin targets of the King George VI Chase at Kempton on Boxing Day and the Cheltenham Gold Cup in March.

In all there were twenty-five races in Grade One in the 1994–95 season, with sixty-five supporting events in Grade Two, and fifteen in Grade Three: this last group includes the big handicap hurdles and chases.

National Hunt Flat Race

There are National Hunt races which spare the runners the inconvenience of clearing obstacles. These races – popularly known as 'bumpers' – are an increasingly valuable testing ground for young jumping horses. They are confined to four-, five- and six-year-olds who have not run under the Rules of Racing except in NH Flat Races. Garrison Savannah, winner of the 1991 Cheltenham Gold Cup, is just one example of a well-known chaser who started his racing career in bumpers: he won a National Hunt Flat Race at Kempton Park as a four-year-old in February 1987 at 25–1.

The racing programme allows for variations on the basic categories of race. There are races in which all the riders are apprentices or conditional jockeys, or ladies, or amateurs; in which the runners can only be fillies, or colts, or mares – or (as in the case of a steeplechase at Warwick) horses aged ten years or over. Occasionally there are what may be termed 'novelty races', for

At the Garth and South Berks Hunt point-to-point at Tweseldown on 15 January 1995 (the first Sunday race meeting with cash betting) Prince Rockaway leads Double U Dee. Many people's experience of racing begins with or is confined to a visit to their local point-to-point meeting, where racegoers can often see old favourites from steeplechasing under Rules, or promising young horses who will later became household names: Norton's Coin ran in point-to-points before embarking on a career under Rules (as 'official' racing is known) which led to 100–1 Gold Cup glory in 1990, pulling up on his first appearance 'between the flags', refusing on his second and being beaten a distance on his third before finding the winning touch. Point-to-point meetings, usually held on farmland and staged to benefit a hunt, retain a very strong local flavour.

GRADE ONE RACES OVER JUMPS, 1994–95

Tingle Creek Chase
Sandown Park: 2 miles

Long Walk Hurdle
Ascot: 3¼ miles

Feltham Novices' Chase
Kempton Park: 3 miles

King George VI Chase
Kempton Park: 3 miles

Christmas Hurdle
Kempton Park: 2 miles

Finale Junior Hurdle
Chepstow: 2 miles

Challow Hurdle
Newbury: 2½ miles

Tolworth Hurdle
Sandown Park: 2 miles

Cleeve Hurdle
Cheltenham: 2½ miles

Scilly Isles Novices' Chase
Sandown Park: 2½ miles

Comet Chase
Ascot: 2½ miles

Supreme Novices' Hurdle
Cheltenham: 2 miles

Arkle Chase
Cheltenham: 2 miles

Champion Hurdle
Cheltenham: 2 miles

Sun Alliance Novices' Hurdle
Cheltenham: 2½ miles

Queen Mother Champion Chase
Cheltenham: 2 miles

Sun Alliance Chase
Cheltenham: 3 miles

Festival Bumper
Cheltenham: 2 miles

Triumph Hurdle
Cheltenham: 2 miles

Stayers' Hurdle
Cheltenham: 3 miles 1 furlong

Cheltenham Gold Cup
Cheltenham: 3¼ miles

Maghull Chase
Aintree: 2 miles

Melling Chase
Aintree: 2½ miles

Sefton Novices' Hurdle
Aintree: 3 miles

Aintree Hurdle
Aintree: 2½ miles

celebrities or 'golden oldie jockeys' or some such: at Kempton Park in June 1990 there was a ladies' race in which every rider had to be the wife, daughter or secretary (why not the mother?) of a trainer; the Shadwell Estates Private Handicap, opening event of Ascot's annual charity fixture in September 1992, gave Brough Scott his first winner for twenty-one years, and John Oaksey his last race-ride in public; and the Aintree curtain-raiser on Grand National Day 1995 was a race in which all jockeys had to have won the Grand National – Maurice Barnes, hero of the 1979 National on Rubstic, landed a highly popular novelty event on Chinour.

The great variety of types of race is another of the enduring attractions of British racing.

THE PATTERN

Pattern races, or Group races, are the elite contests of Flat racing: a series of tests for the best horses at all ages and at different distances, together they give the season its carefully constructed form, ensuring top-class and competitive racing on a Europe-wide scale.

The idea was born in the mid-1960s in response to worries about the lack of balance between British and French racing, and the Duke of Norfolk's Pattern of Racing Committee recommended in 1965 a system to embrace England, Ireland and France. (Germany and Italy joined later.) The aim of the Pattern was not to invent races but to grade existing races in such a way, according to the report of the Committee, as 'to ensure that a series of races over the right distances and at the right time of the year are available to test the best horses of all ages and . . . to ensure that the horses remain in training long enough and race often enough to be tested properly for constitution and soundness.'

In addition to this noble aim in pursuit of the excellence of the Thoroughbred breed, the existence of the Pattern guarantees enthusiasts a constant stream of high-class racing throughout the season and makes it

GROUP ONE RACES ON THE FLAT IN 1995 (IN GREAT BRITAIN)

Madagans Two Thousand Guineas
Newmarket: 1 mile, for three-year-old colts and fillies

Madagans One Thousand Guineas
Newmarket: 1 mile, for three-year-old fillies

Lockinge Stakes
Newbury: 1 mile, for four-year-olds and upwards

Vodafone Oaks
Epsom Downs: $1\frac{1}{2}$ miles, for three-year-old fillies

Vodafone Coronation Cup
Epsom Downs: $1\frac{1}{2}$ miles, for four-year-olds and upwards

Vodafone Derby
Epsom Downs: $1\frac{1}{2}$ miles, for three-year-old colts and fillies

St James's Palace Stakes
Royal Ascot: 1 mile, for three-year-old colts and fillies

Coronation Stakes
Royal Ascot: 1 mile, for three-year-old fillies

Gold Cup
Royal Ascot: $2\frac{1}{2}$ miles, for four-year-olds and upwards

Coral-Eclipse Stakes
Sandown Park: $1\frac{1}{4}$ miles, for three-year-olds and upwards

July Cup
Newmarket: 6 furlongs, for three-year-olds and upwards

King George VI and Queen Elizabeth Diamond Stakes
Ascot: $1\frac{1}{2}$ miles, for three-year-olds and upwards

Sussex Stakes
Goodwood: 1 mile, for three-year-olds and upwards
International Stakes

York: 1 mile $2\frac{1}{2}$ furlongs, for three-year-olds and upwards

Aston Upthorpe Yorkshire Oaks
York: $1\frac{1}{2}$ miles, for three-year-old fillies and upwards

Nunthorpe Stakes
York: 5 furlongs, for two-year-olds and upwards

Sprint Cup
Haydock Park: 6 furlongs, for two-year-olds and upwards

Teleconnection St Leger
Doncaster: 1 mile 6 furlongs 132 yards, for three-year-old colts and fillies

Queen Elizabeth II Stakes
Ascot: 1 mile, for three-year-olds and upwards

Fillies' Mile
Ascot: 1 mile, for two-year-old fillies

Cheveley Park Stakes
Newmarket: 6 furlongs, for two-year-old fillies

Middle Park Stakes
Newmarket: 6 furlongs, for two-year-old colts

Dewhurst Stakes
Newmarket: 7 furlongs, for two-year-old colts and fillies

Dubai Champion Stakes
Newmarket: $1\frac{1}{4}$ miles, for three-year-olds and upwards

Racing Post Trophy
Doncaster: 1 mile, for two-year-old colts and fillies

---

difficult for the best horses from several countries to avoid meeting each other regularly.

The recommended system was finally implemented in 1971, with the Pattern races divided into three groups:

Group One: Classics and other races of major international importance.
Group Two: Races of international importance but at a level just below championship standard.
Group Three: Primarily domestic races regarded as preparatory contests for the higher groups (such as Classic trials).

Group One races are always run without penalties on a weight-for-age-and-sex basis, whereas penalties can apply in Groups Two and Three races, based on previous performance in Pattern races.

Below Group races are **Listed races**, a set of races designed to identify racehorses of superior merit but below Group standard.

The Pattern is fluid, allowing the status of a particular race to be altered if appropriate: thus the Lockinge Stakes at Newbury was upgraded from Group Two to Group One in 1995 to provide an early-season opportunity for the cream of the older milers, whereas Doncaster's Flying Childers Stakes was downgraded from Group One to Group Two in 1979 following its consistent failure to bring together the best sprinting two-year-olds.

The idea is to space out the best races over similar distances for horses of particular age groups. So a four-year-old ten-furlong specialist might have the season mapped out around three Group One peaks: the Eclipse Stakes at Sandown Park in July, the International Stakes at York in August and the Champion Stakes at Newmarket in October.

There were 107 Pattern races scheduled for 1995 in Great Britain, with twenty-five at Group One level, twenty-seven at Group Two, and fifty-five at Group Three. Of the twenty-five races designated Group One, sixteen were scheduled to be covered by Channel Four.

When winning the Jockey Club Cup at Newmarket in October 1994, Further Flight made history as the first horse to land the same Group race in Britain four years in a row.

THE CLASSICS

The five Classics – the One Thousand Guineas, Two Thousand Guineas, Derby, Oaks and St Leger – are the landmarks of the Flat season. They offer to three-year-old colts and fillies the challenge of having the speed to beat the best of the generation over a mile at Newmarket in the spring, the agility to do so again over one and a half miles of very different terrain at Epsom in the summer, and the stamina and resilience to win over a mile and three-quarters at Doncaster in the autumn.

But they were not planned as a series. The five races were founded individually in the late eighteenth and early nineteenth centuries in response to the growing inclination to race horses at younger ages and over shorter distances than hitherto. Their grouping together into the Classic programme evolved later; and in the modern era, when specialization in racing is on the increase, for any colt to take the Triple Crown by winning the three legs of the Classic programme for which he is eligible (the One Thousand Guineas and the Oaks are for fillies only) is a remarkable feat. For many people the Classics are still the ultimate test of the Thoroughbred.

No horse has ever won all five Classics. In 1868 Formosa won the Two Thousand Guineas (dead-heating), One Thousand Guineas, Oaks and St Leger. In 1902 Sceptre won the same four races outright, and finished fourth in the Derby.

The One Thousand Guineas

Run over 1 mile at Newmarket, for three-year-old fillies only, carrying 9 stone.

The One Thousand Guineas, which under the sponsorship of Madagans became in 1995 the first English Classic to be run on a Sunday, is the youngest of the five races; the first running in 1814, when a field of only five runners went to post (from an initial entry of ten, each paying 100 guineas to enter – hence one thousand guineas), was won by Charlotte. In its early years the race was run over the Ditch Mile, a course much flatter and therefore less demanding than the Rowley Mile, to which the race was transferred in the early 1870s.

It is customary for One Thousand Guineas winners to be aimed for the second fillies' Classic, the Oaks, and several have won both races. But only the grey filly Tagalie in 1912 has ever won the One Thousand and the Derby: she took the Newmarket race at 20–1 and won at Epsom at 100–8. Two days after the Derby she was well beaten in the Oaks at 2–1 on.

Recent winners have included many outstanding fillies, including Pebbles, who in 1984 won the first sponsored running.

The Two Thousand Guineas

Run over 1 mile at Newmarket, for three-year-old colts and fillies: colts carry 9 stone, fillies 8 stone 9 pounds.

The Two Thousand Guineas has the distinction of holding the record for the number of entries in one race: 1,001 horses were entered for the 1974 running. Just twelve of them went to post.

In 1809 Wizard beat seven rivals in the first Two Thousand Guineas (twenty-three entries at 100 guineas each – roughly two thousand guineas!), and the race has been run on the Rowley Mile ever since, except during the Second World War, when both Guineas races were transferred to the July Course, the Rowley course being requisitioned by the RAF. Like the One Thousand, it was first sponsored – by General Accident – in 1984.

The Two Thousand Guineas is the high point of the early part of the Flat season, and has produced some memorable races. In 1971 it provided one of the most hotly contested events of the post-war era, the top three in the betting going off at

6–4 Mill Reef
2–1 My Swallow
11–2 Brigadier Gerard

in a field of six. Brigadier Gerard swept past his rivals in the closing stages to win by an easy three lengths from Mill Reef on the only occasion that these two famous horses ever met.

In 1984 El Gran Senor powered home from Chief Singer, 1986 saw Dancing Brave trounce Green Desert, and in 1989 Nashwan announced his arrival in the top bracket and landed a hefty gamble. But these notable performances were rivalled – if not eclipsed – by the powerhouse performance in 1993 of Zafonic, who stormed up the hill to beat Barathea by three and a half lengths (see pages 180–2).

And the 1995 renewal saw one of the great Two Thousand Guineas occasions, as Pennekamp swooped to explode the Triple Crown aspirations of Celtic Swing by a head.

The 1995 Vodafone Derby at Epsom Downs: Lammtara (Walter Swinburn, left) collars Tamure (Frankie Dettori, white cap) close home, with Presenting (Cash Asmussen, white colours with green hoop) third and Fahal (Richard Hills, right) fourth.

The Derby

Run over 1½ miles at Epsom Downs for three-year-old colts and fillies: colts carry 9 stone, fillies 8 stone 9 pounds.

No event in the world compares with Derby Day; a great sporting occasion, it is also very much more than that, as tens of thousands of people gather on Epsom Downs, just a few miles outside London, to indulge in what has been called Britain's greatest annual celebration. What they are celebrating is not only the running of what still claims to be the most famous horse race in the world, a race which has given its name to imitations around the globe, but also the Derby as a social institution: it is a day when class differences are traditionally forgotten, or at least disregarded, as the entire spectrum of society from the Royal Family down joins together for a day at the races.

This tradition goes back a long way. In the middle of the nineteenth century, the halcyon days of the Derby as pure festivity, the *Illustrated London News* noted:

On Derby Day the patrician puts his pride into the pocket of his gossamer paletot [loose coat] and is perfectly ready to be hail fellow well met with the humblest of the working classes. None save the most ill-conditioned curmudgeons lose their temper at the witticisms levelled at them on the Hill or in coming and going. If things are thrown at you, just throw them back. But there are limits – oranges and lobster claws are just all right but not bags of flour or bad eggs.

For many decades in Victorian times parliament suspended business on Derby Day so that MPs could join the tumultuous throng on the Downs.

Such an occasion would have been far from the thoughts of the twelfth Earl of Derby and Sir Charles Bunbury when they hatched the plan which led to the first running of the race on 4 May 1780, and whether or not the story is true that they tossed a coin to see which man's name would be given to the race, it seems that the Earl was the principal proponent of the idea. For it was he who had organized the first running of the Oaks the previous year, an experiment considered such a success that it was decided to repeat the formula of a race at Epsom for three-year-olds, this time for both colts and fillies and to be run over a mile. (The distance was not increased to a mile and a half until 1784.)

That first Derby was won – fittingly – by Sir Charles Bunbury's Diomed, and Bunbury was to win it twice more, with Eleanor and Smolensko.

The Derby was run at Newmarket during both World Wars, and was first sponsored (by Ever Ready) in 1984, when El Gran Senor, apparently coasting to victory halfway up the straight, had to give best to Secreto by a short head after a desperate struggle. Many runnings of the race have featured thrillingly close finishes, and the whole history of the Derby is full of spectacle, heroism and drama . . .

1844

The first horse past the post had been entered as the three-year-old Running Rein. He was, in fact, a four-year-old named Maccabeus, who had come under extreme suspicion the previous year when winning a two-year-old race at Newmarket as a three-year-old, the intrigue being masterminded by his owner Goodman Levy. A group of prominent Turf figures headed by Lord George Bentinck tried to prevent 'Running Rein' taking part in the Derby, but the Stewards decided that he should be permitted to run. He won from Orlando, whose owner duly sued Mr Wood, in whose name Running Rein had competed. The judge in the case, remarking that 'if gentlemen condescended to race with blackguards, they must condescend to expect to be cheated,' found against Wood, and the race went to Orlando.

It is almost incidental to record the other happenings in this Derby. Another runner, Leander, was struck into by Running Rein and broke his

'The Derby is a little like your first experience of sex – hectic, strenuous, memorably pleasant and over before you know it.'
BILL BRYSON

The oldest jockey to win the Derby was John Forth, who was over sixty when riding Frederick to victory in 1829. The youngest – at least this century – was Lester Piggott, eighteen when winning on Never Say Die in 1954. Walter Swinburn was an older eighteen when taking the 1981 race on Shergar. John Parsons is believed to have been sixteen when winning on Caractacus in 1862, but this has not been verified.

The Oaks

Run over 1½ miles at Epsom Downs, for three-year-old fillies carrying 9 stone.

The Oaks is the second oldest of the Classics, having been first run in May 1779, three years after the first St Leger. The twelfth Earl of Derby, whose name was soon to be immortalized by the greater Epsom Classic launched the following year, instituted the Oaks and named it after his house near Epsom. His own Bridget won the inaugural running.

Four fillies have won the Derby as well as the Oaks: Eleanor (1801), Blink Bonny (1857), Signorinetta (1908) and Fifinella (1916), though even to attempt the double would be practically unthinkable today.

Pawneese and Time Charter were recent Oaks winners who went on to win Britain's most important middle-distance race open to older horses, the King George VI and Queen Elizabeth Diamond Stakes, but even their achievements do not match the extraordinary record of Cherimoya, who in the 1911 Oaks won a Classic in the only race of her life (a feat matched by the 1838 Derby winner Amato). She was ridden by Fred Winter, father of the great National Hunt jockey and trainer.

The Oaks was run at Newmarket during both World Wars, and was first sponsored in 1984.

The St Leger

Run over 1 mile, 6 furlongs, 132 yards at Doncaster, for three-year-old colts and fillies: colts carry 9 stone, fillies 8 stone 9 pounds.

The St Leger, the oldest Classic, was first run on Cantley Common, Doncaster, in 1776, transferring to its present stage on the Town Moor two years later. Named after a prominent local sportsman, Lieutenant Colonel Anthony St Leger, it was run over two miles until 1813, when its distance was shortened to one mile, six furlongs, 193 yards. Those 193 yards were reduced to 132 in 1826 and further down to 127 in 1969 before reverting to 132. Pushed around the country by the wars, the St Leger was run at Newmarket from 1915 to 1918, at Thirsk in 1940, Manchester in 1941, Newmarket in 1942–44 and York in 1945. In 1989 subsidence in the Doncaster straight caused the St Leger to be abandoned and moved up to Ayr, where it was run a week after its originally scheduled date and won by Michelozzo.

The only Classic run in the north, the St Leger has always attracted huge local support and is one of the highlights of the later part of the Flat season. Its prestige became rather dented for a while in the 1970s and there was even talk of opening it to older horses (as happened with the Irish St Leger), but the temptation was resisted, and although its proximity to the running of the Prix de l'Arc de Triomphe means that it is no longer automatically on the autumn agenda of the top three-year-olds, it has regained much of its lost reputation by attracting many top-class horses, not all of whom have been successful. Shergar's defeat in 1981 (he was fourth to Cut Above at 9–4 on) was a major sensation, and Alleged, who was to win the Arc twice, went down by a length and a half to the Queen's Dunfermline in 1977 after a protracted duel up the straight. Other notable occasions in recent years were the victories of Sun Princess (1983), Oh So Sharp (1985) and User Friendly (1992), all of whom had won the Oaks; of Reference Point, a brilliant Derby winner, in 1987; and of Commanche Run, whose neck victory over Baynoun in 1984 in the first sponsored running gave Lester Piggott his record-breaking twenty-eighth Classic.

But a local triumph in the St Leger is what really raises the Doncaster roof, and when Apology won the race in 1874 (her third Classic win) ridden by Yorkshire jockey John Osborne, the cheering is said to have been heard at York Minster.

Snurge, trained by Paul Cole and winner of the St Leger in 1990, holds the record for prize money by a European-trained horse, with earnings officially calculated as the equivalent of £1,283,794 accrued over six seasons' racing and in six different countries – Britain, Ireland, France, Italy, Germany and Canada.

THE INTERNATIONAL SCENE

As an example of how racing has become truly international, take Barathea, winner of the Breeders' Cup Mile in 1994. He was born in Ireland, by the great stallion Sadler's Wells, who himself was born in the USA. Barathea's co-owner Sheikh Mohammed is from Dubai. The horse's breeder and other co-owner Gerald Leigh is based in Northamptonshire. His trainer Luca Cumani is Italian but trains at Newmarket in Suffolk. Barathea was ridden to Breeders' Cup glory at Churchill Downs by Lanfranco Dettori, who is also Italian. In his previous races during 1994 Barathea had been ridden by the Irish champion jockey, Mick Kinane; in the 1993 Breeders' Cup Mile he had been partnered by the American rider Gary Stevens, and in other races that year by Michael Roberts (South African) and Pat Eddery (Irish). He raced in England, Ireland, France and the USA.

Breeding Thoroughbreds has long been carried out on an international basis, and with the ease of modern transport it is becoming increasingly common for horses' racing campaigns to be planned on a global, rather than a national, basis. The following are the major countries with which British racing is involved.

IRELAND

Ireland produces some of the world's finest Thoroughbred stock, especially steeplechasers, and although many of the best young chasing horses are sold to race in Britain, the continuing success of Irish bloodstock wherever it races pays eloquent tribute to the excellence of Irish breeding. In Ireland racing is a way of life, and it is no surprise that the Irish influence is widely felt in other areas of the sport: many Flat jockeys now based in England are Irish or of Irish extraction, and there is a long and honourable tradition of jumping jockeys from Ireland – notable current examples including Richard Dunwoody (from Ulster, though in racing terms there is no border), Adrian Maguire and Norman Williamson. The country boasts twenty-seven racecourses, the grandest of which is The Curragh, situated on a vast plain about thirty miles outside Dublin and home of all the Irish Classics.

Other courses which are often seen on British television include Leopardstown, in suburban Dublin, on which are run the Irish Champion Stakes, the Hennessy Gold Cup (Ireland's equivalent of the Cheltenham Gold Cup and not to be confused with the Hennessy at Newbury), the Ladbroke Hurdle and several other good jumping races; Fairyhouse,

The field for the 1993 Budweiser Irish Derby at The Curragh makes its way across to the start.

north-west of Dublin, home of the Irish Grand National, run on Easter Monday; and Punchestown, venue of the great three-day festival meeting in April.

The major Irish races are:

Irish Grand National
Fairyhouse, 3 miles 5 furlongs

First run in 1870, the Irish Grand National bears little relation to its Liverpool counterpart but has been won in its time by some famous horses – notably Arkle, who carried 12 stone to victory in 1964 as a seven-year-old after his first Cheltenham Gold Cup triumph over Mill House. Flyingbolt won the race in 1966, and Brown Lad won it three times. The only horse since the war to have won both the Irish and the Liverpool races is Rhyme 'N' Reason, who won at Fairyhouse in 1985 when trained by David Murray Smith and Liverpool in 1988 from the stable of David Elsworth, who in 1990 sent out Desert Orchid to take the Irish event – the horse's only steeplechase outside England.

Irish Two Thousand Guineas
The Curragh, 1 mile

Often the next stop for horses who have run in the Two Thousand Guineas at Newmarket, this is always a high-class race. Triptych was the first filly ever to win when taking the race in 1985, and Don't Forget Me in 1987 the first horse to do the Newmarket–Curragh double since Right Tack in 1969. Don't Forget Me's trainer Richard Hannon repeated the feat with Tirol in 1990, and Lester Piggott completed the double on Rodrigo de Triano in 1992. Other notable performances in the race in recent years came in 1991, when Fourstars Allstar became the first American-trained horse ever to win a European Classic, and in 1994, when Robert Sangster's Turtle Island won by the astonishing margin of fifteen lengths.

Irish One Thousand Guineas
The Curragh, 1 mile

This race, too, often sees runners coming on from Newmarket, though to date no filly has ever won the Irish race after triumphing on the Rowley Mile. Recent winners have included very high-class fillies such as Cairn Rouge (1980), Katies (1984), Al Bahathri (1985), Sonic Lady (1986), Forest Flower (1987), Kooyonga (1991) and Marling (1992).

Irish Derby
The Curragh, 1½ miles

One of the major international events of the Flat season, the Irish Derby is always an important contest. In 1962 the race received a massive injection of cash through its connection with the Irish Sweeps – that year the Irish Derby was worth £50,027, the Epsom Derby £34,786 – and today it is a natural target for the Epsom winner: since 1970 Nijinsky, Grundy, The Minstrel, Shirley Heights, Troy, Shergar, Shahrastani, Kahyasi, Generous and Commander In Chief have added the Irish Derby to victory in the English race. Salsabil in 1990 was the first filly to win since Gallinaria in 1900, and Balanchine in 1994 emulated Salsabil by winning the Irish Derby in the wake of victory in the Oaks at Epsom. Often the Irish Derby has the extra spice of staging the first meeting between the winners of the English and French Derbies – as was the case when Generous beat Suave Dancer in 1991 and Commander In Chief beat Hernando in 1993.

Irish Oaks

The Curragh, 1½ miles

First run in 1895, the Irish Oaks is now a major international contest. A staggering burst of acceleration in this race in 1973 introduced most of the racing world to Dahlia, who went on to become one of the best female racehorses of the modern era. Many winners of the Epsom Oaks have gone on to take the Irish, including Fair Salinia, who won it in 1978 on the controversial disqualification of Sorbus, Diminuendo, who dead-heated with Melodist in 1988, and User Friendly in 1992.

Irish Champion Stakes

Leopardstown, 1¼ miles

First run at Phoenix Park in 1984 and transferred to Leopardstown for the 1991 running after that course shut down, the Irish Champion Stakes has an exceptionally distinguished list of winners: Sadler's Wells took the inaugural running, and the first decade of the race's history was completed by winners Commanche Run, Park Express, Triptych, Indian Skimmer, Carroll House, Elmaamul, Suave Dancer, Dr Devious and Muhtarram. Of those, Carroll House and Suave Dancer went on to win the Prix de l'Arc de Triomphe, while in 1992 Dr Devious and St Jovite produced one of the greatest races of the modern era, locked together in a desperate struggle up the straight until Dr Devious got his head in front on the line by a minute margin.

Irish St Leger

The Curragh, 1¾ miles

The Jefferson Smurfit Irish St Leger run on 8 October 1983 made Turf history as the first running of an English or Irish Classic race open to horses over the age of three – and it was won by the four-year-old filly Mountain Lodge. The decision to open the race to older horses reflected concern at the diminishing status of the race, run as it is so close to the Prix de l'Arc de Triomphe. Vintage Crop won the race in 1993 en route to his historic victory in the Melbourne Cup, and repeated that win in 1994.

FRANCE

There are no bookmakers in France, and the betting monopoly of the Pari-Mutuel totalisator system allows a large proportion of the money wagered to be ploughed back into the sport, keeping the level of prize money high. So French races are very much on the agenda for British-trained horses, and not only the very best ones: many trainers like to take their early-season types to race at the seaside track of Cagnes-sur-Mer in February in order to get them into trim before the home season on turf starts the following month.

France is of course a much larger country than Britain and this has led to a more centralized pattern of racing. There are two major training centres not far from Paris, at Chantilly and Maisons-Laffitte; race meetings are held regularly at Longchamp (in the Bois de Boulogne in Paris) and Saint-Cloud, not far from the centre of the city, and just outside the capital at Evry, Maisons-Laffitte and Chantilly. In August almost the whole racing community decamps to Deauville, on the Normandy coast, for the meeting which climaxes in the valuable one-mile race the Prix Jacques le Marois.

French racehorses have made many telling raids on the big British Flat races, and in the last few years the enterprise of trainer François Doumen has seen major jumps prizes crossing the Channel: Nupsala caused a shock when winning the King George VI Rank Chase at Kempton Park in 1987, and his stablemate The Fellow captured the same prestigious race twice, in 1991 and 1992. In the Cheltenham Gold Cup, The Fellow was short-headed twice – by Garrison Savannah in 1991 and Cool Ground in 1992 – and

Derby decider at The Curragh in 1993: Epsom hero Commander In Chief (Pat Eddery) holds off Chantilly winner Hernando (Cash Asmussen) in the Budweiser Irish Derby.

finished fourth in 1993 before finally coming triumphantly good in the 1994 renewal, staying on up the run-in to beat Jodami and give French racing one of its greatest moments in Britain.

The major French races in which British horses seek revenge are:

Poule d'Essai des Poulains
Longchamp, 1 mile
The French equivalent of the Two Thousand Guineas, this race has been won by many brilliant horses, such as Blushing Groom in 1977. In 1981 Recitation, trained by Guy Harwood, provided a rare British win.

Poule d'Essai des Pouliches
Longchamp, 1 mile
This is the French equivalent of the One Thousand Guineas, and the list of winners is glittering: it includes Allez France, Ivanjica, Dancing Maid, Three Troikas, Miesque, Ravinella and East of the Moon.

Prix du Jockey-Club
Chantilly, $1\frac{1}{2}$ miles
The French Derby, the Prix du Jockey-Club usually determines the identity of the best three-year-old in France. Since the war it has been won by such notable performers as Scratch II, Sicambre, Herbager, Right Royal, Val de Loir, Reliance, Sassafras, Youth, Acamas, Bikala, Assert, Caerleon (both trained in Ireland, Assert – the first foreign-trained winner – by David O'Brien and Caerleon by his father Vincent), Bering, Suave Dancer and Hernando. The first victory in the race by a British-trained runner came in 1989 when Sheikh Mohammed's Old Vic powered to a seven-length success under Steve Cauthen, the second in 1990 when Pat Eddery drove Sanglamore to a hard-fought win over Epervier Bleu, and the third in 1995 when Kevin Darley and Celtic Swing battled home from Poliglote and Winged Lore.

Prix de Diane
Chantilly, 1 mile $2\frac{1}{2}$ furlongs
This is popularly known as the French Oaks, though it is shorter than its Epsom equivalent: its distance proved an attraction for Henry Cecil's Indian Skimmer, who slammed Miesque in the race in 1987. Cecil won again with Rafha in 1990. Other notable recent winners have been Pawneese, who won after taking the Epsom Oaks in 1986, and Highclere, who won for the Queen in 1974 after winning the One Thousand Guineas at Newmarket.

Grand Prix de Saint-Cloud
Saint-Cloud, 1 mile $4\frac{1}{2}$ furlongs
This is one of the major middle-distance targets in mid-season. Sea Bird II won it in 1965, Rheingold took it twice, and Teenoso won on his way to victory in the King George VI and Queen Elizabeth Diamond Stakes in 1984. User Friendly, Oaks and St Leger winner in 1992, won in 1993.

Prix Royal-Oak
Longchamp, 1 mile $7\frac{1}{2}$ furlongs
Although nominally the French equivalent of the St Leger, the Prix Royal-Oak has been open to four-year-olds and upwards since 1979, and has since then been won by good stayers such as Gold River and Ardross. Moonax in 1994 became the first horse to complete the St Leger–Prix Royal-Oak double.

Prix de l'Abbaye de Longchamp

Longchamp, 5 furlongs

Just as the Prix de l'Arc de Triomphe is the culmination of the European season for middle-distance horses, so the Prix de l'Abbaye, run the same afternoon, is the sprinters' end-of-season target. There have been plenty of British successes in the race in recent years, with horses such as Gentilhombre, Double Form, Moorestyle, Marwell, Sharpo, Habibti, Double Schwartz and Silver Fling. But perhaps the most scintillating performances over the last few runnings have been those of Dayjur – who scorched home in 1990 – and of Lochsong, whose two pillar-to-post victories in 1993 and 1994 set the rafters ringing and gave the huge British contingent at Longchamp on Arc day something extra to invest on the big one. Not that this contingent can ever see much of the race in detail: it is run over a straight course so remote from the stands that it makes the sprint course at Sandown Park seem positively intimate.

Carnegie in 1994 was the first Prix de l'Arc de Triomphe winner to be out of an Arc winner: his dam Detroit won the race in 1980.

Prix de l'Arc de Triomphe

Longchamp, $1\frac{1}{2}$ miles

The Prix de l'Arc de Triomphe is the most important race run in Europe during the Flat season, for it brings together the cream of several generations. It invariably attracts an international field of the highest quality and provides a wonderful spectacle as the runners charge into the straight. Ribot took it twice, as did Alleged, and since Sea Bird II's stunning victory over Reliance in 1965 such horses as Vaguely Noble, Mill Reef, Rheingold, Allez France, All Along, Rainbow Quest and Suave Dancer have confirmed their greatness in the race. Dancing Brave's famous triumph in 1986 is described on page 177–8.

The climax of the 1994 Forte Prix de l'Arc de Triomphe, with Carnegie (Thierry Jarnet) hitting the front.

INTERNATIONAL CLASSIFICATIONS

The system of International Classifications, which commenced in 1977, is a way of presenting annually an agreed framework of ratings of Flat horses which have been competing in the major racing countries of Europe – Britain, France, Ireland, Italy and Germany (the last two countries joined the scheme in 1985). A board of handicappers from the five participating countries meets and subsequently publishes its ratings – usually thereby triggering much discussion and controversy.

The Classifications, divided by age and by category of race distance, are a way of providing objective comparisons between different generations of racehorse. For example, Celtic Swing's rating of 130 for his juvenile career in the 1994 Classifications makes him the highest rated two-year-old on turf form since the scheme began, the only other juvenile rated as high as 130 being Arazi in 1991, a mark based on his Breeders' Cup Juvenile run on dirt. On the other hand, Balanchine's 1994 rating of 130 makes her the joint worst-rated top three-year-old (with Zafonic in 1993) in the history of the scheme.

UNITED STATES OF AMERICA

Thoroughbred racing is the biggest spectator sport in the USA, though the atmosphere at many courses is closer to that of greyhound racing in Britain than to any British race meeting. The tracks are comparatively uniform in shape, and there is much less emphasis on the horse itself than there is in Britain: 'paddock inspection' is normally a fairly cursory activity, not the lingering study of the horses before the race which the British racegoer enjoys. Most tracks are left-handed ovals, most races are run on dirt and the whole sport is geared towards betting: although there are no on-track bookmakers, some states allow off-track betting at the odds determined on the course by the totalisator system in operation. (Some states – such as South Carolina, home of the Colonial Cup steeplechase – do not allow betting but still stage horse races.)

But it would be unfair to characterize the American racing fan simply as a gambler, for certain horses do reach celebrity status, and these stars – Kelso, for instance, who was Horse of the Year five times from 1960 to 1964, or John Henry – are wildly feted. John Henry, foaled in 1975, won thirty-nine of the eighty-three races he contested, including twenty-five Stakes races (the equivalent of European Group races), and the Arlington Million in 1981 and 1984. His career total of earnings was $6,597,947. Perhaps the greatest of all American racehorses was Secretariat, who won the Triple Crown in 1973, capping the three-race sequence with a 31-length victory in the Belmont Stakes, causing the distinguished Turf writer Charlie Hatton to observe: 'He could not have moved faster if he had fallen off the grandstand roof.'

The US Triple Crown is the backbone of the American racing year, and consists of:

Kentucky Derby: *$1\frac{1}{4}$ miles at Churchill Downs, Louisville, Kentucky*
Preakness Stakes: *1 mile $1\frac{1}{2}$ furlongs at Pimlico, Baltimore, Maryland*
Belmont Stakes: *$1\frac{1}{2}$ miles at Belmont Park, Long Island, New York*

Since the war the Triple Crown has been won by Assault (1946), Citation (1948), Secretariat (1973), Seattle Slew (1977) and Affirmed (1978, ridden in all three by Steve Cauthen). Northern Dancer won the Kentucky Derby and the Preakness in 1964, as did Spectacular Bid in 1979 and Sunday Silence in 1989. Alydar, second to Affirmed in all three 1978 races, is the only horse ever to have finished runner-up in all three.

The Triple Crown races are for three-year-olds, are run on dirt and take place early in the season (the Kentucky Derby on the first Saturday in May), but nevertheless the increasing ease of long-distance transport and increasingly enterprising spirit of European trainers have seen several transatlantic challenges mounted in recent years. The first British-trained horse to run in the Kentucky Derby was Bold Arrangement, sent over by the ever-adventurous Clive Brittain to cover himself in glory when runner-up to Ferdinand

THE BREEDERS' CUP

The inauguration of the Breeders' Cup programme in the USA in 1984 changed the face of world Flat racing, for the staging of the richest day's sport anywhere on the globe on Breeders' Cup Day in late October or early November – the timing and venue in America change from year to year – now offers a hugely valuable end-of-season target to the best horses from Europe and elsewhere.

The Breeders' Cup was devised by John Gaines, one of Kentucky's most famous breeders, as a way of combating the decline of racing in America by presenting the Turf equivalent of the Superbowl or World Series – an event to which the whole of the sport would aspire, and to which the rest of the sporting world would pay attention.

The funds needed to finance this extravaganza of racing were raised from breeders, who each make an annual payment of a sum equivalent to the stud fee of each of their stallions and make the foals of these stallions eligible through payment of an additional fee. (The scheme has a reciprocal arrangement with the European Breeders' Fund.) The Breeders' Cup fund puts money into several hundred races, but primarily into the seven races on Breeders' Cup Day.

Although it comes at the end of a long and hard European season, and although problems will remain while horses are allowed to compete in Breeders' Cup events in some states under the influence of drugs banned in Europe, the victories of stars such as Pebbles, Miesque, and Arazi will ensure that European horses continue to grace the richest international showcase that world racing provides.

BREEDERS' CUP RACES

Breeders' Cup Turf
1½ miles on grass
The victory of Pebbles, ridden by Pat Eddery, at Aqueduct in 1985 was at the time the highlight of

English involvement in Breeders' Cup races and signalled the arrival of Breeders' Cup Day as the international championship of racing. But this race also provided Britain's gloomiest moment, when Dancing Brave failed to show his true ability and finished fourth behind Manila in California in 1986.

Breeders' Cup Mile
1 mile on grass
Last Tycoon won this for France in 1986, and Miesque ran out a brilliant winner in both 1987 and 1988. Zilzal flopped in 1989. But Barathea and Frankie Dettori came good in the 1994 running with a blazing three-length victory.

Breeders' Cup Juvenile
1 mile 110 yards on dirt for two-year-old colts and geldings
Usually a benefit for the home horses, but the showcase for one of the greatest performances in racing history at Churchill Downs in 1991 – Arazi! (See pages 16–17.)

Breeders' Cup Juvenile Fillies
1 mile 110 yards on dirt for two-year-old fillies only

Breeders' Cup Classic
1¼ miles on dirt
This race, the richest of the day, produced memorable finishes in 1987, when Ferdinand just beat Alysheba, and in 1989, when Sunday Silence held off Easy Goer – and a result memorable in another way when French-trained Arcangues won in 1993 at odds of 133–1.

Breeders' Cup Sprint
6 furlongs on dirt
Two consecutive performances by British-trained horses stand out. In 1990 the brilliant Dayjur was racing to certain victory at Belmont Park when he jumped over a shadow thrown by the bright sun across the time-keeper's box on top of the stands, lost his momentum and was just beaten by Safely Kept; and more happily, the following year

Sheikh Albadou, trained by the late Alex Scott and ridden by Pat Eddery, came right away from his rivals to record only the second victory by a British-trained horse in a Breeders' Cup race. The 1992 running was marred by the death of Richard Hannon-trained Mr Brooks, whose fatal fall on the bend left Lester Piggott with severe injuries.

Breeders' Cup Distaff
1 mile 1 furlong on dirt for fillies and mares only
No European successes, but a race that lingers in racing's collective memory: the 1990 running at Belmont Park when Go For Wand and Bayakoa locked into a head-to-head battle round the turn and into the straight. Inside the final furlong Go For Wand fell, sustaining injuries from which she was immediately put down.

BREEDERS' CUP VENUES

1984	Hollywood Park, Los Angeles, California
1985	Aqueduct, New York
1986	Santa Anita, Los Angeles, California
1987	Hollywood Park, California
1988	Churchill Downs, Louisville, Kentucky
1989	Gulfstream Park, Florida
1990	Belmont Park, New York
1991	Churchill Downs, Kentucky
1992	Gulfstream Park, Florida
1993	Santa Anita, California
1994	Churchill Downs, Kentucky
1995	Belmont Park, New York
1996	Woodbine, Toronto

Breeders' Cup glory for Pebbles (Pat Eddery) in the 1985 Turf, as she powers clear of Strawberry Road (Steve Cauthen).

HONG KONG

There are two race tracks in Hong Kong – Happy Valley, where racing has taken place since 1846 and where night racing under floodlights has been an immensely popular feature since its introduction in 1973; and Sha Tin, built on reclaimed land and opened in 1978. Attendance at these tracks averages over 40,000 people per day, and the level of betting is massive, both on-course and in the numerous off-course betting centres around the territory, with over £1,750 million staked annually – over £1 million per race. Many British Flat jockeys ride in Hong Kong during the winter, and our big races such as the Grand National and Derby are broadcast live into the colony's racetracks.

in 1986. Dr Devious, winner of the 1992 Derby at Epsom, had run seventh in the Kentucky equivalent – the same race that saw the desperately disappointing eclipse of the French-trained Arazi; My Memoirs, trained by Richard Hannon, was second to A.P. Indy in the Belmont Stakes in 1992. The first European-trained horse ever to win one of the Triple Crown races was Go and Go in the 1990 Belmont Stakes; trained in Ireland by Dermot Weld and ridden by Michael Kinane, he made his mark on racing history by eight and a quarter lengths.

Two other countries belong to the European Pattern system – **Germany** and **Italy** – and horses from Britain, Ireland and France often raid the best races in these countries: for many trainers, the Classics in Italy provide much easier pickings than those at home.

Several Western horses travel to **Japan** for the Japan Cup, an invitation race over a mile and a half held in Tokyo in late November or early December. It was first run in 1981; the 1986 Cup attracted horses from Britain, the USA, Canada, New Zealand and France as well as local runners, and in a driving finish Jupiter Island, trained by Clive Brittain and ridden by Pat Eddery, beat another British challenger, Allez Milord, by a head to carry off a first prize equivalent to £448,276. Prize money to the winner of the Japan Cup in 1994 was £1,023,498, making it the richest race in the world.

Japan is exerting its influence on racing in the West in ways other than just offering tempting prizes for our horses. Big Japanese owners have been making their presence felt through hefty buying at the yearling sales and building up strings of top-class horses – Kooyonga and White Muzzle, to name but two, were familiar Japanese-owned performers – and Japanese breeders are vigorously importing European stallions, including Dancing Brave (reportedly sold to Japan for £3 million, after his original syndication to stand in Britain valued him at £14 million), recent Derby winners Dr Devious, Commander In Chief and Erhaab, and top-class middle-distance horse Opera House.

The major race in **Australia** (where there are bookmakers on the course but not off) is the Melbourne Cup, a two-mile handicap run at Flemington. Its most famous winner remains the legendary Phar Lap, who triumphed under 9 stone 12 pounds in 1930, but Dermot Weld's Vintage Crop made a huge breakthrough in international racing when becoming the first European-trained winner of the race in 1993: ridden by Mick Kinane, he started at 14–1 and won by three lengths.

Dubai, home of the Maktoums (see pages 97–9) has a state-of-the-art racecourse at the Nad Al Sheba track, one of five courses overseen by the United Arab Emirates Racing Association, founded in 1993.

THE RACING YEAR

The range of events, occasions and moods which horse racing provides all the year round is one of the sport's abiding attractions, and although the advent of all-weather racing and summer jumping have effected changes in the formal structure of the sport – so that the Flat season, for example, formally commences on 1 January and concludes on 31 December – the ebbs and flows of the currents of the racing year remain strong.

New Year's Day is the official birthday of all racehorses as well as the official start of the Flat, but on the racing front the mood in **January** and **February** is primarily one of anticipation of the big Cheltenham meeting in March, and every major event is viewed through the prism of what that race means in terms of Cheltenham prospects. The Anthony Mildmay, Peter Cazalet Memorial Chase at Sandown Park in January and the Racing Post Chase at Kempton Park the following month are major chases of the period, while Newbury's Tote Gold Trophy in mid-February is a handicap hurdle which traditionally provides one of the big betting races of the National Hunt year. The other landmark date at this time is of more interest to stallions than to horses in training – 15 February, start of the covering season.

The appetizer to Cheltenham in **March** is another handicap hurdle, the Imperial Cup at Sandown Park, but in reality the great National Hunt Festival overshadows all else, not only at this time but throughout the jumping season – and, for many aficionados, throughout the whole racing year: three days of racing of the highest class played out in the wonderful setting of Prestbury Park, every event a major race, a huge crowd revelling in the sport, a maelstrom of excitement, quality racing, and sheer celebration of the horse. Although each day of the Festival has its central event – Champion Hurdle on Tuesday, Queen Mother Champion Chase on Wednesday, Gold Cup on Thursday – the standard of racing is so high that the day is not dominated by that race, and often races such as the Arkle Trophy or the Sun Alliance Chase are anticipated every bit as keenly as the more familiar triple peaks.

In the afterglow of the Festival, it often escapes the attention that the Flat season on turf begins towards the end of March, with the one-mile Lincoln Handicap at Doncaster providing the season's first big race.

The Flat may have started in earnest, but jumping still holds centre stage in early **April** with the festival meeting at Aintree, these days second only to Cheltenham as a feast of National Hunt racing. Each day features a race over the National fences – the John Hughes Memorial Trophy on the Thursday, the Foxhunters' on the Friday, and the Grand National itself on the Saturday – but the interest is sustained throughout the three days by top-class sport on the Mildmay Course, including on the Friday the Melling Chase over two and a half miles, which in 1995 produced the memorable race between Viking Flagship, Deep Sensation and Martha's Son, and the Aintree Hurdle, again over two and a half miles, immediately before the Grand National.

The Irish Grand National at Fairyhouse on Easter Monday often sees Aintree also-rans out for a consolation prize, and then attention switches firmly to the Flat with the three-day Craven Meeting at Newmarket – with significant Classic trials in the Nell Gwyn Stakes for fillies, the Free Handicap and the Craven Stakes – and the Newbury Spring Meeting also focusing on Classic aspirants in the Fred Darling Stakes for fillies and the Greenham Stakes (in 1995 a pre-Guineas prep for Celtic Swing).

But jumping still has plenty of ammunition in April, with the Scottish National at Ayr and, late in the month, the great three-day festival meeting at Punchestown in Ireland and the Whitbread Gold Cup at Sandown Park.

Early **May** features the Guineas meeting at Newmarket, with the first two Classics – Two Thousand Guineas and One Thousand Guineas – while over in the USA the first leg of the American Triple Crown, the Kentucky

The essence of the Cheltenham Festival (1): Klairon Davis (Francis Woods, stripes) and Sound Man (Charlie Swan) inseparable at the last fence in the 1995 Guinness Arkle Challenge Trophy.

Derby, is always held at Churchill Downs on the first Saturday of May, with the Preakness at Pimlico two weeks later.

Back at home the jumping season enters its final phase around the 'gaff' tracks, the small courses which provide the backbone of sport over the sticks, while the Flat circus moves on to the great May meeting at Chester – featuring Derby and Oaks trials in the shape of the Chester Vase and Cheshire Oaks, and a famous old staying handicap in the Chester Cup. Then comes the year's first big York meeting – Musidora Stakes for Oaks hopes, Dante Stakes for Derby, plus the Yorkshire Cup. Derby and Oaks trials are completed at Lingfield Park and Goodwood later in the month.

June is busting out all over with big racing occasions, none more important than the Epsom Summer Meeting, with its highlights of the Derby, Oaks and Coronation Cup. The US Triple Crown is completed with the Belmont Stakes in New York. In mid-June comes the social highlight of the racing year in the elegant shape of Royal Ascot, a four-day feast of prancing about for the nobs and racing straight out of the top drawer: St James's Palace Stakes, King Edward VII Stakes, Coronation Stakes, Gold Cup, Royal Hunt Cup, Ribblesdale Stakes, King's Stand Stakes, Hardwicke Stakes and Wokingham Stakes.

The jumping season formally ends in June, then almost immediately started again in 1995 with a summer jumps programme at six courses (Perth, Worcester, Market Rasen, Uttoxeter, Southwell and Stratford).

As June turns into **July**, the pace of the racing year is fast and furious. There's the Irish Derby at The Curragh, and the Eclipse Stakes at Sandown Park – the first time the cream of the middle-distance Classic generation meet their elders. The July Meeting at Newmarket, three days of relaxed sociability in sylvan surroundings and high-class racing, culminates in the July Cup, the first Group One sprint of the year in Britain. There's Britain's top middle-distance race of the Flat season, the King George VI and Queen Elizabeth Diamond Stakes at Ascot, and there's Glorious Goodwood – the July Meeting (which often spills over into August), famously described as a garden party with racing tacked on and featuring such famous races as the Stewards' Cup, a mad downhill dash of a six-furlong sprint, the Sussex Stakes, which attracts the best milers in Europe, and the Nassau Stakes for fillies.

Bad news for stallions in July: the covering season finishes on the 15th. Good news for breeders: the world's first major yearling sales of the year take place at Keeneland, Kentucky.

August is dominated on the racing front by the great York meeting in the middle of the month, for many people the best Flat meeting of the whole year. Each of the three days has a Group One race – International Stakes on Tuesday, Yorkshire Oaks on Wednesday, Nunthorpe Stakes on Thursday – with the big betting race of the week, the Ebor Handicap, on the middle day, and significant two-year-old races in the form of the Lowther Stakes for fillies and the Gimcrack Stakes.

If you've had a good year on the betting front, August is the time to make for the yearling sales at Deauville.

By **September** the Flat season is entering its late phase, with the final Classic of the season, the St Leger, heading the four-day Doncaster meeting which also hosts the Doncaster Cup – third leg (after Ascot and Goodwood) of the stayers' Triple Crown – and important two-year-old races such as the Champagne Stakes. In mid-month, the Irish Champion Stakes represents class and the Ayr Gold Cup a huge betting medium, and the Ascot September Meeting features the last big mile race of the season in Britain, the Queen Elizabeth II Stakes, as well as vital races for juveniles: the Fillies' Mile and the Royal Lodge Stakes.

The first of the two big Newmarket meetings which stand like gateposts to the way out of the Flat season culminates in the Cambridgeshire, but for purists and for those looking forward to the following year's Classics the meeting is more significant for two Group One two-year-old races – the Cheveley Park Stakes for fillies and the Middle Park Stakes.

The day after the Cambridgeshire, on the first Sunday of **October**, comes Europe's greatest race of the season, the Prix de l'Arc de Triomphe at Longchamp, and on the same afternoon the Paris track hosts the culmination of the European sprinting year in the form of the Prix de l'Abbaye – won in 1993 and 1994 by the flying filly Lochsong.

Back at Newmarket in mid-month comes the Houghton Meeting, with the most important two-year-old race of the year, the Dewhurst Stakes, and on the Saturday one of the best Flat fixtures of the season, with the Champion Stakes offering the last Group One middle-distance race in the country, and the Cesarewitch a marathon handicap, after the Cambridgeshire the second leg of the Autumn Double.

Britain's major yearling sales take place at Tattersalls in Newmarket in late September/early October.

Until the last few years the racing year on the Flat effectively ended – at least as far as the best horses were concerned – after the Houghton Meeting, with the exception of the Racing Post Trophy over one mile for two-year-olds at Doncaster (the race which in 1994 started all those Triple Crown ideas for Celtic Swing). But all that has changed since the Breeders' Cup, staged in late October or early November, became established as the world championships of racing (see page 85), and as soon as the Arc is over, attention focuses fervently on European prospects in the USA.

November forms the cusp between the Flat and jumping codes. Although the Melbourne Cup in Australia on the first Tuesday of the month now captures a great deal of European interest, and the November Handicap at Doncaster provides a late-season medium for a gamble, for many racing fans the Flat loses its appeal once the Breeders' Cup is over, and attention switches to the jumping scene as the season gathers pace with its first big races: the Mackeson Gold Cup at Cheltenham, the Becher Chase over the Grand National fences at Aintree, and the Hennessy Cognac Gold Cup at Newbury.

By **December** the top Flat horses will already have been packed off to stud or be tucked up at home for a quiet winter as connections plan the plunder of the world's top prizes next year, and with the minor distraction of all-weather racing on the Flat, the jumping crowd have the stage to themselves, with the Tripleprint Gold Cup and Bula Hurdle heading a good Cheltenham fixture early in the month, and one of the sport's busiest times just after Christmas, with Kempton's festival meeting featuring the King George VI Chase – second only to the Cheltenham Gold Cup as a prestige target for staying chasers – and Christmas Hurdle, and the Welsh National at Chepstow a valuable and historic mid-season handicap chase.

On New Year's Eve the Flat season officially ends. The next one starts the following day.

The essence of the Cheltenham Festival (2): Norman Williamson and Master Oats return to glory after winning the 1995 Tote Cheltenham Gold Cup.

Owners,
Trainers,
Jockeys

OWNERS

There is a story of an owner who, on being told by his trainer that his horse was still green, replied, 'He was brown the last time I saw him.'

Most racehorse owners, though, belie the outdated image of the rich but ignorant nuisance who owns horses simply for social reasons, and the nature of ownership over the last two decades has changed immensely. On the one hand, ownership of the very best horses on the Flat is mostly confined to a very small number of immensely rich people who build up huge strings of superbly bred horses by their own breeding operations and by shelling out unconscionable amounts of money at the yearling sales, so that big race after big race after big race is being fought out by jockeys sporting the colours of one of the Maktoum brothers, or Khalid Abdullah, or Robert Sangster. On the other hand, regulations concerning syndicates and racing clubs mean that thousands of 'ordinary' people can now enjoy a genuine involvement with ownership for a fairly small outlay. Racing clubs (whose members make a one-off payment for a share) are increasingly popular among those with limited means but aspirations to rub shoulders with Sheikh Mohammed in the parade ring.

An extra dimension has been added to ownership – and an extra grotesquerie to the naming of horses (see page 33) – by allowing commercial companies to own racehorses, sometimes (though not always) for advertising purposes: 1994 Two Thousand Guineas winner Mister Baileys, for example, was named by owners G. R. Bailey Ltd to promote their Baileys Horse Feeds.

There are over 18,000 owners registered with the Jockey Club. When registration (which in 1995 cost £42.00 plus VAT for an individual) is accepted the owner deposits money in an account with Weatherbys. To this will be added winnings, and from it will be deducted entry fees and fees to the jockey. (Training fees are paid directly to the trainer.) When deductions exceed additions the owner must top up the account.

But what are the chances of making a profit by owning a horse? Few owners are in it for monetary gain, and many are well aware that the odds are stacked against their prospering from this pursuit. The basic training fee per horse will be upwards of £150 per week, to which must usually be added charges for the attentions of the vet and the farrier, entry fees, transport costs, insurance premiums, jockeys' fees and various registration fees. In very round numbers it will cost at least £10,000 a year to keep a horse in training – considerably more if the animal is with one of the top Flat trainers. Even with the minimum race value (that is, the total to be won by all placed horses) standing in 1995 at £3,250 for a flat race, £3,250 for a steeplechase and £2,400 for a hurdle, a horse at the lower level is clearly unlikely to pay its way, and around two-thirds of all horses in training fail to win a race at all.

It is a tribute to the allure of British and Irish racing that it has attracted the involvement of many owners from overseas – not only the Maktoums and the Japanese, but also famous American figures such as the late Raymond Guest, owner of Derby winners Larkspur and Sir Ivor and of the great chaser L'Escargot, or Paul Mellon, whose Mill Reef is one of the Turf's immortals, and whose black and gold colours are still a familiar sight in British races. Grundy, winner of the Derby in 1975, was owned by the Italian aristocrat Carlo Vittadini, Pebbles in her early racing career by the Greek shipping magnate Marcos Lemos, who also owned Petingo, sire of Troy; Bolkonski and Wollow, who won the Two Thousand Guineas in successive years, were owned by the Italian Carlo d'Alessio; and Secreto, who pipped El Gran Senor in the 1984 Derby, by Luigi Miglietti from Venezuela.

RACING COLOURS

Racing colours must be registered annually with Weatherbys – the fee for 1995 was £23.00 (plus VAT) – and once registered cannot be taken by any other person. You do not actually have to own a racehorse to have racing colours: you could register in the expectation of future ownership in order to prevent anyone else from taking that combination of colours.

In bygone years subtle shades of colour could be registered. Lord Howard de Walden's colours are 'apricot', and the Duke of Devonshire's have been 'straw' since colours were first used on jockeys in 1762 'for the greater convenience of distinguishing the horses in running, as also for the prevention of disputes arising from not knowing the colours worn by each rider'. Nowadays the Jockey Club specifies eighteen basic colours in which new registrations must be made (white, grey, pink, red, maroon, light green, emerald green, dark green, light blue, royal blue, dark blue, mauve, purple, yellow, orange, beige, brown and black), and as all possible registrations in single colours have been claimed a new owner will now have to accept a combination of at least two. The Jockey Club has also standardized the design of the colours, so that only a combination of the designs reproduced opposite will be allowed.

Previous spread:
Trainer David Loder, jockey Mick Kinane and owner Sheikh Mohammed at York, May 1994.

JACKET

1 Plain	2 Seams	3 Epaulets	4 Stripe	5 Braces	6 Stripes	7 Hoop
			4" centre strip	2" vertical strip	Alternate 2" vertical stripes	4" hoop
8 Hoops	9 Halved	10 Quartered	11 Sash	12 Cross Belts	13 Chevron	14 Chevrons
Alternated 2" hoops	Vertically only sleeves reversed		4" diagonal stripe from left shoulder to right hip	4" diagonal stripe from each shoulder	One large "V"	Alternate 2" chevrons
15 Check	16 Diamonds	17 Spots	18 Stars	19 Cross of Lorraine	20 Diamond	21 Star
1"-1½" squares	4" vertical diamonds	Spots 2½" in diameter	Stars 3" in diameter	10" solid cross	10" vertical diamond	10" solid star
22 Disc	23 Inverted Triangle	24 Diabolo	25 Large Spots	26 Triple Diamond	27 Hollow Box	
10" solid disc	10" triangle	Triangles of same size	4" spots from right shoulder to left hip	6" vertical diamond	10" box	

SLEEVES

1 Plain	2 Armlet	3 Hooped	4 Striped
5 Chevrons	6 Seams	7 Stars	8 Spots
9 Halved	10 Diabolo	11 Diamonds	12 Check

CAP

1 Plain	2 Hooped	3 Striped
4 Check	5 Spots	6 Quartered
7 Star	8 Diamond	9 Stars
4" centre to apex	4" centre to apex	
10 Diamonds		

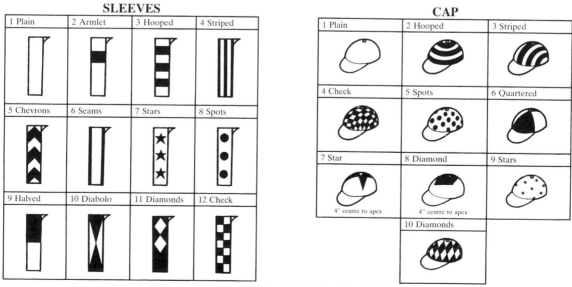

THE OFFICIAL DESIGNS FOR RACING COLOURS, AS SPECIFIED BY WEATHERBYS

DOROTHY PAGET

Dorothy Paget.

One of the great eccentrics of the century, Dorothy Paget raced on a vast scale between the wars, financing her operation with the fortune she had inherited at the age of twenty-one. Once an accomplished horsewoman herself, riding side-saddle in point-to-points, her curious lifestyle included obsessive eating, and she soon weighed in at over 20 stone. She disliked human company – especially men, whose proximity reportedly inclined her to vomit – and surrounded herself with a bevy of female minders.

She kept odd hours, dining at 7 a.m., sleeping through the day and getting up for breakfast at 8:30 p.m., then spending the night consuming vast meals and phoning her trainers. She expected them to be adaptable to such eccentricities, but (not surprisingly) her tyrannical ways led to friction: horses would be shuffled around between trainers at her whim. But her nomadic string included some star performers, notably Golden Miller, who won the Cheltenham Gold Cup five times from 1932 to 1936 and remains the only horse to have won the Gold Cup and Grand National in the same year: 1934. (When she planted a kiss on Golden Miller's nose after one of his victories, a racegoer suggested that this was probably the first occasion on which she had kissed a member of the opposite sex: 'And he's a gelding,' pointed out another.) She owned 1940 Gold Cup winner Roman Hackle, Insurance, twice winner of the Champion Hurdle, and two other Champion Hurdle winners: Solford, ridden to victory by one Sean Magee in 1940, and Distel in 1946. She also owned Straight Deal, who took the wartime Derby at Newmarket in 1943, and Mont Tremblant, winner of the Cheltenham Gold Cup as a novice in 1952.

Another of her horses, Tuppence, does not figure in the records of great races but was the subject of one of the oddest gambles of modern times. He was backed from odds as long as 200–1 in the week before the 1933 Derby, and started at 10–1 – a 'steamer' to end all steamers – to finish nineteenth of twenty-four runners behind Hyperion. (Tuppence later dead-heated for a race at Hamilton Park, netting his owner £56.) Presumably much of the money bringing his Derby odds tumbling so dramatically was Miss Paget's, for she was an inveterate punter: her largest stake was reputed to have been £160,000, on an 8–1 on chance. To say that it duly obliged (which it did) seems to underplay the magnitude of the wager.

But her curious daily routine made orthodox punting rather awkward, and such was the trust with which she was regarded by one of her bookmakers that he allowed her to phone him in the evening and bet on races which had already taken place.

Stories of Dorothy Paget's eccentricity are legion, but one which would appeal to any racing fan whose afternoon's sport has been spoiled by the car breaking down on the way to the races concerns an incident shortly after the war. En route to a race meeting, accompanied by her secretary, her car seized up. The only other vehicle in sight was a butcher's delivery van; this she instructed her secretary to purchase on the spot, and was reported to have arrived at the racecourse sitting between two carcasses. She had been alarmed by the breakdown, and thereafter never drove anywhere without a second car following her in case of a repetition. For long journeys a third car would follow the second, just in case the back-up vehicle broke down as well.

Dorothy Paget – truly a big owner – died in 1960.

ROYALTY

Racing has for long been known as the Sport of Kings, and today the active involvement of the Royal Family is one of the great boons of the sport. Her Majesty the Queen has some thirty horses in training (with Lord Huntingdon and Ian Balding), the Queen Mother's passion for National Hunt racing has been one of jumping's greatest joys, and the riding exploits of the Princess Royal have borne witness to a new generation of Royal participation in the sport.

Charles II, the first English king to show a real enthusiasm for organized racing, holds the distinction of being the only reigning monarch to ride the winner of an official horse race. His patronage of Newmarket established the town as the centre of British racing, and Charles won The Plate there in 1671 and 1674: 'I do assure you the king won by good horsemanship,' wrote Sir Robert Carr of his second victory.

William of Orange owned and bred racehorses, winning a match at Newmarket with the engagingly named Stiff Dick.

It was Queen Anne who next exerted great royal influence on the Turf, establishing Ascot racecourse in 1711: the Queen Anne Stakes remains the traditional opening race at Royal Ascot. George II's third son, the Duke of Cumberland, bred Herod and Eclipse, and George IV instituted the Royal Procession at Ascot. Queen Victoria bred the winners of eleven Classics, though she never set foot on a racecourse after the death of Prince Albert. Her son the Prince of Wales founded the Sandringham Stud and bred Persimmon, who won the Derby for him in 1896, and Diamond Jubilee, who repeated the feat in 1900. As King Edward VII he won his third Derby with Minoru in 1909. George V was less keen than his father, though he won the One Thousand Guineas in 1928 with Scuttle, but George VI, who had little interest in racing until his accession, won five Classics: in 1942 the brilliant Sun Chariot took the One Thousand Guineas, Oaks and St Leger; in the same year the King won the Two Thousand Guineas with Big Game and in 1946 the One Thousand again with Hypericum.

In Queen Elizabeth II the British racing scene has a patron who is not only highly knowledgeable about the sport (especially about breeding) but also a keen racegoer. Success as an owner came early in her reign, her Aureole running second to Pinza in the Derby in 1953 shortly after the Coronation. Aureole matured into a top-class four-year-old, winning the King George VI and Queen Elizabeth Stakes in 1954 (having again found Pinza too good for him in the 1953 running), and had a fine career at stud, siring the 1960 Derby and St Leger winner St Paddy and two other winners of the St Leger in Aurelius and Provoke.

Colours of Her Majesty Queen Elizabeth II

Colours of Her Majesty Queen Elizabeth the Queen Mother

Royalty and racing: Her Majesty the Queen Mother with Queen Elizabeth II at a gathering at Ascot in October 1994 to celebrate the Queen Mother's 400th winner. The horse paying respects is Lunabelle, trained by Ian Balding (left).

WINSTON CHURCHILL

Sir Winston Churchill was seventy-five before he first registered as an owner, but he had long been a keen racing enthusiast. He became a member of the Jockey Club and owned several renowned horses, notably the grey Colonist II, who won thirteen races (including the Jockey Club Cup and – appropriately – the Winston Churchill Stakes), and came second in the Ascot Gold Cup. High Hat was one of the best middle-distance horses of his generation, beating Petite Etoile at Kempton Park and finishing second to St Paddy in the Jockey Club Stakes; he was fourth in the Prix de l'Arc de Triomphe in 1961. Vienna won six races and was placed in the St Leger, Coronation Cup, Hardwicke Stakes, Champion Stakes and Prix Ganay, and became the sire of the great Vaguely Noble. Sir Winston's racing colours – pink, chocolate sleeves and cap – live on in the scarf of Churchill College, Cambridge.

Sir Winston Churchill with jockey Tommy Gosling at Hurst Park, May 1951.

The Queen's first Classic winners were Carrozza, who snatched the Oaks by a short head under Lester Piggott in 1957, and Pall Mall, winner of the Two Thousand Guineas in 1958. Highclere, grand-dam of Nashwan, won the One Thousand Guineas in 1974 and then took the Prix de Diane at Chantilly. In 1977, the Queen's Jubilee year, Dunfermline fittingly provided two more English Classic victories in the Oaks and – after an unforgettable duel with Alleged – the St Leger.

Although Her Majesty rarely has a runner in the Classics these days, in June 1995 she showed that her horses can still hold their own at the top level of the sport when her Phantom Gold, trained by Lord Huntingdon and ridden by Frankie Dettori, won the Ribblesdale Stakes at Royal Ascot – her first winner at the Royal meeting since Colour Sergeant landed the Royal Hunt Cup in 1992.

If a triumph in the Queen's colours excites any Flat meeting, the Queen Mother holds a very special place in the affections of the National Hunt community: for she, more than any other individual, was responsible for raising the status of the jumping game from that of a poor relation to the Flat to the position it enjoys today. A succession of famous horses have carried the 'blue, buff stripes, blue sleeves, black cap, gold tassel' to victory in top races: Manicou, The Rip, Makaldar, Laffy, Double Star, Gay Record, Antiar, Oedipe, Escalus, Inch Arran, Colonius, Isle Of Man, Game Spirit, Sunyboy, Tammuz and The Argonaut among them. Two others in particular recall notably memorable, and very different, occasions.

Special Cargo, who won the Grand Military Gold Cup at Sandown Park three times, will always be remembered for his last-gasp victory in the Whitbread Gold Cup on the same course in 1984, a race which many people (including Graham Goode: see page 173) regard as the finest steeplechase of all time.

And what of Devon Loch? His fate in the 1956 Grand National will be for ever the epitome of defeat snatched out of the jaws of victory. For having seen off his rivals in the world's greatest steeplechase with a superb display of jumping, Devon Loch (ridden by Dick Francis) was bounding up the Liverpool run-in to certain triumph in front of his owner and the young Queen and Princess Margaret when, fifty yards from the winning post, he seemed to leap at an imaginary obstacle and slid down to the turf, leaving ESB to stride past and take the race. No one can say for sure why he did it: Dick Francis thinks that the crescendo of noise greeting a winner who would have been the most popular victor in the history of the race scared the horse: 'I have never heard in my life such a noise. It rolled and lapped around us, buffeting and glorious, the enthusiastic expression of love for the Royal Family and delight in seeing the Royal horse win.'

Whatever the reason for Devon Loch's sensational slither, the Queen Mother stifled her disappointment: 'Well, that's racing!', she is said to have exclaimed, and wrote a few days later to the horse's trainer Peter Cazalet, 'We will not be done in by this, and will just keep on trying.'

Her 400th winner as an owner came when Nearco Bay, trained by Nicky Henderson and ridden by John Kavanagh, won the Neville Lumb Silver Jubilee Handicap Chase at Uttoxeter on 30 May 1994.

The Prince of Wales rode a few times over fences in the 1980–81 season, taking a well-publicized tumble from Good Prospect at the Cheltenham National Hunt Festival. Under pressure to give up such a dangerous pursuit, he was quoted as saying: 'I wish people could only understand the real thrill, the challenge of steeplechasing. It's part of the great British way of life, and none of the sports I've done bears any comparison.'

The Princess Royal became an accomplished amateur jockey under the tutelage of trainer David Nicholson, and rode regularly under both codes. In 1987 she won the top ladies' race of the season, on Diamond Day at Ascot, for Michael Stoute on Ten No Trumps; and the following year she took (appropriately) the Queen Mother's Cup at York on Insular.

THE MAKTOUMS

'When we were small boys we were riding horses,' Hamdan Al-Maktoum explained in a newspaper interview in July 1990 when asked why he and his brothers so loved horse racing: 'It's part of our culture. Our involvement here started as a hobby, and now it's a very strong hobby.'

A very strong hobby indeed. Even though the Maktoum brothers have been part of the racing scene for many years, the facts and figures still boggle the mind. Together they own some 1,500 horses. Sheikh Mohammed has about 600 in training, Sheikh Hamdan 300. Sheikh Mohammed, Hamdan Al-Maktoum and Maktoum Al Maktoum filled the first three places in the table of leading owners on the Flat in 1994, with win and place prize money respectively of £2,666,730, £2,637,366 and £1,216,405. (In fourth place was Khalid Abdullah with the comparative small change of £730,992.) The youngest of the brothers, Sheikh Ahmed, was twelfth. But that does not tell the whole story: in tenth place was Godolphin, the Maktoum-owned racing and breeding operation which takes selected horses to Dubai during the winter, returning them to Britain to race: Godolphin numbered ten winners from its twenty-four horses – notably Oaks and Irish Derby winner Balanchine. The first English Classic winner trained outside Europe, Balanchine was formally in the charge of her Dubai handler Hilal Ibrahim. In 1995 the Godolphin horses had a new trainer in Saeed Bin Suroor, and the idea is to use Dubai as a base from which horses can be shipped to all the far-flung corners of the racing globe – including Europe (where in Great Britain, for example, the horses will be based in Godolphin's own yard in Newmarket, Moulton Paddocks), Australia, Japan and the USA. (See page 99.)

Mwah! Sheikh Maktoum Al Maktoum (left) receives the trophy and a fraternal peck from Hamdan Al-Maktoum after the victory of Hatoof in the 1993 Dubai Champion Stakes at Newmarket.

So the four brothers plus Godolphin earned over £7 million in prize money – and that in Britain alone, without taking into account Maktoum wins in the Irish Derby, Prix de l'Arc de Triomphe, Breeders' Cup Mile and all sorts of other big overseas races. Seems like a lucrative hobby.

It's an expensive hobby as well. Each of the four brothers owns a breeding operation, and each spends heftily at the yearling sales. But whatever they cost, the achievements of the horses who have run in one set or other of the Maktoum colours are legion: Nashwan, Oh So Sharp, Salsabil, Pebbles, Indian Skimmer, Musical Bliss, Soviet Star, Touching Wood, Wassl, Mtoto, Shadeed, Shareef Dancer, Ma Biche, In The Wings, Unfuwain, Al Bahathri, Dayjur, Diminuendo, Carnegie, King's Theatre, Erhaab, Shadayid, Mtoto, Balanchine, Barathea, Pennekamp, Moonshell Lammtara . . .

Colours of Hamdan Al-Maktoum

The Maktoum brothers are the sons of the late Sheikh Rashid bin Saeed Al-Maktoum, ruler of Dubai, the tiny oil-rich state which forms part of the United Arab Emirates. Maktoum Al Maktoum (colours: royal blue, white chevron, light blue cap) is the oldest of the four and has been ruler of Dubai since his father's death in 1991; he was the first to own a Classic winner when Touching Wood, second to Golden Fleece in the 1982 Derby, went on to win the St Leger. Sheikh Maktoum Al Maktoum followed up with Ma Biche in the 1983 One Thousand Guineas and Shadeed in the 1985 Two Thousand; his Shareef Dancer won the Irish Sweeps Derby in 1983, and Hatoof the One Thousand Guineas in 1992 and Champion Stakes in 1993, and he has also owned fine sprinters in Green Desert and Cadeaux Genereux as well as Ezzoud, winner of the International Stakes in 1993 and 1994 and of the 1994 Eclipse. Maktoum Al Maktoum's bloodstock interests include the Gainsborough Stud near Newbury.

Colours of Sheikh Mohammed

With the achievements of Nashwan, Salsabil, Dayjur, Shadayid, Erhaab and countless other familiar names, the second oldest brother Sheikh Hamdan has challenged the younger Sheikh Mohammed for the position of leading light among the brothers, and in 1994 was only just beaten by his brother for the owners' title. Before Nashwan his best horses had been Unfuwain and the filly Al Bahathri, beaten a short head by Oh So Sharp in the 1985 One Thousand Guineas and a game winner of the Irish One Thousand. His colours of royal blue, white epaulets, striped cap, have become a familiar sight in big races all over the world: he won the Melbourne Cup with At Talaq in 1986 and Jeune in 1994. Sheikh Hamdan's breeding operation is run as the Shadwell Estate Company, the flagship of which is the Nunnery Stud near Thetford in Norfolk: here Nashwan, Unfuwain and Green Desert took up stud duties.

Colours of Maktoum Al Maktoum

Sheikh Mohammed races and breeds on the grandest scale, with 200 or so broodmares in addition to his 600 horses in training around the world. He started developing his racing interests in earnest in the late 1970s, but had to wait until 1985 for his first Classic winner when Oh So Sharp, whom he had bred, took the One Thousand Guineas: she then won the Oaks and the St Leger. Sheikh Mohammed bought Pebbles after she had won the One Thousand Guineas in 1984, and she went on to win the Eclipse Stakes (the first filly to do so), the Champion Stakes (sponsored since 1982 by the Maktoum family) and the Breeders' Cup Turf in 1985 – the year that Sheikh Mohammed first became leading owner. Other good fillies to have raced in his colours (maroon, white sleeves, maroon cap, white star) include the winners of the 1987, 1988 and 1993 Oaks in Unite, Diminuendo and Intrepidity, the 1989 One Thousand Guineas winner Musical Bliss and the brilliant Indian Skimmer (see page 18). Moonax gave him a second St Leger when winning at 40–1 in 1994, Sheikh Mohammed's first victory in an English Classic with a colt. Three weeks later he won his first Prix de l'Arc de Triomphe with Carnegie, and in May 1995 his first Two Thousand Guineas with Pennekamp. He has even made an impact on the National Hunt scene, his Kribensis winning the 1990 Champion Hurdle. Like his brothers, Sheikh Mohammed maintains his own international breeding interests – notably at the Dalham Hall Stud, Newmarket, and the Kildangan Stud in Ireland – but he still buys widely at the yearling sales.

Sheikh Ahmed (yellow, black epaulets) is the youngest of the four brothers. His best-known horses have been Wassl, winner of the Irish Two Thousand Guineas in 1983, and Mtoto, who took the Eclipse Stakes in 1987 (from Reference Point) and 1988 (from Shady Heights) before winning the King George at Ascot. Sheikh Ahmed, who won the Irish Oaks in 1991 with Possessive Dancer, owns the Aston Upthorpe Stud in Oxfordshire, where Mtoto stands.

With so many hundreds of horses in training and a control of so many of the best bloodlines, the Maktoums dominate British (and indeed world) Flat racing, and their grip looks set to become even firmer after the sensational achievements of Godolphin – the Dubai-based training scheme masterminded by Sheikh Mohammed – in the spring and early summer of 1995: one weekend in mid-May, Vettori won the Poule d'Essai des Poulains (the French Two Thousand Guineas) at Longchamp, Flagbird the Group One Premio Presidente della Repubblica in Rome, and Heart Lake the Yasuda Kinen (worth over £600,000 to the winner) in Tokyo. Even better was to come in June with Moonshell in the Vodafone Oaks, and then Godolphin's greatest moment of all – Lammtara's sensational victory in the Vodafone Derby. Lammtara ran in the colours of Maktoum Al Maktoum's nineteen-year-old son Saeed Bin Maktoum Al Maktoum – whose uncle Sheikh Mohammed fittingly led the horse into the winner's enclosure.

Colours of Khalid Abdullah

KHALID ABDULLAH

Khalid Abdullah is a Saudi prince who has become one of the biggest owner–breeders in modern racing. His Known Fact was the first Arab-owned English Classic winner when taking the 1980 Two Thousand Guineas on the disqualification of Nureyev, and his colours of green, pink sash and cap, white sleeves have since then been carried by many well-known horses, among them the brilliant milers Rousillon and Warning; Rainbow Quest, who won the 1985 Coronation Cup and Prix de l'Arc de Triomphe; and Zafonic, whose explosive victory in the 1993 Two Thousand Guineas marked him out as an exceptional horse (see pages 180–2). Khalid Abdullah's Dancing Brave was one of the outstanding horses of the post-war period, winning in 1986 the Two Thousand Guineas, Coral-Eclipse, King George VI and Queen Elizabeth Diamond Stakes and a memorable Prix de l'Arc de Triomphe (described on pages 177–8). Dancing Brave was controversially beaten in the 1986 Derby, and Abdullah was also placed in the Epsom Classic with Damister (third in 1985) and Bellotto (third in 1987). But he finally won the race with Quest For Fame in 1990, three days after his Sanglamore had won the French equivalent, the Prix du Jockey-Club, and three years later followed up with Commander In Chief, who went on to win the Irish Derby. Khalid Abdullah has more than 150 horses in training in Britain, and his Juddmonte Stud operation has bases in Berkshire, County Meath and Kentucky.

Colours of the Aga Khan

THE AGA KHAN

The Aga Khan, Imam (spiritual leader) of the Shia Muslims, was born in 1936, grandson of the Aga Khan who was a major figure in European racing in the middle part of the century, winning the Triple Crown in 1935 with Bahram and the Derby on four other occasions, with Blenheim, Mahmoud, My Love and Tulyar. The present Aga Khan built up his racing interests during the 1970s and enjoyed spectacular success throughout the following decade. He won the Derby, Irish Derby and King George VI and Queen Elizabeth Diamond Stakes in 1981 with the ill-fated Shergar, and the Derby twice more with Shahrastani in 1986 and Kahyasi (who carried his second

Colours of Robert Sangster

Robert Sangster greets jockey John Reid after the victory of Turtle Island in the Scottish Equitable Gimcrack Stakes at York in August 1993.

SHOW BUSINESS

Racing is a great entertainment, and has long had close links with show business, with many actors and actresses, singers and other entertainers drawn to the British racing scene – among them King Edward VII's friend Lily Langtry, whose horses were raced under the name of 'Mr Jersey'; Gregory Peck, who owned some good steeple-chasers, including Owens Sedge and Different Class, third in the 1968 Grand National; and James Bolam, whose best horse has been Credo's Daughter, a game chasing mare of the 1970s (see pages 22–3). Bing Crosby owned a part of Meadow Court, winner of the King George VI and Queen Elizabeth Stakes in 1965: when the horse won the Irish Derby, Crosby regaled the crowd in the grandstand at The Curragh with an impromptu rendition of 'When Irish Eyes Are Smiling'.

Singer Billy Fury owned Anselmo, fourth in the 1964 Derby, while Gainsay won the Ritz Club National Hunt Chase at the 1987 Cheltenham Festival for Errol Brown of the group Hot Chocolate. Comedian Freddie Starr struck Grand National gold in 1994 with Miinnehoma, a horse he had himself bought at the sales, registering his bids by sticking his tongue out. Other familiar entertainers who have indulged in ownership include such diverse talents as Frankie Vaughan, Sting, Des O'Connor, Frazer Hines, Enn Reitel, Henry Kelly and Rick Wakeman.

And it's not only in ownership that the showbiz connections can be found. George Formby was an apprentice jockey before embarking on his legendary singing career: he rode in Lord Derby's colours at the age of ten.

colours, the green and chocolate hoops made famous by his grandfather) in 1988: his first colours (green, red epaulets) were carried in that race by Doyoun, who had added to the Classic haul by taking the 1988 Two Thousand Guineas. But the victory of his Aliysa in the 1989 Oaks had a real sting in the tail: Aliysa failed the post-race dope test, being adjudged to be positive to a derivative of camphor. Her owner protested at what he perceived to be flaws in the testing methods used at the Horserace Forensic Laboratory, and after lengthy legal representations had failed to bring about a reconciliation of views between the Aga Khan and the Jockey Club, he removed all his horses from Britain in 1991. In late 1994 it was announced that changes to the British testing procedures announced by the Jockey Club had satisfied the Aga Khan, and his colours returned to a British race-course on Adjareli in the St James's Palace Stakes at Royal Ascot in June 1995.

ROBERT SANGSTER

Emerald green, royal blue sleeves, white cap, emerald green spots – how many famous horses have carried those colours! The Minstrel, El Gran Senor, Golden Fleece, Alleged, Detroit, Assert, Sadler's Wells, Caerleon, Solford, Pas De Seul, Hawaiian Sound, Lomond, Rodrigo de Triano, Las Meninas, Turtle Island – all have played their part in building up Robert Sangster's massive international owning and breeding interests. His first success as an owner was a far cry from the exploits of those star names: Chalk Stream, trained by Eric Cousins, won a small race at Haydock for the 24-year-old Sangster in 1960. After that humble beginning he acquired more horses, and in the early 1970s decided to become involved in the breeding side. In partnership with John Magnier he founded the Coolmore Stud in County Tipperary, and in 1975 formed a syndicate of big owners (including Stavros Niarchos and Danny Schwartz) to breed and race horses to be trained by Vincent O'Brien at Ballydoyle. The first crop – not all of which raced in Sangster's colours – included The Minstrel, Be My Guest, Artaius, Godswalk and Alleged. Sangster's own Swettenham Stud has bred many fine horses (such as Dibidale, El Gran Senor and Sadler's Wells), but his breeding interests range all over the world. It was the international spirit of Sangster's operation, particularly his widespread importation of the best American blood, which helped to change the character of racing, and the global nature of his owning interests was epitomized by the victory of his Beldale Ball in the 1980 Melbourne Cup. In 1984 he purchased the famous training establishment at Manton in Wiltshire, with first Michael Dickinson (who departed in 1986) and then Barry Hills as his trainer; Hills returned to Lambourn at the end of the 1990 season, to be replaced at Manton by Sangster's stepson-in-law Peter Chapple-Hyam, in whose hands the stable has sent out a stream of big winners in the Sangster colours, including Rodrigo de Triano – who, partnered by Lester Piggott, won the Two Thousand Guineas, Irish Two Thousand Guineas, International Stakes and Champion Stakes in 1992. Sangster's Las Meninas, trained in Ireland by Tommy Stack, won the One Thousand Guineas in 1994.

Victor Morley Lawson, owner of several good horses including Popsi's Joy, was sixty-seven when he rode his first winner, Ocean King at Warwick in October 1973.

The joy of winning: jockey Shane Broderick, trainer Michael Hourigan and owner Tom Doran broach the bubbly after Doran's Pride's victory in the BonusPrint Stayers' Hurdle at Cheltenham in March 1995.

TRAINERS

Be they Hamdan Al-Maktoum or a 'fun' owner who can only afford one-hundredth of a less-than-classically bred animal trained on the wrong side of Newmarket's Hamilton Road, owners need trainers. And although the owner–trainer relationship can be a fraught one, the onus is on the trainer to make it work: in the words of the Jockey Club rule, 'Every trainer shall conduct his business of training racehorses with reasonable care and skill and with due regard to the interests of his owners and to the safety of his employees and agents and of the horses in his charge.'

There are around 850 trainers in Great Britain licensed by the Jockey Club. Of this number, some 300 are 'permit holders', licensed to train for steeplechases, hurdle races and National Hunt Flat races only horses which are the property of the trainer or his (or her) immediate family. Horses are trained all over the country and in a variety of settings: Red Rum's stable was behind a second-hand car showroom on a busy street in Southport, and he galloped on the local beach. ('If a horse has ability,' said his trainer Ginger McCain, 'you can train it up the side of a mountain or down a mineshaft.') A complete contrast is the magnificent training estate of Manton in Wiltshire. And there are towns and villages which revolve around racehorse training. The major one in Britain is Newmarket, which houses around sixty trainers and about 2,300 horses in training. Lambourn in Berkshire is the home of some forty trainers; the Yorkshire towns of Malton and Middleham are other major centres.

The number of horses which a trainer has in his care varies enormously. Henry Cecil had 208 horses listed as being in his charge in *Horses in Training* for 1995; John Dunlop had 157; Michael Stoute 159. The top jumping trainers tend to maintain smaller establishments than their equivalents on the Flat: Martin Pipe had 66 horses, David Nicholson 90. Many trainers had only a couple.

Breaking in. This young lady, being long-reined near John Dunlop's stable in Sussex, certainly learned well enough: it's Salsabil, winner of the One Thousand Guineas, Oaks and Irish Derby in 1990, here being taught the ropes as a yearling in 1988.

VINCENT O'BRIEN

The retirement in 1994 of Vincent O'Brien brought to an end the glorious career of probably the greatest trainer that European racing has ever produced.

Born in County Cork in 1917, O'Brien started his training career with greyhounds before taking out a licence to train racehorses in 1943 (before that he had been contemplating opening a butcher's shop). A big gamble on the Irish Autumn Double in 1944 – of his two 20–1 shots, one dead-heated for first place and the other won outright – provided the funds to establish himself, and by the end of the decade success was coming thick and fast.

O'Brien won the Cheltenham Gold Cup three times in a row from 1948 to 1950 with Cottage Rake, and the Champion Hurdle in 1949, 1950 and 1951 with Hatton's Grace. In the space of eight years (1952–59) he won ten divisions of the Gloucestershire Hurdle at what we now call the Cheltenham Festival, and in 1952 added another Gold Cup with Knock Hard. He won three consecutive Grand Nationals with three different horses – Early Mist (1953), Royal Tan (1954) and Quare Times (1955) – but towards the end of the Fifties started to turn his attention more to the Flat. The exploits of the staying mare Gladness – with whom O'Brien began his famous association with Lester Piggott – and the great Ballymoss (winner of the St Leger in 1957 and the Coronation Cup, Eclipse, King George and Arc in 1958) placed him at the forefront of his profession, a position he maintained for the next thirty years, with a stream of famous horses being produced from his yard at Ballydoyle, near Cashel in County Tipperary. He won sixteen English Classics, including the Derby six times – with Larkspur (1962), Sir Ivor (1968), Nijinsky (1970), Roberto (1972), The Minstrel (1977) and Golden Fleece (1982) – and twenty-seven Irish Classics; and he won the Prix de l'Arc de Triomphe three times, with Ballymoss in 1958 and Alleged in 1977 and 1978. Among the other famous horses he trained were El Gran Senor, Be My Guest, Artaius, Solinus, Sadler's Wells, Jaazeiro, King's Lake, Caerleon and Royal Academy – whose Breeders' Cup Mile victory under Lester Piggott at Belmont Park in 1990 set the seal on O'Brien's incomparable training career.

Vincent O'Brien leads in his last Royal Ascot winner – College Chapel, ridden by Lester Piggott, after the Cork and Orrery Stakes in 1993.

THE FARRIER

George Windless may not be a name familiar in the annals of the Turf, but his importance in Charlottown's 1966 Derby victory cannot be overrated. For Charlottown, a well backed third favourite for the Epsom Classic, trod on his own off-fore foot when being mounted in the paddock by Scobie Breasley, and wrenched off the shoe. He had 'spread a plate'. As trainer Gordon Smyth's farrier, George Windless had the delicate task of replacing the offending shoe on a horse that suffered from thin-soled feet, so that Charlottown could take his place in the field.

Windless did his job adeptly, as – a few minutes later – did horse and jockey.

A farrier's role is usually less dramatic, and less public, but no less important for that. For without being comfortably shod a racehorse cannot race.

The racing 'plate' which a horse wears in the race is normally made of aluminium – light but sturdy – as opposed to the iron-based shoes which it will wear about the stable and for exercise. Trainers differ in how long before a race they will have the horse fitted with its racing plates: some will have them put on several days before the race, others leave it until the actual day. Whenever it is done, the farrier's skills are vital, for the shoe is attached by thin nails driven into the wall of the hoof, and a nail hammered in a centimetre off target can ruin months or even years of preparation.

Horses with particularly sensitive feet may wear special 'stick-on' shoes, attached to the hoof not by nails but by adhesive: Royal Academy sported such hoofwear when taking the Breeders' Cup Mile at Belmont Park, New York in 1990.

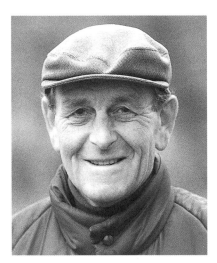

John Dunlop, who won his second Derby with Erhaab in 1994, after Shirley Heights in 1978. Other well-known horses to have come from his Arundel yard include English Classic winners Quick As Lightning (1980 One Thousand Guineas), Circus Plume (1984 Oaks), Moon Madness (1986 St Leger), Salsabil (1990 One Thousand and Oaks, plus the Irish Derby) and Shadayid (1991 One Thousand Guineas); 1974 Ascot Gold Cup winner Ragstone; and the brilliant sprinter Habibti. In June 1995 he sent out five winners at Royal Ascot.

Whatever the size of the operation, the key to the art of training any racehorse is to combine a regular routine with a carefully worked out programme of exercise and feeding in order to bring the horse to its peak at just the right moment – to have it 'trained to the minute'. A horse cannot be kept at its best for long stretches of time, nor can it be expected to be at maximum fitness for every single race it runs, so the trainer will run it in lesser races in order to bring it to top fitness for the really important occasions. When its racing season has finished it will be 'roughed off' and probably turned out in a field to relax after the rigours of training.

The cycle of the Flat trainer's year begins in the autumn, when the stable receives the new intake of yearlings from studs and from the sales. Most of these will have learnt the basics of what is required of them (see 'Breaking in' panel opposite) by the turn of the year, though the trend nowadays is to bring the best horses along more slowly, so that a horse being thought of as a candidate for the Derby (run two seasons after it arrives in the stable as a yearling) might not race until the autumn of its two-year-old season, and thus will not need to be hurried. Humbler yearlings will be taught their trade more quickly with the aim of winning races early the following year before the cream of the crop starts racing.

THE TRAINER'S TEAM

The personnel which a trainer normally has under his command are:

Assistant trainer

Often an amateur jockey and usually working in the stable in order to learn the skills of the job before setting up as a trainer himself, he is the trainer's understudy. Assistant trainers often move around from one yard to another (sometimes going abroad in order to gain a breadth of experience), and most well-known trainers have spent time as an assistant: John Gosden and Michael Kauntze each learned his trade at the feet of Vincent O'Brien; Guy Harwood was assistant to Bryan Marshall, Roger Charlton to Jeremy Tree, and Henry Cecil to his stepfather Cecil Boyd-Rochfort. Peter Scudamore is assistant trainer to Nigel Twiston-Davies.

BREAKING IN

The timing of when a horse is 'broken in' – taught how to be ridden – depends on when it will go into training. A horse destined to run on the Flat will be broken towards the end of its second year, whereas a horse which will be kept as a 'store' for racing over jumps without racing on the Flat will not be broken until much later: Arkle was not broken until he was nearly four.

The horse will have worn a halter and been led from its days as a very young foal and will be used to human company, but nevertheless breaking in is a tricky and crucial operation, usually entrusted to a highly experienced stable lad.

The whole process normally takes two to three weeks. The horse must get used to the feel of a bit in its mouth, and is introduced to this peculiar sensation by means of a mouthing bit, to the mouthpiece of which are attached jangling 'keys' with which the youngster can fiddle with its tongue. To this bit are attached long reins: the lad walks behind the horse and gets it used to feeling the signals coming through the reins to its mouth, and then teaches it to lunge – to walk and trot in circles on the end of a single long rein. Then comes the roller, a padded girth fitted in the position where there will later be a saddle: the reins are fitted through rings on the roller to replicate the feel of the rider's hands on the reins. Next the roller is replaced by a saddle, so that the horse can become accustomed to a larger item on its back. At each stage the horse will continue to be lunged and will be taken walking with the unfamiliar equipment to get it used to these strange sensations.

Eventually comes the big moment when it will be 'backed' – when for the first time it will feel a human being on its back. A lad will lean across the horse, then lay across its back for a few moments, then for longer – all the while making the horse amenable to the new sensations – and before long he will sit quietly and loosely astride it. Then the horse will be lunged with the lad sitting astride and, when it is clear that it accepts as normal the presence of the rider, the lungeing rein will be removed and the horse will be properly ridden – quietly at first by walking and trotting, but soon getting used to the company of other horses by engaging in a gentle canter up the gallops, usually with an older horse to show the way.

A horse which will run on the Flat must also be introduced to starting stalls. The yearling is loaded into the stalls and at first will walk out, then trot out, when the front doors are opened. When it is used to that it will be ridden out of the stalls more forcefully and be allowed to canter for a few hundred yards.

The more advanced education comes when the horse is taught how to keep itself balanced while negotiating bends and how to stretch out at the gallop. It is not until these crucial stages that the trainer will learn the potential racing ability of the new racehorse.

Head lad

The head lad (a very big establishment might have several) is a crucial person in the yard, ensuring the smooth running of the place in all aspects relating directly to the horses and to the stable lads and stable lasses who look after them. The job demands an exceptionally high level of knowledge of horses and the training business, and it is not surprising that many of today's top trainers once served as head lads – Barry Hills with John Oxley, for instance, and Clive Brittain with Noel Murless.

Travelling head lad

To the travelling head lad falls the vital responsibility of seeing that the stable's runners get to the races and supervising the horses' stay at the course. He will often represent the trainer if the latter cannot attend himself.

Stable lad

The lad (or lass) knows the individual horse better than anyone, as he or she spends time grooming it and generally looking after it in its box. The lad will not necessarily ride it in its work: often a more experienced lad or a work rider will do this. A stable lad will normally look after ('do') several horses, and a brief spasm of fame can come to those who have a household name in their charge – witness Desert Orchid's dedicated attendant Janice Coyle. Notoriously underpaid yet devoted to the horses in their charge, stable lads are the unsung heroes and heroines of racing.

Peter Chapple-Hyam, trainer in 1992, only his second season with a licence, of two English Classic winners – Rodrigo de Triano in the Two Thousand Guineas and Dr Devious in the Derby. He has also won the Irish Two Thousand Guineas with Rodrigo de Triano (1992), Turtle Island (1994) and Spectrum (1995).

FOOD AND DRINK

A horse which consumes its food enthusiastically and shows the benefit is known as a 'good doer', and any horse's intake of food is carefully adjusted according to its individual needs and tastes and to its racing and training programme.

The traditional basic diet is corn – oats (too much of which can get a horse over-excited) and bran (what is left when the flour is milled from wheat) – and hay. Many trainers now feed their charges on 'racehorse cubes', manufactured compounds which ensure a balanced diet of high-quality feed. The drawback of cubes is that they can be contaminated by prohibited substances, and the trainer feeding cubes has less control over exactly what he is giving his horses.

Other common foodstuffs are dried sugar beet, maize, boiled barley, linseed, molasses, and carrots and apples. A bran mash is a sort of porridge in which the bran is supplemented by oats, treacle or other ingredients to make it more appetizing, and perhaps some Epsom salts as a laxative.

Other additives are more bracing. Arkle's basic feed when in training was a mixture of mash and dry oats mixed up with six eggs and supplemented by two bottles of Guinness, and Mandarin enjoyed a Mackeson: on his retirement he had two bottles a day delivered to him from the local pub in Lambourn, courtesy of the late Colonel Bill Whitbread, whose company sponsors the famous handicap chase

in which he was thrice runner-up. But unsupervised eating can cause problems: the good hurdler No Bombs once filched his lad's Mars Bar, ingesting a prohibited substance which the 'work, rest and play' delicacy contains. He ran, won, failed the dope test and lost the race.

There are also, in horses as in humans, fussy eaters: when the yearling Nijinsky arrived at Ballydoyle from Canada, Vincent O'Brien discovered that he would not eat oats, so O'Brien had to send across the Atlantic for supplies of the horse nuts which the pernickety young horse was used to. By the time the nuts arrived in County Tipperary, Nijinsky had taken to eating the oats!

The unmistakable outline of Richard Hannon supervising his string. Hannon, who first took out a licence in 1970, was champion trainer for the first time in 1992. Among his best-known horses have been Two Thousand Guineas winners Mon Fils (1973), Don't Forget Me (1987) and Tirol (1990), and sprinters Mr Brooks and Lyric Fantasy.

Newmarket: the all-weather gallop up Warren Hill.

Clive Brittain singing in the rain as the weather gods deliver the right going for User Friendly in the 1992 St Leger at Doncaster. User Friendly was Newmarket-based Brittain's sixth English Classic winner, following her own victory in the 1992 Oaks, One Thousand Guineas success for Pebbles (1984) and Sayyedati (1993), the Two Thousand Guineas with Mystiko (1991) and the St Leger with Julio Mariner (1978). He was the first British trainer to win a Breeders' Cup race – with Pebbles in the 1985 Turf.

Stable jockey

Should it have one, the stable's retained jockey is a vital member of the team and will work closely with the trainer in planning the campaign of each horse, riding work, advising on the purchase of fresh horses, and so on.

Apprentice

The stable apprentice will 'do his two' (in practice, probably four or five) like the other stable lads while pursuing his aim of learning the art of race riding.

Stable secretary

The secretary is partly an accountant (looking after the yard's books, arranging the payment of wages, sending accounts to owners), partly a record keeper, and partly a personnel officer.

In addition, a big yard might have its own feedman (responsible for the feeding routine of each horse) and tackman (who would maintain the equipment). And it would certainly have its own farrier (see page 104).

A STABLE'S DAY

Everyday stable routine is a vital part of the training business, and has changed little in 200 years. Horses for the most part enjoy routine and can become keyed up – for good or ill – if it is disturbed: in the later part of his spectacular career Arkle (see pages 14–16) would become overexcited when his mane was plaited before a race, and in order to cut down on this unnecessary expenditure of nervous energy his mane was left unplaited for what turned out to be his final two races.

The daily timetable varies depending on the time of year (horses cannot work in the dark), but the routine in a fairly large stable might be approximately as follows:

6:30 a.m.

The head lad opens the yard and gives each horse its first feed of the day. He checks the horses for any problems which have have occurred or developed during the night, and the stable lads arrive to muck out the boxes and give the horses a light grooming before saddling up the 'first lot' – the first string of horses which will go out for exercise.

7:30 a.m.

When first lot are mounted the trainer will probably ask the lads to walk them around the stable yard so that he can see if they are walking sound (the head lad having already reported any special problems to him); as soon as they are ready they move off.

Racehorses undergo many different forms of exercise, walking for miles around the roads, especially when building up towards the new season, and trotting and cantering as they are brought towards true fitness. They will seriously gallop ('work') no more than twice a week when they are in full training, either on grass or on purpose-built gallops of peat, woodchip or other surfaces specially designed to be resistant to the vagaries of the weather. (They will also benefit from the occasional swim – excellent exercise without putting stress on the legs.)

Often a trainer will get permission to gallop a horse on a racecourse after racing: although horses like routine they also appreciate a change, and many horses will work better or more informatively at a racecourse than they would on the familiar home gallops. Going to the racecourse also helps accustom inexperienced horses to the travel involved.

The training routine has to be tailored to the particular quirks of the horse: Master Oats proved when winning the Tote Cheltenham Gold Cup in 1995 that he can gallop pretty effectively, but because of the fear of the horse breaking blood vessels, trainer Kim Bailey keeps him to an exercise regime based on quiet cantering.

Work is timed to fit in with a horse's next race, its main pre-race gallop normally taking place four or five days before the event, with a 'pipe opener' two days before the race to clear its wind. The trainer will position himself in a spot from where he can see as much of the gallop as possible and will assess each horse as it comes by, usually expecting his working horses to start off at half speed and gradually increase the pace towards the end of the gallop. A trainer can discover how good a horse is before he races it by galloping it with another horse whose ability he is well aware of, at carefully calculated weights, and word of a trial that shows up something special can often get round very rapidly: Nashwan became favourite for the Two Thousand Guineas in 1989 on the strength of reports of one spectacular gallop at Dick Hern's West Ilsley stable.

Jumping horses will be 'schooled' over hurdles or fences in addition to their usual work, but many trainers do not school a horse once its season has begun (unless its racing performance suggests that it needs a refresher course).

9:00 a.m.

The return from exercise is a crucial moment, for the lads will have to report to the trainer any occurrence of the dreaded cough. Each horse that has been exercised is settled in its box with a net of fresh hay, and the lads then go off for their own breakfast.

10:00 a.m.

Second lot goes out. Often this includes horses who are not in serious work, either because they are backward or because they have recently run in a

André Fabre, whose Pennekamp became his fourth English Classic winner when taking the 1995 Madagans Two Thousand Guineas from Celtic Swing. Based in Chantilly, near Paris, Fabre won the 1991 St Leger with Toulon and the 1993 Two Thousand Guineas with Zafonic and Oaks with Intrepidity. Carnegie in 1994 was his third win in the Prix de l'Arc de Triomphe, following Trempolino (1987) and Subotica (1992).

François Doumen, who sent shock waves through British steeplechasing when sending 25–1 shot Nupsala over from France to win the 1987 King George VI Chase at Kempton Park, and went on to land that race four times in eight years with the subsequent victories of The Fellow in 1991 and 1992 and Algan in 1994. The Fellow, short-headed in the Cheltenham Gold Cup in 1991 and in 1992, finally won chasing's most prestigious prize in 1994 when beating Jodami.

Henry Cecil on his hack on Newmarket Heath.

Jenny Pitman (below) is to date the only woman to have trained the winner of the Grand National (Corbiere in 1983 and Royal Athlete in 1995) and likewise the only woman to have trained the winner of the Cheltenham Gold Cup (Burrough Hill Lad in 1984 and Garrison Savannah in 1991).

But no longer is the sight of a lady trainer in the winner's enclosure in any way unusual. Since ladies were first given the right to hold licences in 1966, many have made their mark on both codes of racing: Mrs Pitman, Mercy Rimell (the first woman to train a Champion Hurdle winner: Gaye Brief in 1983) and Monica Dickinson led the way under National Hunt Rules, while on the Flat Criquette Head became the first lady to saddle the winner of an English Classic when Ma Biche took the One Thousand Guineas in 1983: she won the same race with Ravinella in 1988 and Hatoof in 1992.

Other notable members of the ranks of lady trainers include Mary Reveley, a phenomenally successful handler under both codes, Celtic Swing's trainer Lady Herries, and Lynda Ramsden.

race: once a horse is fit it will maintain that fitness for a while, but if it has no imminent engagements after running it will be 'let down' before being built up to its next peak.

11:30 a.m.

Second lot returns. This leaves only a few horses with special needs to go out: some horses may be exercised individually because of temperament or a particular condition.

Meanwhile the contingent which is to go racing is getting prepared. The travelling head lad is responsible for ensuring not only that the stable's runners are ready, but that they are accompanied to the course by all the necessary accoutrements – such as the owner's colours and the horse's passport (see page 164) – before supervising the loading of the runners into the horsebox and setting off for the races.

12:30 p.m.

The horses receive their lunchtime feed, under the watchful eye of the head lad, who will take a quick look at each horse as the feed goes round.

2:00 p.m.

Early afternoon is the quiet time in a racing stable, and the lads have a couple of hours off – or a couple of hours doing stable tasks, such as clipping or weighing the horses, for which there is not time during the rest of the day.

4:00 p.m.

Evening stables. As the third feed of the day is served, the trainer (or, if he is away at the races, the assistant trainer) and the head lad go round all the horses and discuss the condition of each with its stable lad. Is there any heat in its legs (a sign of tendon strain)? Is it eating up? Is it giving off any of the tell-tale signs which advertise an unhappy horse – crib biting, weaving (that is, swaying from side to side while standing in its box), box walking?

DICK HERN

Few results in 1995 were more popular than the victory of Harayir in the Madagans One Thousand Guineas, for the filly's decisive defeat of Aqaarid brought Major W. R. Hern his first Classic victory since he trained Nashwan to win the 1989 Derby – and his sixteenth in all. The first came with Hethersett in the 1962 St Leger, and in between the Hern roll of Classic honour had included such great horses as Brigadier Gerard, whose victory in the 1971 Two Thousand Guineas was among his seventeen wins in an eighteen-race career; the Queen's Highclere (1974 One Thousand); Bustino (1974 St Leger, and runner-up to Grundy in the famous 1975 King George); the Queen's great filly Dunfermline (1977 Oaks and St Leger); Sun Princess (1983 Oaks and St Leger); and Hern's first two Derby winners, Troy (1979) and Henbit (1980). He also trained top middle-distance horses Ela-Mana-Mou and Petoski, and the phenomenally fast sprinter Dayjur, and was champion trainer in 1962, 1972, 1980 and 1983.

The lads finish work at about 6 p.m., and tranquillity descends on the stable. Not that the trainer's day is done: there are future races to study and entries to arrange, for placing horses to compete in and to win races suitable to their true ability is a key part of the trainer's job. There are owners to phone, with good news or bad, queries from the racing press to deal with, and a hundred other tasks.

A trainer never stops, but there is something magical about a racing stable, with its air of efficient calm contrasting with the hectic excitement of the racecourse. 'The nicest thing about training is going out with the horses in the morning and going round them in the evening,' says Henry Cecil, one of many great trainers of the last few years . . .

HENRY CECIL

Henry Richard Amherst Cecil was born on 11 January 1943, ten minutes before his identical twin brother David. A fortnight before his birth his father had been killed in action in North Africa. In 1944 his widowed mother married Captain Cecil Boyd-Rochfort, who the previous year had been appointed trainer to King George VI: he continued as Royal trainer after the accession of Queen Elizabeth II, preparing many of the Queen's horses for big-race victories. Henry Cecil became his assistant trainer in 1964 and took charge of the famous stables at Freemason Lodge in 1968 on Boyd-Rochfort's retirement. His first winner came when Celestial Cloud prevailed by a short head in the Newby Maiden Stakes for amateur riders at Ripon on 17 May 1969; in the same season he won the Eclipse Stakes with Wolver Hollow and the Observer Gold Cup with Approval.

Since those early days Henry Cecil has established himself at the very peak of his profession. He won his first English Classic with Bolkonski in the 1975 Two Thousand Guineas and took the race again with Wollow in 1976, the first year he was champion trainer. On the retirement of Sir Noel Murless (whose daughter Julie he had married ten years earlier: they divorced in 1990 and she is now a Newmarket trainer in her own right), he moved his horses into Murless's stables at Warren Place in Newmarket. Leading trainer again in 1978 and 1979, he set a twentieth-century record for winners trained (128) in 1979, the year he took the One Thousand Guineas with One In A Million and pulled off the Cup treble at Ascot, Goodwood and Doncaster with Le Moss (who repeated the achievement the next year). He won the 1980 St Leger with Light Cavalry for Jim Joel and the 1981 One Thousand Guineas for the same owner with Fairy Footsteps, but had to wait until 1985 for his first victory in the Derby, Steve Cauthen powering home aboard Slip Anchor. The same year Cecil sent out Oh So Sharp to win three Classics and became the first trainer in British Turf history to saddle the winners of races worth over £1 million – £1,148,189 in all. In 1987 Reference Point gave him his second Derby and third St Leger: that year he set a fresh record of winners trained – 180. Diminuendo won him another Oaks in 1988, and Michelozzo a fourth St Leger in 1989, in which year his Old Vic won the Irish Derby and the Prix du Jockey-Club. In 1990 Rafha won the Prix de Diane (the French Oaks), with another Cecil horse Moon Cactus second, and the King George brought a memorable moment in his extraordinary career when his pair Belmez and Old Vic fought out a rousing duel up the Ascot straight to finish first and second, separated by a neck. His third Derby came with Commander In Chief in 1993, but the winner was the less fancied of Cecil's two runners in the race – the other being 5–4 on favourite Tenby, who flopped.

Other horses to come under Cecil's magic spell include Ardross, Kris, Buckskin, Indian Skimmer and King's Theatre.

MICHAEL STOUTE

Born in Barbados in 1945, Michael Stoute moved to Britain at the age of nineteen to join the Yorkshire stable of Pat Rohan, following this with spells at Newmarket with Doug Smith and Tom Jones before setting up there on his own account in 1972. Classic success came with Fair Salinia in the 1978 Oaks (she also won the Irish and the Yorkshire Oaks), and in 1981 he was leading trainer for the first time, principally through the memorable exploits of Shergar, whom he sent out to win five races that year, including the Derby, Irish Derby and King George. Stoute also won the Irish Derby in 1983 with Shareef Dancer (who had been beaten in a handicap at Sandown on Whitbread Gold Cup Day in April), and took his third English Classic with Shadeed in the 1985 Two Thousand Guineas. Shahrastani brought him his second Epsom Derby and third Irish Derby in 1986; he won the Oaks again with Unite in 1987, the Two Thousand Guineas with Doyoun in 1988 and his first One Thousand Guineas with Musical Bliss in 1989. (He thus became the first trainer this century to win an English Classic in five successive seasons.) In 1993 Stoute achieved a noteworthy treble with Sheikh Mohammed's five-year-old Opera House – the Coronation Cup, Eclipse Stakes and King George VI and Queen Elizabeth Diamond Stakes – and in 1994 he was champion trainer for the fourth time, with win and place prize money of £1,917,462.

MARTIN PIPE

Martin Pipe, son of a West Country bookmaker, took out his first training licence in 1977 and landed his first big race when Baron Blakeney won the Daily Express Triumph Hurdle at Cheltenham in 1981 at 66–1. But it was towards the end of the 1980s that his extraordinary dominance of National

'The Duke' – David Nicholson, who became champion jumps trainer for the first time in 1993–94 and repeated the feat in 1994–95. Trainer of 1988 Gold Cup winner Charter Party and a host of other good horses including What A Buck, Broadsword, Very Promising, Waterloo Boy, Another Coral, Mysilv, Barton Bank, Dubacilla, Mighty Mogul, Moorcroft Boy and the indefatigable Viking Flagship, Nicholson was a successful jockey – winning the 1967 Whitbread on Mill House – before taking out a trainer's licence in 1968, and is now based at a state-of-the-art yard at Jackdaw's Castle, near Stow-on-the-Wold in Gloucestershire.

Martin Pipe, perched on the bicycle which is his habitual means of conveyance round the yard, discussing tactics with his 1991 Hennessy Cognac Gold Cup winner Chatam.

Hunt training was felt most strongly, culminating in the remarkable 1988–89 season when for the first time he was champion trainer, winning nearly £600,000 in prize money from 208 winners: the previous record had been 120 winners trained by Michael Dickinson in 1982–83. Pipe's totals for the next six seasons were 224 (1989–90), 230 (1990–91), 224 (1991–92), 194 (1992–93), 126 (1993–94) and 137 (1994–95), and he has been champion trainer five times. Numerical domination was one thing, but Pipe had to silence the critics by producing winners of big races – and did so with the likes of Granville Again (1993 Champion Hurdle), Miinnehoma (1994 Grand National) and Cache Fleur (1995 Whitbread Gold Cup), horses joining Beau Ranger, Bonanza Boy, Strands of Gold, Sabin du Loir and Carvill's Hill in the list of the best Pipe has trained.

Martin Pipe built his reputation on a famous devotion to detail, paying much more attention to such matters as blood-testing and the chemical balance of the equine metabolism than had hitherto been common, and his version of 'interval training' – working horses uphill, then letting them walk down before cantering or galloping up again – has produced exceptionally fit runners.

Middleham trainer Mark Johnston with his 1994 Madagans Two Thousand Guineas winner Mister Baileys, the first northern-trained Classic winner since One Thousand Guineas heroine Mrs McArdy in 1977. His second Group One winner was 1995 Ascot Gold Cup hero Double Trigger – the first northern winner of the Royal meeting's showpiece for over seventy years.

JOCKEYS

Pity the poor jockey. What other sportsman so regularly exposes himself to the merciless attentions of thousands of spectators – millions when the race is on television – who know for a fact that they could do his job as well as he, and who have invested money in the expectation of his displaying his skills with a proper regard for that investment? He should have kicked on earlier . . . he shouldn't have gone for that gap . . . he came too soon . . . he left it too late . . . he got boxed in. Disgruntled punters are free with their advice to a jockey who has deprived them of profit, yet half an hour earlier, when everything was going to plan, that same jockey was the hero of the race. Hero or villain, the jockey plays the most public human role in racing.

There are around 120 professional jockeys licensed to ride on the Flat, plus another 230 or so apprentices. Over jumps some 130 hold full licences, while there are around 200 'conditional' jockeys. In addition there are about 600 registered amateur riders. (See page 117.)

A select few professional jockeys are paid a 'retainer' by a particular stable, which allows that trainer first call on his services. Sometimes a jockey's retainer is with an owner, as with Willie Carson's to ride horses belonging to Sheikh Hamdan Al-Maktoum. A top jockey might have more than one retainer, but if so they will be in a strict order of priority. The amount of each retainer must be registered at Weatherbys' Racing Calendar office: Lester Piggott's demand for the 1982 season for a sum of £45,000 from trainer Henry Cecil's owners over and above his registered retainer of £10,000 set in motion the events which led to his imprisonment for tax fraud. (Some jockeys have arrangements with trainers to ride their horses but are not formally retained to do so, which allows them more flexibility to take up other opportunities: neither Peter Scudamore nor Richard Dunwoody had a contractual arrangement with Martin Pipe – rather an understanding that they would ride his horses.)

The retainer is quite separate from riding fees, and an agreement must not be based on a jockey riding for a lower fee than that laid down in the Jockey Club Rules. These stipulate that from the summer of 1994 a jockey riding on the Flat will earn £58 per ride, over jumps £80 per ride, plus VAT if applicable. (In addition, the owner must pay a percentage of the fee into the Professional Riders' Insurance Scheme.) If an amateur rider is put up, the fee is normally paid by the owner to the British Horseracing Board (so that an owner cannot save money by avoiding the use of professional jockeys). A jockey may also expect a 'present' from a winning owner, and top jockeys may negotiate an arrangement whereby they receive a share in the stallion value of the winners they ride in Group races. But few jockeys are rich, and against all their earnings are set considerable expenses – primarily travel: in Britain alone a professional jockey may have to cover between 50,000 and 60,000 miles per year, by car, aeroplane and helicopter.

As an example, consider Richard Dunwoody's itinerary for a week in April 1994:

Monday afternoon: Hexham
Tuesday afternoon: Wetherby
Tuesday evening: Ascot
Wednesday afternoon: Punchestown (in Ireland)
Wednesday evening: Cheltenham
Thursday afternoon: Punchestown
Friday afternoon: Newton Abbot
Friday evening: Bangor-on-Dee
Saturday afternoon: Uttoxeter
Saturday evening: Plumpton

Hard graft. Yet a very select handful of jockeys can become among the top

APPRENTICES

An apprentice is a young Flat jockey who is tied by annually renewed contract to a licensed trainer, under whom he (or she) will learn the skills of race-riding. A boy or girl can become an apprentice at sixteen, but can no longer ride as an apprentice jockey once the age of twenty-five has been reached. An apprentice may claim a weight allowance – that is, the horse he or she rides in a race will carry less weight than it would if ridden by a fully fledged jockey, in order to compensate for the rider's lack of experience. (In certain races the claiming of allowances is not permitted.)

The allowances are:

7 pounds until he has won 20 races; thereafter
5 pounds until he has won 50 races; thereafter
3 pounds until he has won 95 races.

Given the weight allowances, it can be very tempting for an owner and trainer to put up a good apprentice on a horse in a competitive handicap where to carry less weight would confer an important advantage. But many apprentices find it a struggle to get rides once they have lost their claim, as they then have to compete on equal terms with more experienced jockeys.

LADY JOCKEYS

Women were first allowed to ride under Jockey Club Rules in 1972, and the first ladies' race was run at Kempton Park on 6 May, when the Goya Stakes was won by Meriel Tufnell on Scorched Earth at 50–1. Some 229 runners were ridden by ladies that year, and not all the criticism levelled at the early female style of race-riding came from Male Chauvinist Pigs: Louie Dingwall, one of the famous female trainers and then in her eighties, threatened to apply for a jockey's licence because she could 'ride the backside off these girls'. Since 1975 women have been allowed to ride as professional jockeys, and with the Sex Discrimination Act becoming law that year they generally have to ride against men, though there are still some races confined to lady jockeys – notably the race run at Ascot as a curtain-raiser to the King George VI and Queen Elizabeth Diamond Stakes in July. Lady jockeys are now such an established part of the racing scene that a winner ridden by a girl rarely excites comment, though there have been recent landmarks in the move towards riding emancipation: Gay Kelleway was the first woman to ride a Royal Ascot winner when partnering Sprowston Boy in the 1987 Queen Alexandra Stakes, and in 1991 Alex Greaves became the first lady jockey to win the Lincoln Handicap when taking the race on Amenable.

Women riding over fences was a much less novel idea than lady riders on the Flat, for ladies' races have long been an important element in point-to-point racing. Women were first allowed to ride under National Hunt Rules in 1976, the first winning lady rider being Diana Thorne at Stratford on 7 February. Since then lady jump jockeys have made such a significant impact that it is no longer a cause for much comment if a runner in a big race is ridden by a woman. The first woman to ride in the Grand National was Charlotte Brew – her mount Barony Fort refused four fences out in the 1977 running – and the closest a lady rider has come in the National was fifth: Rosemary Henderson on Fiddlers Pike in 1994. The first woman to win a race over the Grand National course at Liverpool was Caroline Beasley, who won the Fox Hunters' Chase on Eliogarty in 1986. On the same horse in 1983 she had scored the first female riding triumph at the Cheltenham National Hunt Festival, where Gee Armytage rode two winners in 1987. In 1984 the Irish Grand National at Fairyhouse was won by Mrs Ann Ferris on Bentom Boy, and her sister Rosemary finished third.

Maxine Cowdrey, one of the top lady jockeys, after winning the Colenso Diamond Stakes at Ascot in July 1993, her fourth victory in the race which she was to land for a record-breaking fifth time in 1994. (She won the race under three different names: Maxine Carvalho, her first married name, then Maxine Juster, her maiden name, then Maxine Cowdrey, her name following her second marriage.) Her father-in-law Sir Colin Cowdrey is married to trainer Lady Herries, to whom Maxine is assistant trainer.

earners in sport, and it is not hard to see why. Their skills can make the difference between a horse winning and losing a race, and if that race is the Derby or the Prix de l'Arc de Triomphe or one of a few other top events, winning will increase the value of the horse to mind-boggling sums.

But what is the essence of their skills? It is a commonplace of racing that the good jockey is the one who makes fewer mistakes than the ordinary one, rather than the one who will win races which the other will not.

Jockeys do not win races: horses win races. But most races are won by the jockey's complementing the horse's ability in making it as straightforward as possible for the horse to win by responding to the particular manner of that horse's style of racing. Thus a good jockey does not set the pace on a horse with doubtful stamina, but keeps it covered up until the right time to produce it for its run to the winning post. Some horses have instant acceleration, some take longer to work up to top speed (and some, of course, have no acceleration at all). Some horses 'stop' when they find themselves in the lead, so have to get their heads in front at the last possible moment, while some like to lead all the way. The trainer will point out such foibles to the jockey before the horse is mounted, and will instruct the jockey on the best way of riding the race. Sometimes a trainer's pre-race instructions may not fill the jockey with confidence: trainer Tim Forster's usual instruction to his jockeys before the Grand National is supposedly: 'Keep remounting.'

A good jockey will also be a shrewd judge of pace (that is, he will know whether the runners are moving too slowly or too fast, given the distance of the race, the course and the condition of the going), and will be able to adapt to the way a race is run, so that if no jockey wishes to make the pace he may decide to put his horse in front in order to ensure a true gallop, even though that was not the original intention. A jockey riding up the inside rail may find that he is surrounded by other runners at the moment he needs to make his run: does he pull back so as to be able to get round to the outside of the field, or sit tight in the hope that one of the runners in front may tire and roll away from the rails, thus creating a gap?

Such decisions must be made in a split second during a race which is being run at about 35 m.p.h., and call for iron nerve and acute judgement: get it wrong and there's no shortage of vociferous advice from racegoers as you dismount.

Nor can most jockeys drown their sorrows in a few pints of bitter and a Cornish pasty, for the constant battle against weight which many jockeys have to wage forms an austere backcloth to everyday existence. The carefully structured and controlled range of weights which horses are set to carry in Flat races harks back to an age when people generally (and, indeed, horses) were significantly smaller than they are today. Thus today's jockeys need to be uncommonly light in order to ply their trade. Top weight in a Flat race is likely to be somewhere between 9 and 10 stone, with the bottom weight in a handicap around $7\frac{1}{2}$ stone – so, given the preponderance of horses towards the bottom of the handicap, the lighter a jockey can ride at, the more rides he will be able to get.

This means that most jockeys have to subject themselves to fierce discipline in order to keep their weight low: the traditional diet by which a jockey keeps appetite at bay consists of champagne and cigars, though in reality most exist on a very small breakfast of tea and toast, no lunch (though perhaps a bar of chocolate for energy) and a light supper. (The weight range in National Hunt races is around 2 stone higher than for the Flat, reflecting the jumping game's origins in the hunting field, where underfed riders are not a common sight.) These days many racecourse changing rooms have saunas in which jockeys can lose the last few pounds.

The aim, of course, is to keep to a starvation diet and at the same time keep the body fit and strong, for to control over 1,000 pounds of horseflesh through a race demands a level of athleticism which participants in many other sports would envy, and a jockey's body needs to be at maximum fitness to minimize the effects of the injuries which may blight a riding life.

A National Hunt jockey can expect to fall roughly once every eleven or twelve rides, though only 4 per cent of falls result in a significant injury (the most common one being a broken collar bone), and it is a source of constant amazement how easily jump jockeys seem to shrug off the effects of falls. Falls on the flat – under either code – are often far worse on account of their suddenness and the speed at which the horses are travelling. Occasionally injury has a permanent effect, and the history of the profession is peppered with instances of jockeys whose riding careers were brought to an unscheduled end through mishap.

Some jockeys have paid the ultimate price which their highly dangerous profession can exact, including Manny Mercer (brother of Joe), killed at Ascot in September 1959 when thrown on the way to the start, Joe Blanks, killed at Brighton in 1981, Brian Taylor, who died as a result of a fall at the end of a race in Hong Kong in December 1984, Steve 'Samson' Wood, killed at Lingfield Park in May 1994, and jump jockeys Doug Barrott, who died after a fall at Newcastle in 1973, Viv Kennedy, who suffered fatal head injuries in a hurdle race at Huntingdon in August 1988, and Philip Barnard, killed by a fall from Sayyure at Wincanton on Boxing Day 1991.

Every jockey must obtain a Medical Record Book from the Jockey Club, in which his injuries are recorded: this should be shown to the Medical

AMATEUR JOCKEYS

There are two categories of licensed riders who take part in races without receiving a fee. Category A amateur riders may ride in any Flat or National Hunt event confined to amateur riders, while category B riders may ride against licensed professional jockeys under National Hunt rules (on the Flat there are no events, other than novelty races, in which male amateurs may ride against professionals). Many top jump jockeys have begun their riding careers as amateurs. (Amateur jockeys are designated 'Mr' (or indeed 'Miss' or 'Mrs') in the list of jockeys in a race.)

CONDITIONAL JOCKEYS

The conditional jockey is National Hunt racing's equivalent of the Flat apprentice. A conditional jockey must be under the age of twenty-five, and may claim allowances in certain races as follows:

7 pounds until he has won 15 races; thereafter
5 pounds until he has won 30 races; thereafter
3 pounds until he has won 55 races.

Officer at the race meeting before the jockey weighs out. A jockey who has a bad fall can be barred from riding until such time as the Medical Officer specifies, and such restrictions are noted in his Medical Record Book.

Fred Archer, the most famous jockey to ride in Britain before Gordon Richards, succumbed not to injury but to the battle against weight. Archer was unusually tall for a jockey, and although he weighed only 6 stone when taking his first Classic, the Two Thousand Guineas on Atlantic in 1874 – the first year he was champion jockey, at the age of seventeen – he gradually found keeping himself to a reasonable riding weight a terrible struggle. He used an extremely strong purgative, known as 'Archer's Mixture' ('I tried it myself when I was riding races,' wrote the trainer George Lambton, 'and from my own experience I should say it was made of dynamite'), and the effort of wasting took its toll on him mentally and physically. But his riding record was phenomenal: 2,748 winners from 8,084 rides, including twenty-one Classics. (Among his five wins in the Derby was the 1880 victory of Bend Or, whom Archer rode with one arm strapped to a steel brace under his silks, having been savaged by a horse at Newmarket less than a month before.) In October 1886 he wasted fiercely in order to ride St Mirrin in the Cambridgeshire at Newmarket, but he put up one pound overweight and the horse was beaten by a head. Archer's wasting had brought on a fever. He rode for a few more days, going down to Lewes for what turned out to be his last ride, then returned to Newmarket for medical attention. On 8 November 1886 he shot himself in a fit of delirium.

A lesser jockey of the period shortly after Archer, but one arguably of more lasting influence, was the American **Tod Sloan**. For he it was who revolutionized British race riding by popularizing what is now the universal jockey's seat based on very short stirrup leathers, the jockey crouched up over his mount's neck rather than – as Archer would have ridden – in a much more upright posture (though contemporary photographs of Sloan riding show that his length of stirrup leather was still very much longer than is common in today's Flat jockeys). 'He rides like a monkey on a stick,' wrote the famous contemporary society magazine *Vanity Fair*, 'but he wins races.' Sloan had not invented the style (which was deemed to be effective as it cut down wind resistance on a jockey during a race), but he made it a common sight on English racecourses, and he enjoyed a good deal of success. He was a brilliant judge of pace and a fine tactician, and mastered the art of riding a race from the front: to 'do a Tod Sloan' became rhyming slang for going out on your own – hence 'on your Tod'. Between 1897 and 1900 Sloan rode 254 winners (including one Classic winner – Sibola in the 1899 One Thousand Guineas) from 801 mounts in England, and in 1899 had earned the huge retainer of £5,000 from Lord William Beresford. But he fell foul of the Jockey Club on account of his betting, and his licence to ride was not renewed. He was deported from England in 1915 for running an illegal gaming house in London, and died in the charity ward of a Los Angeles hospital in 1933. At the height of his career in England *Vanity Fair* had said of him: 'He is a great little jockey who is popular; but he is hardly so polite as a good American should be.'

More popular, and much more polite, was **Steve Donoghue**, who dominated the jockeys' championship during and following the First World War, taking the title annually from 1914 until 1923, when he tied with the then apprentice Charlie Elliott; and the cry of 'Come on, Steve!' was a familiar shout for long after. Donoghue rode the winners of fourteen Classics, including the Derby six times, on Pommern, Gay Crusader, Humorist, Captain Cuttle, Papyrus and Manna. His name will for ever be associated with two other immortals of the Turf – The Tetrarch, who ran only as a two-year-old but whose achievements in that one year (1913) give him a claim to be the fastest horse ever seen in England, and Brown Jack, on whom Donoghue won the Queen Alexandra Stakes at Royal Ascot for six consecutive years from 1929 to 1934. Their final victory gave rise to some of

Mick Kinane – son of Tommy Kinane, who won the 1978 Champion Hurdle on Monksfield – was thrust into the limelight in 1989 when winning the Prix de l'Arc de Triomphe on Carroll House, and the following year took the Two Thousand Guineas on Tirol and the King George VI and Queen Elizabeth Diamond Stakes at Ascot on Belmez, not long after he had partnered Go And Go to victory as the first ever European-trained horse to win a leg of the American Triple Crown when landing the Belmont Stakes. Irish-born Kinane won the 1993 Derby on Commander In Chief after Khalid Abdullah's then retained jockey Pat Eddery had opted for odds-on favourite Tenby, and consolidated his position as one of the great international jockeys with victory on Dermot Weld's Vintage Crop in the Melbourne Cup the same year. He won a second King George in 1994 on his second ever mount in the race – King's Theatre.

The end of a great career: Peter Scudamore returns to unsaddle Sweet Duke at Ascot in April 1993 after his 1,678th victory.

the most emotional scenes ever seen on a British racecourse: 'Never will I forget the roar of that crowd as long as I live,' wrote Donoghue; 'All my six Derbys faded before the reception that was awaiting Jack and myself as we set out to return to weigh in. I don't think I was ever so happy in my life.'

Gordon Richards was the most successful jockey in the history of British racing. His career total of 4,870 winners from 21,843 rides has never been in danger of being exceeded; he was champion jockey twenty-six times and rode the winners of fourteen Classics.

Born in Shropshire on 5 May 1904, one of twelve children of a miner, he had his first ride in public in 1920 and his first winner, Gay Lord, in an apprentice race at Leicester, in 1921. (On returning to unsaddle he was asked why he had taken the horse so wide round the bends, and he replied that he had been told that Gay Lord needed a longer trip.) He was champion jockey for the first time in 1925, and for the 1932 season accepted a retainer from the immensely powerful Fred Darling stable at Beckhampton: he subsequently rode for the stable until Darling's retirement in 1947.

In 1933 Richards's seasonal total of winners was a record-breaking 259. On 3 October that year he won on his last ride at Nottingham, then all six races at Chepstow the next day, and the first five at Chepstow the day after. In the sixth race he was aboard a 3–1 on shot called Eagle Ray: 'I did not think that I could possibly be beaten,' he wrote, but Eagle Ray finished third, beaten a head and a neck. Gordon Richards had ridden the winners of twelve successive races, still a world record.

Another memorable Richards year was 1947, when his total of 269 winners set a fresh record which has never been beaten. The same year, though, saw one of his most sensational defeats, on Tudor Minstrel in the Derby. Tudor Minstrel had won the Two Thousand Guineas by eight lengths and seemed a certainty for the Epsom race, starting at 7–4 on. In his autobiography *My Story*, Gordon Richards recalled the race:

I have never, in the whole of my life, had such an uncomfortable ride at Epsom. Every time I held him up, he fought me. Every time I let him down to go, he shot off to the right. Either way, he was making certain that he lost the race. The whole race was a nightmare, but he still finished fourth.

Then the letters began to arrive. Hundreds of them, and telegrams as well. Some incredibly impertinent people even telephoned. I was told that I had pulled the horse's head off. The kindest suggested that I was incapable of riding a donkey.

As a matter of fact, I find donkeys very difficult to ride.

Lack of stamina combined with his refusal to settle caused Tudor Minstrel's downfall, but Richards finally got his desperately sought-after victory in the Derby with Pinza in 1953, just after he had been knighted in recognition of his services to racing – the first and to date the only jockey to have been so honoured. Pinza and Richards went on to win the King George VI and Queen Elizabeth Stakes, but in 1954 Richards was forced to retire after the Queen's filly Abergeldie reared and fell on him in the paddock at Sandown Park on Eclipse Stakes day, causing severe injuries.

His career as a trainer produced several very good horses, including Pipe of Peace, winner of the Middle Park Stakes in 1956 and third to Crepello in both the Two Thousand Guineas and the Derby the following year; Court Harwell, second to Ballymoss in the 1957 St Leger; and Reform, who beat Taj Dewan and Royal Palace in the Champion Stakes in 1967. His final year of training was 1969, after which he acted as racing manager for Sir Michael Sobell and for Lady Beaverbrook. Gordon Richards died on 10 November 1986.

He had an unorthodox riding style, more upright than today's jockeys and often with a loose rein. Yet his mounts did not get unbalanced and horses ran extremely straight for him. He used his whip as an encouragement, not a punishment, yet was rarely pipped in a close finish. A model of integrity and modesty, he was loved by the racing community and punters alike.

But we must not forget the exploits of the great jockeys in the other code,

Fred Archer, as caricatured by Vanity Fair's 'Spy' in 1881.

The youngest jockey to ride in a recorded race was Frank Wootton, who rode in South Africa at nine years and ten months. He was champion jockey in England from 1909 to 1912.

the riders whose names adorn the annals of the winter game. Before the
Second World War jumping was very much the inferior code, but three
jockeys stood out: **Fred Rees** and **Billy Stott**, who each won the jockeys'
championship five times, and **Gerry Wilson**, who won it six times just
before the war and rode Golden Miller when that great horse won the
Cheltenham Gold Cup and the Grand National in 1934, winning the Gold
Cup again on him in 1935. (Golden Miller was ridden by four different
jockeys for his five Gold Cup victories.) The immediate post-war period was
dominated by **Tim Molony**, champion jockey from the 1948–49 season
until 1951–52 and again in 1954–55; and the Fifties belonged to **Fred
Winter**, champion four times: 1952–53 and 1955–56 to 1957–58. He rode to
victory in the Grand National on Sundew (1957) and Kilmore (1962) and was
to win it twice more as a trainer in the 1960s, with Jay Trump in 1965 and
Anglo the following year; his greatest feat as a jockey was to steer Mandarin
to victory in the Grand Steeplechase de Paris in 1962, a race described on
page 171. **Stan Mellor**, champion in 1959-60, 1960–61 and 1961–62,
became the first jump jockey to ride more than 1,000 winners, and twice-
champion **Jonjo O'Neill**'s record of 149 winners in a season in 1977–78
stood until Peter Scudamore's 1988–89 term, the early Eighties having seen
keen rivalry between Scu and **John Francome** – 'The Greatest Jockey'
(John McCririck's highly appropriate nickname for him), who rode 1,138
winners during his career, from Multigrey at Worcester on 2 December 1970
to Gambler's Cup at Huntingdon on 8 April 1985. John Francome never
rode a Grand National winner – he was second on Rough and Tumble in
1980 – but took the Gold Cup on Midnight Court in 1978 and the Champion
Hurdle on Sea Pigeon in 1981, and was champion seven times (including
one shared).

    Peter Scudamore retired laden with records after riding Sweet Duke to
victory at Ascot on 7 April 1993. His career tally of 1,678 winners is a record
for a National Hunt jockey, and his total of 221 in the phenomenal 1988–89
season a record for a single term. Like Francome he never won the Grand
National (he was third on Corbiere in 1985), nor could he crown his great
career with Gold Cup victory, but he landed the Champion Hurdle twice –
on Celtic Shot in 1988 and Granville Again in 1993. He was champion
jockey a record eight times, including the title shared with John Francome
in 1981–82. Another telling Scudamore statistic: 792 of his 1,678 winners
were for trainer Martin Pipe.

    Great jockeys all, but none so dear as the one who will bring home your
next winner.

LESTER PIGGOTT

Lester Piggott was twelve when scoring his first victory, on The Chase, at
Haydock Park on 18 August 1948, and as he approached sixty in 1995 he was
still riding winners.

    He took the jockeys' championship eleven times, winning a record
number of English Classics and hundreds of other big races at home and
abroad. His record makes him the second most successful jockey (behind
Gordon Richards) in British Turf history. In addition, he won twenty races
over hurdles and over 800 races overseas. He 'retired' first in 1985, and
trained for a couple of seasons before being convicted of tax fraud and being
sent to prison in October 1987; he was released on parole in 1988, and
formally released the following year. Then, to pile sensation upon sensation,
he returned to race-riding in October 1990 – not as some bit player on the
fringe of his erstwhile profession, but as a major operator: the week
following his return, he won the Breeders' Cup Mile at Belmont Park, New
York, on Royal Academy, with as brilliant a ride as he had ever produced.

    The bare facts of Piggott's extraordinary life in racing do little to convey
the magic he wove during his riding career. Bred for the sport (his father
Keith was a trainer and jockey, his grandfather had ridden the winners of

Gordon Richards.

two Grand Nationals, his mother was a member of the famous jockey-producing Rickaby dynasty), he was the complete rider: a superb judge of pace, fearless, almost unbeatable in a close finish, hard on a horse when he thought it necessary yet unsurpassed at coaxing the best out of a reluctant or non-staying partner, completely cool yet fiercely competitive. This last aspect of his character led him into trouble on many occasions, not least when at the age of eighteen in 1954 he fell foul of the Royal Ascot Stewards for his riding of Never Say Die (on whom he had won his first Derby that year) in the King Edward VII Stakes. Piggott had supposedly ridden dangerously in going for a gap just after the turn into the home straight, and the incident is still, over forty years later, the subject of debate and

LESTER PIGGOTT'S CLASSIC WINNERS

Two Thousand Guineas
Crepello 1957
Sir Ivor 1968
Nijinsky 1970
Shadeed 1985
Rodrigo de Triano 1992

One Thousand Guineas
Humble Duty 1970
Fairy Footsteps 1981

Derby
Never Say Die 1954
Crepello 1957
St Paddy 1960
Sir Ivor 1968
Nijinsky 1970
Roberto 1972
Empery 1976
The Minstrel 1977
Teenoso 1983

Oaks
Carrozza 1957
Petite Etoile 1959
Valoris 1966
Juliette Marny 1975
Blue Wind 1981
Circus Plume 1984

St Leger
St Paddy 1960
Aurelius 1961
Ribocco 1967
Ribero 1968
Nijinsky 1970
Athens Wood 1971
Boucher 1972
Commanche Run 1984

The old guard and the new: Lester Piggott with Frankie Dettori at Ascot.

disagreement. He was suspended from riding until further notice, the Stewards of the Jockey Club (to whom the case was referred) advising him that they had 'taken notice of his dangerous and erratic riding both this season and in previous seasons, and that in spite of continuous warnings, he continued to show complete disregard for the Rules of Racing and for the safety of other jockeys.'

Piggott himself calmly put such reversals behind him, and in 1955 replaced Sir Gordon Richards (who had retired in 1954) as jockey to Noel Murless – the top riding job in British racing. The partnership won several Classics and saw Piggott take his first jockeys' title in 1960, but it was not a formal arrangement, and when in 1966 Piggott decided to ride Vincent

Lester Piggott wins his thirtieth Classic – the 1992 Two Thousand Guineas on Rodrigo De Triano. Pursuing him here is fourth-placed Silver Wisp (Paul Eddery); runner-up Lucky Lindy and third-placed Pursuit Of Love are out of the picture.

Of all the myriad Lester Piggott stories, a favourite which combines his deafness and his fabled carefulness with money concerns a stable lad who was still waiting for the customary 'present' from Piggott after leading up a winner he had ridden. After waiting some weeks he encountered the jockey at the racecourse.

'How about a pound for that winner I did you?'

'Uhhh?'

'How about a pound for that winner I did you?'

'I can't hear you – that's my bad ear. Try the other side.'

The stable lad goes to the other ear.

'How about a couple of quid for that winner I did you?'

'Still can't hear you. Go back to the one-pound ear!'

O'Brien's Valoris in the Oaks rather than the Murless runner, Varinia, Murless announced that their partnership was over.

Valoris duly won the Classic, and Piggott and Murless patched up their differences, enabling the jockey to ride several other big winners for the stable. In 1967 he won the jockeys' championship as a freelance, and in 1968 deepened his already close association with the Vincent O'Brien stable, putting in one of his most brilliant performances in producing Sir Ivor with a dazzling burst of finishing speed to win the Derby.

In 1970 he landed the Triple Crown with Nijinsky, though he was criticized by some riders in the stand for coming too late on the colt in the Prix de l'Arc de Triomphe when beaten a head by Sassafras. Controversy surrounded Piggott again before the 1972 Derby, in which he replaced Bill Williamson as rider of Roberto. Whether this was a case of Piggott's jocking off the other rider or whether he was an innocent bystander as the owner exercised his right to have whichever partner he could get for his horse, Piggott produced one of his most inspired finishes to get Roberto home by a short head from Rheingold – and the same determination was in evidence when he drove The Minstrel home a neck ahead of Hot Grove in the 1977 Derby, having won his seventh Derby on the French-trained Empery in 1976.

Towards the end of the 1980 season O'Brien and Piggott parted company, and in 1981 Piggott became stable jockey to Henry Cecil at Warren Place, the Newmarket yard where he had had such a long association with Noel Murless. The new arrangement got off to a flying start when Piggott rode Fairy Footsteps to take the One Thousand Guineas – just days after he had been dragged under the front door of the Epsom stalls by Winsor Boy, an accident which left the jockey with a severely injured ear. He was champion jockey for the last time in 1982, and for what was announced as his final season in 1985 Piggott returned to freelance status. (Cecil snapped up four Classics that year with his new stable jockey, Steve Cauthen.)

Many other famous horses apart from his own Classic winners in Britain had benefited from the Piggott touch: dual Arc winner Alleged, Dahlia, Shergar (on whom he won the 1981 Irish Derby in a canter), Ardross, Park Top, Sagaro, Moorestyle, Rheingold, Aunt Edith, Meadow Court, Zucchero, Zarathustra. But Piggott was as determined and as effective in a small race on a mediocre horse as in any Derby, and it was this quality which made him a man to have on your side. Hence the devotion he attracted from punters.

That devotion was transferred to his new career. In 1986, his first year as a trainer at Eve Lodge, Newmarket, he sent out thirty winners, including Cutting Blade in the Coventry Stakes at Royal Ascot, and the following year won the Italian Oaks with Lady Bentley. But while on the surface the future looked bright, disaster was waiting in the wings.

Lester Piggott had always been an enigmatic character, and stories of his carefulness with money were part of the fabric of racing gossip for decades. But few people were prepared for the revelation that he was being investigated for possible tax fraud, and the shock when he was convicted and sentenced to three years in prison in October 1987 reverberated throughout the racing world. His OBE, awarded in the 1975 New Year Honours, was stripped from him. He was released on parole on 24 October 1988, a year and a day after conviction, and that seemed to be that – a sad coda to an extraordinary sporting career.

One of the many surprises surrounding his return to the saddle in October 1990 was how well kept was the secret. Suddenly, it seemed, Lester was back – persuaded in large measure by his old ally Vincent O'Brien. It was a measure of Piggott's standing in the sport that once the racing world had recovered from the shock, it seemed to accept his presence as completely normal – despite the fact that when on 15 October 1990 he had his comeback ride at Leicester he was three weeks short of his 55th birthday. The following day he rode Nicholas, trained by his wife Susan, to win a six-furlong race at Chepstow, and the winner-machine was back in action.

On the Saturday of the following week he was at Belmont Park to replace the injured John Reid on Vincent O'Brien's Royal Academy, and showed that the old magic was still very potent when bringing the colt with an exquisitely timed late run on the outside to get up and win by a neck.

In May 1992 he won his thirtieth English Classic when Rodrigo de Triano took the Two Thousand Guineas, and although the name L. Piggott no longer figured high in the list of leading jockeys come the end of the season (he rode just nineteen winners in Britain in 1994), his very presence continued to defy the norms of the sport – as he had been doing for so long.

WILLIE CARSON

William Hunter Carson was born in Stirling on 16 November 1942. His first winner was Pinker's Pond – a six-length victory in an apprentice handicap at Catterick on 19 July 1962 – and he has hardly looked back since. He was champion jockey for the first time in 1972 (following eight successive championships by Lester Piggott), repeating the feat in 1973, 1978, 1980 and 1983.

Hands up who's won the Derby! Willie Carson and Erhaab return after their virtuoso performance at Epsom in 1994.

He won his first Derby on Troy in 1979, his second on Henbit a year later, his third in 1989 on Nashwan and his fourth on Erhaab in 1994. On Nashwan he also won the Two Thousand Guineas (to add to High Top in 1972, Known Fact in 1980 and Don't Forget Me in 1987), the Eclipse (which he would land again on Elmaamul in 1990) and the King George VI and Queen Elizabeth Diamond Stakes (following victories on Troy in 1979, Ela Mana Mou in 1980 and Petoski in 1985). He won the Oaks on Dunfermline for the Queen in 1977, on Bireme in 1980, on Sun Princess in 1983 and on Salsabil in 1990; the One Thousand Guineas on Salsabil and Shadayid (1991); and the St Leger on Dunfermline, Sun Princess and in 1988 on Lady Beaverbrook's Minster Son, whom he had bred himself. At Newcastle on 30 June 1990 he became only the third jockey this century to notch up six victories at one fixture, entering the record books alongside Gordon Richards's 1933 feat at Chepstow (see page 120) and Alec Russell's in 1957 at Bogside. Less than two months later he was rearranging the record books again: his victory on Joud at Newmarket on 24 August 1990 brought his career total of wins in Great Britain to 3,112, taking Carson past Doug Smith's total to make him the third most successful jockey in British racing history, behind Gordon Richards and Lester Piggott.

PAT EDDERY

Pat Eddery.

Pat Eddery had his first winner at the age of seventeen when riding Alvaro to victory at Epsom in April 1969. Apprenticed to 'Frenchie' Nicholson, the greatest tutor of young jockeys (who also gave a start to Paul Cook, Tony Murray and Walter Swinburn), Eddery first displayed his exceptional talents when riding five winners from seven mounts at Haydock Park one Saturday in August 1970, and was leading apprentice in 1971 with 71 winners. His apprenticeship over, he joined Peter Walwyn, becoming champion jockey for the first time in 1974, the year he also won his first Classic, the Oaks on Polygamy. He retained the title for the following three seasons. The high point of his time with Walwyn was the 1975 summer campaign of Grundy, who won the Derby and Irish Derby before beating Bustino in the King George VI and Queen Elizabeth Diamond Stakes at Ascot, widely held to be the race of the century.

Eddery's riding of Grundy that day was testament to his great qualities as a jockey – acute judgement of pace with the ability to read the rapidly changing circumstances of a race, strength and determination in a close finish and a wonderful rhythmical drive to help his horse see out the punishing final stages.

Eddery's next English Classic win was on Scintillate for Jeremy Tree in the 1979 Oaks, and in 1980 he won the Prix de l'Arc de Triomphe on Robert Sangster's Detroit. That year he started riding for Vincent O'Brien, and in 1981 he won the Irish Two Thousand Guineas and Sussex Stakes for the stable on King's Lake. The following year he won his second Derby on Golden Fleece (who never ran again), in 1983 the Two Thousand Guineas on Lomond, and 1984 was marked by his association with El Gran Senor, on whom he won the Two Thousand Guineas and the Irish Derby but whose failure by a short head to get back at Secreto in the Derby after a ding-dong struggle through the last furlong brought upon the jockey charges of over-confidence from the riders in the stand.

But in 1985 he really asserted himself on the international stage by taking the Irish Derby on Law Society, the Coronation Cup and Prix de l'Arc de Triomphe on Rainbow Quest, and the Champion Stakes and Breeders' Cup Turf on Pebbles. He won the St Leger for John Dunlop on Moon Madness in 1986 and in the same year took over from Greville Starkey the ride on Dancing Brave, winning the King George and the Arc. His association with this great horse led to a lucrative retainer with Dancing Brave's owner Khalid Abdullah, for whom he rode such fine horses as Warning, the English and French Derby winners of 1990, Quest For Fame and Sanglamore, and

1991 St Leger winner Toulon. More Breeders' Cup triumph came on Sheikh Albadou in the 1991 Sprint at Churchill Downs, and in 1994 he landed his third St Leger, on Sheikh Mohammed's Moonax. To date Pat Eddery has been champion jockey ten times, most recently in 1993.

LANFRANCO DETTORI

Frankie Dettori was born in Milan in December 1970, son of the great Italian jockey Gianfranco Dettori, who had won the Two Thousand Guineas on Bolkonski in 1975 and Wollow in 1976.

Frankie's first winner came at Turin in 1986, but it was when he moved to England to serve his apprenticeship at Newmarket with fellow Italian Luca Cumani that the flame of his career really started to blaze. In 1989 he was champion apprentice, with seventy-five winners; and the following year, at the age of nineteen, he became the first teenager to ride a century of winners in Britain since Lester Piggott – an older nineteen – in 1955. That season he came fourth in the jockeys' championship with 141 wins to his credit, and he kept up the momentum in the following years, scoring 94 in 1991, 101 in 1992 and 149 in 1993 (third in the championship behind Pat Eddery and Kevin Darley). It was an extraordinary start to a riding career, the more so because along with quantity was coming quality. His association with the great sprinting filly Lochsong in 1993 and 1994 captivated the racing public, securing an affection that public was already predisposed to bestow on account of Dettori's naturally ebullient demeanour. His avowed

Frankie Dettori winning in the royal colours on Her Majesty the Queen's Success Story at Lingfield Park in January 1994.

intention was to be champion jockey, and he achieved that feat in 1994 with a rare vengeance.

It had been decreed that all-weather racing would count towards the title; so, rather than wait for the turf season to commence in March, Dettori made a concerted effort to put runs on the board while his main rivals were still sunning themselves or fulfilling lucrative riding contracts overseas, and by dint of unrelenting application on the unglamorous all-weather circuits in January and February built up such a lead that Pat Eddery, the other major contender, never had the chance to get in a blow. By mid-season the only question was whether Frankie could beat Gordon Richards's all-time record of 269 winners, and while the statisticians argued about the merits of comparing the feat with Richards' were he to do so, Dettori carried on totting up the winners. He reached the century on 11 June and the double century on 1 September – both records – and by the end of the season his final tally was a massive 233. Jason Weaver was second on 200. Dettori's tally of mounts was 1,317, a new record and testament to his furious dedication to the task.

But 1994 was also a year of huge achievement on the quality scale, with more big sprint wins on Lochsong (including a second Prix de l'Abbaye), his first win in an English Classic (after being beaten a short head in both Guineas that year!) when Balanchine won the Oaks, a first Irish Derby on the same filly, and then a memorable victory in the Breeders' Cup Mile on Barathea.

In June 1995 he won his second English Classic when Moonshell outstayed Dance A Dream and Pure Grain in the Vodafone Oaks at Epsom.

The phrase 'breath of fresh air' has often been used to describe the effect of Frankie Dettori's enthusiastic approach to his work – and it's a breath which has inspired the last few years on the Flat.

RICHARD DUNWOODY

'The Prince' – Richard Dunwoody.

Born in Belfast in January 1964, Richard Dunwoody first sat on a pony at the age of two, led up a horse at a race meeting at Gowran Park at the age of seven ('Is he not a bit young?', the stipendiary steward asked his father) and had his first ride under Rules in August 1982, with his first winner coming on Game Trust in a hunter-chase at Cheltenham on 4 May 1983. Within just seven years of that initial victory Dunwoody had joined Fred Winter, Willie Robinson and Bobby Beasley as the only jockeys since the war to have won the big treble of jump racing, taking the Grand National on West Tip in 1986, the Cheltenham Gold Cup on Charter Party in 1988 and the Champion Hurdle on Kribensis in 1990. But the horse with whom he became most closely associated was Desert Orchid: taking over the ride on the grey on the retirement of Simon Sherwood, he won seven races on Dessie, including the King George VI Chase in 1989 and 1990. By the time a second Grand National was landed with Miinnehoma in 1994 Dunwoody – respectfully nicknamed 'The Prince' by his weighing-room colleagues – had established himself as one of the great jump jockeys of the age. After three consecutive years as runner-up to Peter Scudamore, he was champion jockey for the first time in 1992–93, and the following term just beat Adrian Maguire after a sensationally close contest which went to the very last meeting of the season. Another landmark was reached in 1994 when he became only the fourth National Hunt jockey in history to ride over 1,000 winners (the others were Stan Mellor, John Francome and Peter Scudamore). Richard Dunwoody stands second only to Scu in the all-time rankings. But figures and records convey little of the magic of Dunwoody in the saddle, for he has been the supreme stylist, a craftsman with riding skills unmatched since the close of John Francome's career. Above all, Dunwoody has shown consummate ability in presenting a horse at a fence – that is, adjusting its stride on the approach so that it jumps fluently – and it is testament to his mastery of this operation that during the 1993–94 season he had so few serious falls that he did not miss a single ride through injury.

ADRIAN MAGUIRE

Adrian Maguire, heir apparent to the jump jockeys' crown, was born in April 1971 and learned his skills around the pony-racing tracks of his native Ireland. Having ridden his first winner under Rules in a bumper at Sligo in April 1990, he first made his mark on the English jumping scene when partnering Martin Pipe-trained Omerta to victory in the Fulke Walwyn Kim Muir Chase at the Cheltenham Festival in March 1991, and followed this up by winning the Irish National on the same horse the following month, beating Cahervillahow by a short head in a barn-storming finish. Maguire moved to England under the tutelage of Toby Balding, for whom he drove home Cool Ground to a 25–1 shock victory in the 1992 Tote Cheltenham Gold Cup by a short head from The Fellow, and that season was eighth in the jockey's championship. In 1992–93 he was third behind Richard Dunwoody and Peter Scudamore, and in 1993–94 – a season highlighted by a brilliant victory on Barton Bank in the King George at Kempton – was narrowly beaten by Richard Dunwoody after a desperately close contest.

That season was his first with trainer David Nicholson, for whom Maguire rode horses of exceptional quality, notably Barton Bank and the redoubtable chaser Viking Flagship, whose greatest moment of 1995 is described on pages 182–3. Injury curtailed Maguire's 1994–95 season – in the jockeys' title race he finished joint runner-up with Norman Williamson behind Richard Dunwoody – but few doubt that he is champion-in-waiting.

Occupational hazard: Mark Richards about to part company from L B Laughs at Ascot in January 1991.

Adrian Maguire.

THE MADAGANS 2000 GUINEAS STAKES (CLASS A)
(Estimated total value £230000)
(Group 1)
ROWLEY MILE
for three yrs old
£150000 added to stakes

CHANNEL FOUR RACING

TOTE TRIO

Distributed in accordance with Order 194 (ii)(c) (Includes a sixth prize) for three yrs old only, entire colts and fillies £500 stake, £1000 extra unless forfeit declared *April 25th, £300 extra if entry confirmed Weights: Colts.9st; fillies 8st 9lb MADAGANS PLC has generously sponsored this race, the value of which includes a trophy value £1000 for the winning owner In addition, Madagans Plc will award mementoes to the winning trainer and jockey, plus a £100 prize for the lad or girl responsible for the best turned out horse in this race THERE WILL BE A PARADE FOR THIS RACE Runners will be assembled in the parade ring in racecard order, and will be released on to the racecourse at approximately ten second intervals to canter to post The Directors of the British Horseracing Board have modified Order 121 (ii)(a) for the purposes of this race The breeder of the winner, if qualified under Order 196,will receive a Breeder's Prize of £3500 75 entries, 60 at £500, 2 at £1500 and 13 at £1800. - Closed March 1st, 1995 **Owners Prize Money. Winner £92880; Second £38018; Third £18906; Fourth £8668; Fifth £4189; Sixth £2497. (Penalty Value £117912) A SS BP**

CLASS 120

Form/Owner	Trainer	Age	st	lb	Draw

1   BAHRI (USA) (14) .... **9   0   (1)**
B c Riverman (USA) - Wasnah (USA) (Nijinsky (CAN))
Mr Hamdan Al Maktoum..(J. L. Dunlop,Arundel)   W. Carson
ROYAL BLUE, WHITE epaulets, striped cap.
2221-2   (Breeder - Shadwell Farm Inc)

CELTIC SWING(9-0) won, with BAHRI(9-0) tracked leaders, steady headway, ran on well, 2nd, beaten 11/4l, Newbury, April 22, good, 7f, 3yo group 3 stakes. Consistent type who ran a cracking race on his seasonal debut, sound claims. Class 120 Rating 126

2   CELTIC SWING (14) .... **9   0   (7)**
Br c Damister (USA) - Celtic Ring (Welsh Pageant)
Mr P. D. Savill..(Lady Herries,Littlehampton)   K. Darley
D   MAROON, LIGHT BLUE sleeves, LIGHT BLUE cap, MAROON diamond.
111-1   (Breeder - Lavinia Duchess of Norfolk)

CELTIC SWING(9-0) tracked leader to halfway, took it up 2 out, kept on well, won, with BAHRI(9-0) 2nd, Newbury, April 22, good, 7f, 3yo group 3 stakes. Yet to put a foot wrong and is the one they all have to beat. Outstanding individual. Class 130 Rating 131

3   CHILLY BILLY (16) .... **9   0   (6)**
B c Master Willie - Sweet Snow (USA) (Lyphard (USA))
Mr G. E. Shouler...(Mrs J. R. Ramsden,Thirsk)   K. Fallon
ROYAL BLUE, WHITE Cross of Lorraine, WHITE cap.
5341-4   (Breeder - W. and R. Barnett Ltd)

PAINTER'S ROW(8-12) won, with Montjoy(8-9) 2nd, beaten a nk, NWAAMIS(8-9) 3rd, CHILLY BILLY(9-0) always prominent, gradually faded latter stages, 4th beaten 5l, Newmarket, April 20, good to firm, 1m, 3yo group 3 stakes. Class 105 Rating 107

4   DIFFIDENT (FR) (17)................................. **9   0   (4)**
Ch c Nureyev (USA) - Shy Princess (USA) (Irish River (FR))
Sheikh Mohammed ....(A. Fabre,France)   M. J. Kinane
C   MAROON, WHITE sleeves, WHITE cap.
11-1   (Breeder - Haras d' Etreham and R. Ades)

DIFFIDENT(9-5) raced in rear, smooth headway, led close home, readily, won, with Harayir(9-7) 2nd, beaten 11/4l, SILCA BLANKA(9-4) behind, Newmarket, April 19, good to firm, 7f, 3yo handicap. Displayed sheer class to score latest, big threat to all. Class 115 Rating 117

5   GREEN PERFUME (USA) (204) .... **9   0   (10)**
B c Naevus (USA) - Pretty Is (USA) (Doonesbury (USA))
Lord Sondes ....(P. F. I. Cole,Whatcombe)   T. Quinn
Sir George Meyrick
BLACK, WHITE triple diamond, halved sleeves, WHITE cap, BLACK star.
221122-   (Breeder - Brereton C. Jones)

PENNEKAMP(9-0) won, with GREEN PERFUME(9-0) raced in rear, moved up to lead, kept on once headed, 2nd, beaten 1l, Newmarket, October 14, good to firm, 7f, 2yo group 1 stakes. Model of consistency last season, no forlorn hope here. Class 115 Rating 117

cont'd over

6 NWAAMIS (USA) (16) 9 0 (5)

B c Dayjur (USA) - Lady Cutlass (USA) (Cutlass (USA))
Mr Hamdan Al Maktoum................................(J. L. Dunlop,Arundel)   R. Hills
C   ROYAL BLUE, WHITE epaulets, BLACK cap.
1-3   (Breeder - Shadwell Farm Inc and Shadwell Estate Co Ltd)

PAINTER'S ROW(8-12) won, with Montjoy(8-9) 2nd, beaten a nk, NWAAMIS(8-9) a
ran on at the finish, 3rd beaten about 1l, CHILLY BILLY(9-0) 4th, Newmarket, Ap
group 3 stakes. Class 105 Rating 108

7 PAINTER'S ROW (IRE) (16) ....

B c Royal Academy (USA) - Road To The Top (Shirley Heights)
Lord Weinstock & The Hon Simon Weinstock ....
....(P. W. Chapple-Hyam,Marlbor
CD   PALE BLUE, YELLOW and WHITE check cap.
11-1   (Breeder - Ballymacoll Stud Farm Ltd)

PAINTER'S ROW(8-12) tracked leader to halfway, took it up 2 out, kept on well, won, with Montjoy(8-9) 2nd,
beaten a nk, NWAAMIS(8-9) 3rd, CHILLY BILLY(9-0) 4th, Newmarket, April 20, good to firm, 1m, 3yo group 3
stakes. Unbeaten and has done nothing wrong so far. Faces his biggest test to date. Class 110 Rating 113

8 PENNEKAMP (USA) (21)................................ 9 0 (11)

B c Bering - Coral Dance (FR) (Green Dancer (USA))
Sheikh Mohammed ....(A. Fabre,France)   T. Jarnet
C   MAROON, WHITE sleeves, MAROON cap, WHITE star.
1111-1   (Breeder - Magalen O. Bryant)

PENNEKAMP(9-2) chased leaders, asserted in the latter stages, won, with Bene Erit(9-2) 2nd, beaten 11/2l,
Evry, April 15, good, 6f, stakes (listed). Unbeaten French ace, stays 12f and has a telling turn of foot. Class
120 Rating 124

9 PIPE MAJOR (IRE) (190) 9 0 (8)

B c Tirol - Annsfield Lady (Red Sunset)
Lord Scarsdale ....(P. C. Haslam,Middleham)   J. Weaver
CD   WHITE, BLACK sash, RED sleeves, YELLOW cap.
1421-   (Breeder - W. Maxwell Ervine)

PIPE MAJOR(8-13) close up, led halfway, headed, regained lead close home, won, with Chief Burundi(8-11)
2nd, beaten 11/4l, Newmarket, October 28, good, 1m, 2yo stakes. Class 100 Rating 105

10 SILCA BLANKA (IRE) (17) 9 0 (2)

B c Law Society (USA) - Reality (Known Fact (USA))
Aldridge Racing Limited ....(M. R. Channon,Upper Lambourn)   R. Hughes
C   ORANGE, BROWN seams, BROWN sleeves, ORANGE seams,
                    ORANGE cap, BROWN spots.
04450-0   (Breeder - Luzi S P A)

DIFFIDENT(9-5) won, with Harayir(9-7) 2nd, beaten 11/4l, SILCA BLANKA(9-4) chased leaders to halfway,
faded, gradually lost touch, behind beaten 8l, Newmarket, April 19, good to firm, 7f, 3yo handicap. Class 95
Rating 100

11 ZEB (IRE) (21) 9 0 (3)

B c Cyrano de Bergerac - Bap's Miracle (Track Spare)
Barouche Stud Ltd................................(B. A. McMahon,Tamworth)   T. Ives
           DARK BLUE, YELLOW braces and armlets, quartered cap.
2260-1   (Breeder - Mrs M. Cross)

ZEB(9-0) always going well, took up the running 1f out, easily, won, with Khamseh(8-9) 2nd, beaten 21/2l,
Haydock, April 15, good to firm, 7f, 3yo maiden stakes. Impressive on seasonal debut but has more to do
here. Class 85 Rating 87

NUMBER OF DECLARED RUNNERS 11 ....(DUAL FORECAST)

Raceform Standard Time: 1 min 37.3 secs Record Time: 1 min 35.08 secs

RESULT: 1st .... 2nd .... 3rd .... 4th ....

DISTANCES ..../ .... TIME ....

1994: **MISTER BAILEYS** 3 9 0 J Weaver 16-1 (M Johnston) 23 ran

The figure in brackets after each horses name indicates the number of days since last ran.

ABBREVIATIONS.
BF - Beaten Favourite. C - Course Winner. D- Distance Winner.

According to the prep-school philosopher Nigel Molesworth, 'every boy ort to equip himself for life by knoing a bit about horse racing,' and he advises his readers how to put their money on: 'You do this with a bookie or the Tote as even a fule kno. What every fule do not kno however is which horse to put the money on and bring back a dividend. To kno this you hav to study form . . . Everything is right. DANDRUFF hav won over the distance, it have two ancestors from the national stud, a french owner, trained on meat, sits up in its stable, lest.. pig.... up, firm going THE LOT. BASH ON THE WINE GUMS.' Dandruff, the 51–1 on favourite in the 3:30 at Sponger's Park, is unplaced in a field of five.

The interpretation of form is not nearly as difficult or mysterious as many people imagine. Form is simply information about a horse's past performances, and by amassing data about the going, the course, the style of running, the jockey, the trainer, the time the race took to run, the distance of the race, the distance between the horse and the other horses, and so on, the student of form can assess which horse in a race has the best chance based on those past performances.

In practice, of course, it is not quite so simple. There is the occasional truly freak result, as when Foinavon won the 1967 Grand National only because he was so far behind the rest of the field before the sensational pile-up at the twenty-third fence that he was able to avoid the mayhem. More usually, there is the factor which might not reasonably be predicted - such as Desert Orchid's defying form book and know-alls in staying three miles to win the 1986 King George VI Rank Chase at Kempton Park, thus causing a rethinking of his preferred trip.

Form is constantly changing, and the more a horse runs, the more your overall picture of it will be coloured in.

The problem, though, is how to interpret form accurately and profitably – how much significance to attach to each of the different pieces which together make up the mosaic. Rather like Sherlock Holmes approaching a case, it is the choice of what is relevant and what is not which makes the study of form so fascinating and (potentially) so rewarding.

Where do you find this vital information? The specialist racing daily newspapers – the *Sporting Life* and the *Racing Post* – will give you a comprehensive and detailed account of the form of each horse in each race. But that takes a great deal of studying if you are to benefit from it fully, so it may be easier to rely on the interpretation which the expert journalists in these and other papers have undertaken on your behalf. Of course, you may disagree with all the experts if your own reading of an earlier race or a particular line of form seems to you to be more convincing, or if you are the beneficiary of solid inside information not available to the pundits.

Form is fact, but it must be tempered by judgement: it can be taken at face value, or amended by personal interpretation, weighted depending upon the circumstances of the race. Whatever the personal input, though, there are certain key factual elements to be taken into account.

DISTANCE OF THE RACE

Most horses have a range of ideal race distances, and what this ideal may be is not always obvious even to those most closely involved with the individual animal. In 1986 Sheikh Mohammed's Ajdal won the top two-year-old race of the season, the Dewhurst Stakes over seven furlongs, then as a three-year-old won the Craven Stakes and disappointed when fourth in the Two Thousand Guineas and third (and subsequently disqualified when his jockey Walter Swinburn failed to weigh in) in the Irish Two Thousand – all races over one mile; his pedigree suggested he might stay further so he ran in the Derby (one and a half miles), only to finish down the field behind Reference Point after being close up two furlongs out – a run which suggested lack of stamina. So he was switched from middle-distance races to sprinting, and proved an instant success, winning three

Previous spread:
The Newmarket racecard form guide for the Madagans Two Thousand Guineas, 6 May 1995.

SOURCES OF INFORMATION

Although some national newspapers give a very brief digest of the form for the major races of the day, the main sources of detailed form are the two racing papers, the *Sporting Life* (established 1859) and the *Racing Post* (established 1986). Both appear daily (though on Sundays only when there is racing) and give a very comprehensive run-down of the form of each runner that day, as well as expert interpretation of that form. In addition to the immediate concern of finding the day's winners, both offer a range of other useful information to anyone interested in racing: results and reports of the previous day's racing in Britain and overseas, entries and weights in future races, profiles of and interviews with leading Turf personalities, articles on all aspects of the sport (both are especially strong on breeding), detailed statistics and a wide range of racing news.

With advances in database and printing technology, both trade papers offer an extremely sophisticated and mind-boggling array of information relating to the form of races. In addition to the specific details on each individual horse, you may expect to find displayed such matters as the records of particular trainers and jockeys in action at each of the day's courses (with course runners and rides since last victory there); lists of trainers' current form (including pertinent matters such as when they last sent out a winner); advance going reports; the performance of favourites at each course; which horses have travelled furthest to each individual meeting; microscopic analysis of ratings; and a whole lot more.

It would be impossible to weigh all that information for every race, so it may be a relief to turn to the advertisements offered by those who have done all the homework for you (and have often supplemented it with inside information from racing stables) and are prepared to divulge their findings for a small consideration, either by post or by recorded telephone message.

For racegoers, an easily accessible and usually comprehensible source of basic form information is the course racecard, which at most tracks these days includes a simple form summary. For example, patrons at the 1995 National Hunt Festival at Cheltenham bought not just a racecard but a document formally designated 'Official Colour Racecard and Form Guide', which contained for each runner a three-line form summary (plus unofficial rating): the Ritz Club National Hunt Chase summary of Rough Quest – 'Has dropped to a handy handicap mark and will win soon' – could have proved more profitable than many hours studying the minutiae of the form in the *Life* or the *Post*, as the horse won at 16–1.

of the major sprint races – the July Cup, the William Hill Sprint Championship and the Vernons Sprint Cup, over six, five and six furlongs respectively.

The first indication of the probable best distance for a horse is its breeding, as stamina, like speed, is hereditary; but racecourse performance is always the most reliable indicator of any aspect of form. Of course, several factors affect how far a particular performance testifies to a horse's stamina – the pace at which the race was run, the state of the going, the nature of the track – and these must be weighed up and interpreted. For instance, any horse which is running on at the end of a truly run race over two miles at Newmarket in heavy going may reasonably be assumed to be able to stay the distance, whereas the winner of a slowly run race over the same distance on firm going around the much tighter and flatter track at Chester could not, on that evidence alone, be said to have the same degree of stamina.

The question of stamina is rarely clear-cut. Some experts think that the Derby course of a mile and a half can suit a horse which truly stays no more than a mile and a quarter, as much of it is downhill: Sir Ivor in 1968 is one instance of a horse who won the Derby but showed that one and a quarter miles was his ideal trip. More curiously, it is often the case that the four-and-a-half-mile Grand National sees fine performances from horses whose optimum trip elsewhere is around two and a half miles: in recent years such old favourites as Classified and The Tsarevich have regularly run well in the National although their best distance was two and a half to three miles, and Gay Trip, winner in 1970, also came into this category. Mention of the Grand National inevitably brings in Red Rum, who won the race race three times and was second twice, yet whose sire, Quorum, never won at further than one mile!

The Timeform organization, based in Halifax in Yorkshire, is the largest concern in the world devoted to the dissemination of information about racing form. It was founded by the legendary Phil Bull, who died in June 1989 at the age of seventy-nine and who had become one of the most influential racing personalities of the century, famed both for his forthright opinions on Turf matters and for the shrewdness of his opinions in interpreting form.

It is said that Bull's father, a Salvation Army captain, was drawn to betting after a religious slogan he had posted on a wall in Doncaster reading 'What shall we do to be saved?' was answered by an anonymous scrawler, 'Back Doricles for the St Leger': Captain Bull took the advice, collected at 40–1, and passed on to his son a love of racing and betting.

Using the pseudonym William Temple, Bull started in the 1930s a service for punters called Temple Racetime Analysis, based on the then revolutionary method of studying the horses' times in races. In the 1940s he began publishing the *Best Horses* series which became the *Racehorses* annuals, now complemented by *Chasers and Hurdlers*.

Timeform offers many other services and publications, including its daily racecards, in which every runner in every race is subjected to close scrutiny, described and given a rating by which its chance in relation to the other runners in the race can be assessed. (Occasionally you may hear one of the Channel Four paddock commentators mention a horse's Timeform rating, and 'a squiggle in Timeform' refers to the sign which accompanies the Timeform rating of an unreliable or difficult horse.)

GOING

Most horses show a liking for a particular state of the ground, though some can act equally well on any going. Preference for a particular kind of going can be passed on from generation to generation, so in the absence of conclusive racecourse evidence useful information will be gleaned from the horse's breeding. In addition, some horses are obviously physically more suited to a certain sort of going by virtue of their action or conformation: a horse with very straight pasterns ('straight in front') will tend to lack suppleness and so may well be uncomfortable on firm ground, which can easily cause jarring.

The size of the feet does not necessarily point to a going preference; more important is the action of the horse, for a horse with a high, round action (that is, one which brings the knees of its forelegs high in each stride) is likely to go well on soft or muddy going, while the animal with a more economical 'daisy-cutting' stride will probably go well on fast ground but will be less effective on soft. And if it seems to 'float' over the ground on good going it may well get stuck in the soft.

Obviously the chances of a horse with an apparent preference for a certain sort of going will be subject to the weather. But having the 'wrong' ground does not of course mean that the horse will not win: Desert Orchid landed the 1989 Cheltenham Gold Cup in very heavy ground, which he was known to dislike; nevertheless in terms of strict form he ran below his best – because of the going. When assessing the chances for any race it is folly to discount the importance of the going: while any horse should be able to act effectively on good ground, on extremes of going – very hard or very heavy – always pay serious attention to the chances of horses who have won or run well on similar going in the past.

CLASS

Form is relative. A close-up sixth in a Classic is probably a much better performance than victory in a lowly race, and it is important that the class of each race which makes up part of the form is taken into account. Detailed form in the specialist racing papers will give the prize money of the past race in question, and will state the level of the race, so the class of the contest can be easily assessed. Generally Group One form on the Flat will be of a very high order, and those who forget the old adage that Classic form is the best form sometimes miss out on a decent winner. On The House won the Sussex Stakes at 14–1 in 1982, the year she took the One Thousand Guineas, and Roberto was 12–1 when supplementing his Derby victory in 1972 with his sensational triumph in the Benson and Hedges Gold Cup – though it hardly seemed a generous price beforehand, as one of his rivals was Brigadier Gerard.

The quality of the form of any race becomes established as the runners proceed to run well subsequently ('frank' or 'advertise' the form) or to disappoint ('devalue' the form), and gradually a picture of the overall quality of the race is built up. The initial impression, for instance, that the 1994 Ever Ready Derby, however exciting, was not a Classic of great quality was borne out by the later performances of the runners that season. The field of twenty-five (including Foyer, who fell at Epsom) subsequently ran in 71 races in 1994 and only managed to notch up ten victories, of which one was a dead heat and just one – King's Theatre in the King George VI and Queen Elizabeth Diamond Stakes at Ascot – was a Group One event.

2.50 Queen Mother Champion Chase (Class A) (Grade 1)
CH4
10 declared *Winner £77,848* — 2m Old

£125,000 added **For** 5yo+ **Weights** 5yo 11st 6lb; 6yo+ 12st **Allowances** mares 5lb **Entries** 15 pay £200 **1st Forfeit** 13 pay£400 **Confirmed** 12 pay £200 **Penalty Value 1st** £77,848 **2nd** £29,032 **3rd** £14,116 **4th** £5,980 **5th** £2,590 **6th** £1,234

1 45-2152 **BRADBURY STAR** 62 CD BF — 10 12-0 P Hide (171)
b g Torus–Ware Princess — J T Gifford — James Campbell

2 3123F64 **DEEP SENSATION** 35 CD — 10 12-0 N Williamson (163)
ch g Deep Run–Bannow Bay — J T Gifford — R F Eliot

3 F-13332 **EGYPT MILL PRINCE** 60 CD — b 9 12-0 W Marston (151)
b g Deep Run–Just Darina — Mrs J Pitman — S R Webb

4 51-163U **KATABATIC** 46 CD — 12 12-0 S McNeill (165)
br g Strong Gale–Garravogue — J T Gifford — Pell-mell Partners

5 11-5121 **NAKIR** (FR) 32 CD — 7 12-0 J Osborne (160)
b g Nikos–Nabita — S Christian — Jim Lewis

6 F22-12F **TRAVADO** 79 CD — 9 12-0 R Dunwoody (164)
br g Strong Gale–Adelina — N J Henderson — Mrs Michael Ennever

7 -14441U **UNCLE ERNIE** 14 D BF — 10 12-0 M Dwyer (151)
b g Uncle Pokey–Ladyfold — J O FitzGerald — Lady Lloyd Webber

8 2-115F2 **VIKING FLAGSHIP** 18 CD BF — 8 12-0 C F Swan (171)
b g Viking–Fourth Degree — D Nicholson — Roach Foods Limited

9 135424- **WILD ATLANTIC** 314 D — 12 12-0 Kevin Jones (91)
b g Welsh Saint–Stonehow Lady — Miss Z A Green — E G Foley

10 42-F222 **SNITTON LANE** 32 D — 9 11-9 D Bridgwater (140)
b m Cruise Missile–Cala di Volpe — W Clay — H D White

1994 (8 ran) Viking Flagship D Nicholson 7 12-0 PM164 — A Maguire 4/1

BETTING FORECAST: 2 Viking Flagship, 11-4 Travado, 7-2 Nakir, 7 Bradbury Star, 9 Egypt Mill Prince, 14 Deep Sensation, 33 Katabatic, Snitton Lane, Uncle Ernie, 1000 Wild Atlantic.

DIOMED

Bradbury Star Better than ever when winning the Mackeson in November for the second time (gaining eighth win here), with Egypt Mill Prince (rec 22lb) third, and has strong claims on that form; however has disappointed both starts since and has gained only three of his 18 career wins in second half of season; successful up to 3m1f but has done most of his winning around 2m4f (only two wins at 2m); has won on soft but ideally suited by better ground.

Deep Sensation Very smart on his day, winner of this race in 1993 and close third last year; again beaten by Viking Flagship and Travado in Grade 1 event at Sandown in December and well below form since; not the strongest of finishers and recent wins have been against lesser opposition; acts on any going.

Egypt Mill Prince Smart 2m-2m4f handicapper; in good form this season and fine second to Martha's Son at Ascot in January, but would be receiving over a stone from the main protagonists if this was a handicap; effective with and without blinkers; acts on any; often makes the running.

Katabatic Winner of this race in 1991, second in 1992, third in 1993 and fifth last year; handled desperate conditions best when reversing Cheltenham placings with Travado over 2m4f at Aintree last spring but this season seems not to be the force he was (let down by jumping last two starts).

Nakir Leading 2m novice chaser last season, winner of Arkle Trophy; made most when accounting for small fields in handicap at Ascot in December and Grade 2 event at Newbury last month (left well clear four out after Viking Flagship fell upsides when seemingly going better); acts on heavy.

Travado Top-class 2m-2m4f chaser, winner of Arkle Trophy in 1993 and pipped by Viking Flagship in this event last year; easy winner at Exeter in November but again beaten by Viking Flagship in Grade 1 event at Sandown in December; has won on soft but ideally suited by less testing conditions; goes well fresh.

Uncle Ernie Smart chaser; has not quite recaptured the form which won him the Martell Aintree Chase last spring by 11l from Viking Flagship (gave 20lb) although has been successful at Haydock (2 ran) and Sandown this season.

Viking Flagship Top-class 2m chaser, beating Travado and Deep Sensation by a neck and a length in this race 12 months ago; gave that pair a bigger beating in Grade 1 event at Sandown on reappearance and easily followed up from Snitton Lane at Wetherby; has blotted his copybook since but possibly finds carrying big weights in very testing ground against him.

Wild Atlantic Hopelessly out of depth here.

Snitton Lane Useful 2m chaser, winner of Grand Annual Handicap off 122 here last year, but lots to find at these weights.

VERDICT: VIKING FLAGSHIP has the best 2m form on offer, but looks sure to go off at a much bigger price than looked possible at the start of the year because of his recent defeats. Conditions should be ideal for him today and he can successfully defend his crown by beating **Travado** again. **Bradbury Star** is an interesting rival, although he has several negatives to overcome.

POSTDATA Viking Flagship — **TOPSPEED** Viking Flagship

READING FORM

This is the card for the 1995 Queen Mother Champion Chase at Cheltenham as published in the *Racing Post*. The race, a Grade One Class A event run over two miles of Cheltenham's Old Course, is due off at 2:50, with ten declared runners, and is being shown live on Channel Four. The Penalty Value (see pages 63–4 above) is £77,848. Then follow the race conditions and details of the entries, and prize money down to sixth place. Bradbury Star will carry number 1. He is a bay gelding by Torus out of Ware Princess, has won over this course ('C') and this distance ('D'), and was beaten favourite in his last race. The form figures '45-2152' give his finishing positions in his last six outings, the most recent (he was second) on the right; the dash indicates the change of season – he was fourth and fifth in his last two outings in 1993–94. It is 62 days since he last ran, and he is a ten-year-old carrying 12 stone. He is trained by J. T. Gifford (a trainer from an overseas base would have his or her home country indicated) and owned by James Campbell, and will be ridden by P. Hide. The figure 171 is his rating in Postmark, the *Racing Post*'s own handicap – a mark which puts him joint top with number 8, Viking Flagship. Looking at the form figures of Bradbury Star's nine rivals, we can see that Deep Sensation fell ('F') three outings ago, and Katabatic unseated his rider ('U') last time out. ('P' would indicate pulled up, 'R' refused and 'B' brought down.) Katabatic's 'CD' indicates that he has won over the distance of this race at this course. The 'FR' after Nakir's name shows that he was foaled in France.

Beneath the card is a note of last year's winner (Viking Flagship won at 4–1 off a Postmark rating of 164) and runner-by-runner analysis of the race by the *Post*'s expert Diomed, plus selections from the paper's other form columns Postdata and Topspeed. Seems like Viking Flagship is a good thing! (He won at 5–2.)

THE ESSENCE OF FORM

The essence of form as information is illustrated in the *Sporting Life*'s guide to Master Oats on the morning of the 1995 Tote Cheltenham Gold Cup. Into this entry is packed an extraordinary amount of data, including:

name, age and weight carried in this race;

finishing position in last fifteen outings (the dash mark indicates the division between the most recent seasons, obliques divisions between earlier seasons);

trainer (K.C Bailey);

breeding (chestnut gelding by Oats out of Miss Poker Face by Raise You Ten);

previous victories, with season, month, course, going, type of race: the novice chase which Master Oats won at Uttoxeter in the 1993–94 season was open to horses officially rated up to 130, the top-weighted horse ran off 124, and Master Oats himself off 107;

total win prize money in career (£98,783) and win prize money this season (£57,843);

details of last five outings, including nature and grade of race, going, weight carried, close-up of running, betting details, and the performances of other runners in that race engaged in the same race now; distances; time of race (with above or below average); speed ratings on a scale 0–100 (83, 67, 70 etc.), and a special 'Racecheck' feature which summarizes subsequent performances (for up to ninety days) by the runners in that race (in this case, one runner in Master Oats's most recent race has since been placed and two have been unplaced) – a good indication of the quality of the form of that race. 'See Miinnehoma' at the foot of the column refers the form student to the separate entry on that horse.

MASTER OATS   **9-12-0**
P/P312/11211F1-111   **K C Bailey**
ch g Oats - Miss Poker Face by Raise You Ten
1991-92 3m ½f ch good (Southwell)
1993-94 (Nov) 3m 2f ch good (Uttoxeter) Hcp [130,124,**107**]; **(Dec) 3m ch soft (Huntingdon)** Hcp [120,114,**114**]; **(Jan) 3m ch heavy (Lingfield)** Hcp [130,125,**125**]; **(Feb) 3m 4½f ch soft (Kempton)** Hcp [op,154,**135**]; **(Apl) 3m ch good/soft (Perth)**
1994-95 (Dec) 3m ch soft (Chepstow) Gr2 Hcp [op,150,**144**]; **(Dec) 3m 6f ch heavy (Newbury)** Hcp [op,153,**148**]; **(Jan) 3m 1½f ch heavy (Cheltenham)** B. **£98,783 (£57,843).**

Jan 28, Cheltenham, 3m 1½f (6-y-o and up) chase B, heavy, £13,615: **1 MASTER OATS** (9-11-6, N Williamson), **held up, pecked ninth, chased leader eleventh, led 16th, clear from three out, impressive.** (6/4 fav op Evens tchd 13/8), **2 DUBACILLA** (9-11-5, D Gallagher), **behind, driven along to stay in touch 16th, ridden and stayed on again from three out, took second run-in, no chance with winner.** (4/1 tchd 5/1), **3 BARTON BANK** (9-11-12, A Maguire), **in touch, challenged seventh, prominent when hit 17th, ridden and one pace from three out.** (2/1 op 9/4 tchd 5/2), **4 YOUNG HUSTLER** (btn 24½l) (8-11-12, T Jenks), **led to 16th, outpaced from three out.** (9/1 op 8/1 tchd 10/1),; 7 Ran. 15l, 3½l, 6l, 2½l. 7m 2.80s (a 46.80s). SR: 83 67 70 64 61.
RACECHECK: Wins 0, pl 1, unpl 2.

Dec 31, Newbury, 3m 6f (5-y-o and up) Hcp chase [open,153], heavy, £24,466: **1 MASTER OATS** (8-11-6, inc 4lb ex, **148**, N Williamson), **held up, headway eleventh, hit 15th, challenged next, not fluent 17th, led approaching four out, clear after three out, easily.** (5/2 jt-fav op 7/4 tchd 11/4), 2 Earth Summit (6-10-12,bl), 3 Party Politics (10-11-5),; 8 Ran. 20l, 25l, ½l, ¾l. 8m 5.70s. RACECHECK: Wins 2, pl 2, unpl 6.

Dec 3, Chepstow, 3m (5-y-o and up) Hcp (Gr 2) [open,150], soft, £17,495: **1 MASTER OATS** (8-11-4, **144**, N Williamson), **held up, mistake seventh, joined leaders next, led 11th, clear approaching three out, steadied and went left last, hard ridden and ran on run-in.** (3/1 op 5/2 tchd 7/2), 2 Party Politics (10-11-7), 3 Cool Ground (12-11-0),; 5 Ran. 4l, dist. 6m 47.10s (a 57.10s). SR: 71 70 -.
RACECHECK: Wins 3, pl 3, unpl 6.

April 22 1994, Perth, 3m (5-y-o and up) chase, good to soft, £7,035: **1 MASTER OATS** (8-12-0, N Williamson), **in touch, joined leader tenth, led 12th, clear after 14th, hit last, very easily.** (4/9 op 2/5 tchd 1/2), 2 Durham Sunset (7-11-3), 3 Ida's Delight (15-11-5),; 5 Ran. 10l, 1¼l, dist. 6m 29.70s (a 32.70s). SR: 13.

April 9 1994, Aintree. See MIINNEHOMA

TIME

The study and use of race times can be immensely complicated, and most casual punters have only a vague notion of how important an element of form the matter of time can be, generally leaving it to the time experts in the racing press to advise them as to what is significant.

Horses do not race against the clock, and compared with human athletes they have shown little improvement in times over the last fifty years. But if record times are not in themselves important, the comparison of the times that different horses take to win different races over the same course can be very significant, and to this end the concept of the standard time has been introduced. The standard time on the Flat is a time for each distance at each course adjusted to a horse carrying 9 stone on good or firm ground, and is calculated by taking the average of the ten fastest runnings over that distance on that course. Courses vary hugely, and standard times will reflect this variety. At Epsom by the end of 1994 the standard time over five furlongs was 54.5 seconds; at Sandown Park, with its stiff uphill finish, the standard time for the same distance was 59.8 seconds. The time of the winning horse will be given in relation to standard, 'above' meaning slower than standard, 'below' faster.

The great advantage of time is that it supplies a completely objective body of evidence which can be used to compare the abilities of horses who have never raced against each other, and many famous professional backers consider the study of race times one of the most significant weapons in their armoury for the battle against the bookmakers.

But the evidence of the clock must be tempered by evidence about the running of that race: was it run at a proper pace, was it run at the end of a day when heavy rain throughout the programme would have transformed the ground, was the horse pushed out to the line or was it easing up? Most of the racing papers and form services have time experts who take much of the mathematical burden away from the punter by compiling ratings based on time.

COURSE

As we saw in the chapter on racecourses (page 38), the notion of 'horses for courses' is a central one when trying to pick a winner, especially on the quirkier tracks such as Chester, Epsom or Windsor. A previous course victory by any horse in a race demands attention, for it shows that the horse in question can act effectively on that track. The exact degree of importance which should be attached to such evidence depends on both horse and course, but remember that although all British racecourses are different, many are alike in some ways, and it pays to know something of the nature of each track: is it right-handed or left-handed, is it flat or undulating, galloping or tight? (See pages 46–57.) Brighton and Lingfield are often good testing-grounds for Epsom, as both are switchback left-handed tracks.

TRAINER AND JOCKEY

The racing press gives detailed statistics about which trainers and jockeys are in good form, and about which are notably successful at a particular racecourse. This can be invaluable information, especially with regard to trainers, for when a stable hits a winning streak it pays to follow it – and similarly, when a stable has hit a thin patch, you would be well advised to be very wary of its runners until its form picks up.

Jockeys too have purple patches, but in any case note who has ridden a horse in previous races: if for the current race Eddery or Dettori or another top jockey is taking the ride on a horse usually partnered by an apprentice or a lesser-known rider, that could be significant. Pay attention also if a top jockey has gone to an obscure meeting to ride for an unfashionable stable: he will not have done so simply for the scenic drive . . .

DRAW

Although at most courses the draw (the order in which the runners in a Flat race line up at the start) is of little import in races over more than a mile, in shorter races it can be of vital importance – again, more so at some courses than others. Always note the effect of the draw in races which are building up the form picture, for the draw will have a bearing on how you interpret the face value of the result.

BETTING

The racing press will give a brief account of the betting movements of each horse in a race, and this can be highly revealing, for a horse whose odds shorten is being backed, while one whose odds lengthen is attracting less money. The *Racing Post*'s brief description of the variations in the price of Doran's Pride before the BonusPrint Stayers' Hurdle at Cheltenham in March 1995 read 'op 7–2 tchd 5–2' – that is, the horse opened in the on-course market at 7–2 and was backed down to 5–2 before easing slightly to his starting price of 11–4. His main rival Cyborgo 'op 2–1' before starting at 3–1. What would you make of this terse shorthand if subsequently you were assessing the form of that race? You would have to conclude that there was

The three phases of form study, as illustrated by racegoers at Cheltenham: extracting it, distilling it, and thinking about it over a glass of beer.

at least hefty confidence – and at best a good old Irish gamble – pushing down the price of Doran's Pride, whereas Cyborgo was not being backed with great conviction: he was 'weak in the market', which does not of course mean that a horse will not win, but is none the less a significant factor to be borne in mind when weighing up that race.

THE RUNNING OF THE RACE

A brief description of the manner in which each horse ran in each race is a crucial element of racing form, as it will tell you whether it was running on at the finish (in which case it has no stamina problems, and might need a longer distance), whether it was able to accelerate, whether it made the pace, whether it encountered any problems in running, and so on. From the depressingly straightforward 'always behind, tailed off' or 'never near enough to challenge' to the equally straightforward 'never headed', these comments will tell you much about each individual running. Watch for 'ran on well', the phrase which tells you that a horse, winning or losing, was keeping going to the end of the race. Mostly such comments are bald and factual, though 'easily' will sometimes offer a value judgement on a winning performance.

TIME SINCE LAST RACE

Form is most valuable when it is fairly recent, and many shrewd punters will not bet on a horse when its form, however good, belongs to a period too far removed from the current race. There are of course exceptions, as when Nashwan was backed down to favouritism for the 1989 Two Thousand Guineas on the strength of glowing reports from the home gallops, despite the fact that he had not raced in public for nearly seven months. With horses who race for season after season, it pays to be aware of whether they tend to need a race or two to get to top form, or whether they are usually ready to do themselves justice first time out.

A feature of the list of runners in most newspapers is a note of the number of days since the horse last ran: a horse that has not run for a very long time could well be rusty and need this race to make it fit. But some horses, especially sprinters, have 'seams' of form lasting for a few closely spaced races, and need to be caught while going through that purple patch.

WEIGHT

Dominating all the other factors of form is the weight which the horse has to carry. However fast it has run, however much it likes the course and the going, in whatever brilliant form its jockey and trainer currently are – all this evidence is meaningless if it appears to have no chance at the weights. In the Classics all horses carry the same weight (except for the allowance to fillies in the races in which they may take on the colts), so weight is not an element in assessing the likely outcome. But in many other races – notably, of course, in handicaps – discrepancies in the weights must be taken into acount. The Weight-for-Age Scale (see page 141) publishes the officially designated differences for horses of different ages over different distances at different times of the year, and naturally the effect of weight variations will not be the same at all distances: if a horse is beaten a neck in a five-furlong sprint it will theoretically dead-heat with its conqueror next time they meet if it carries one pound less weight; in a three-mile steeplechase a pound will be worth a length. Naturally, handicapping is an inexact activity: more credence can be given to the distances separating the first three or four home in a race than the distances between the stragglers, and often a horse will win easily but not by a very long distance: the handicapper (and alert students of form) will make due allowances.

A simple guide for relating finishing distances to weight is as follows.

Flat:
5 furlongs to 7 furlongs: 3 pounds per length;
1 mile to 11 furlongs: 2 pounds per length;
$1\frac{1}{2}$ to 2 miles: $1\frac{1}{2}$ pounds per length;
over 2 miles: 1 pound per length.

National Hunt:
1 pound per length, though over extreme distances further adjustments must be made.

OFFICIAL RATINGS

A detailed form book will tell you the official rating that a horse is running off in that particular race; this can be an invaluable tool for weighing up improvement or decline when compared with another outing by the same horse off a different rating.

So form is a mass of fact, and all you have to do is learn how to read, interpret and use those facts. But remember that form is only one part of the puzzle, and must be accompanied by your judgement of the horse's condition and demeanour before the race. And never forget that the same mass of fact is also available to the bookmakers.

But what if a horse has no form – because it has never run – or the entire field has no form? A field of horses who have never run before is not usually a good betting medium for the casual punter, but if you must have a bet watch how the market moves, as in the absence of form someone – probably someone in the know – will have information and will be backing that information with cash. A good illustration of this was the Wood Ditton Stakes for three-year-olds at Newmarket in April 1989, in which none of the twenty runners who faced the starter had ever run. But the market proved a reliable guide, with the well-backed 7–4 favourite Sabotage beating the 9–4 second favourite Porter Rhodes; the next horse in the betting was 8–1. The betting market had pointed unmistakably towards the two horses with the best chances, and as the runners returned to unsaddle John McCririck proclaimed to Channel Four viewers: 'It's an easy business, this horse racing, if you've got no form book!'

The form student's nightmare is how to interpret a finish like this – in a competitive sprint handicap at York.

WEIGHT-FOR-AGE SCALES

Flat

The scale expresses the number of pounds that it is deemed the average horse in each age group falls short of maturity at different dates and distances. Founded on the scale originally devised by Admiral Rous (see page 61) and revised by him in 1873, it is given here in its current modification.

Distance Furlongs	Age	JAN		FEB		MARCH		APRIL		MAY		JUNE		JULY		AUGUST		SEPT		OCT		NOV		DEC	
		1/15	16/31	1/14	15/28	1/15	16/31	1/15	16/30	1/15	16/31	1/15	16/30	1/15	16/31	1/15	16/30	1/15	16/30	1/15	16/30	1/15	16/30	1/15	16/31
5	2	-	-	-	-	-	47	44	41	38	36	34	32	30	28	26	24	22	20	19	18	17	17	16	16
	3	15	15	15	15	14	13	12	11	10	9	8	7	6	5	4	3	2	2	1	1	-	-	-	-
6	2	-	-	-	-	-	-	-	-	44	41	38	36	33	31	28	26	24	22	21	20	19	18	17	17
	3	16	16	16	16	15	14	13	12	11	10	9	8	7	6	5	4	3	3	2	2	1	1	-	-
7	2	-	-	-	-	-	-	-	-	-	-	-	-	38	35	32	30	27	25	23	22	21	20	19	19
	3	18	18	18	18	17	16	15	14	12	11	10	9	8	7	6	5	4	4	3	2	2	1	1	-
8	2	-	-	-	-	-	-	-	-	-	-	-	-	37	34	31	28	26	24	23	22	21	20	-	-
	3	20	20	19	19	18	17	16	15	13	12	11	10	9	8	7	6	5	4	4	3	3	2	2	1
	4	1	1	-	-	-	-	-	-	-	-	-	-	-	-	-	-	-	-	-	-	-	-	-	-
9	3	22	22	21	20	20	19	18	17	15	14	12	11	10	9	8	7	6	5	5	4	4	3	2	2
	4	2	2	1	1	1	-	-	-	-	-	-	-	-	-	-	-	-	-	-	-	-	-	-	-
10	3	23	23	22	22	21	20	19	18	16	15	13	12	11	10	9	8	7	6	6	5	5	4	4	3
	4	3	3	2	2	1	1	-	-	-	-	-	-	-	-	-	-	-	-	-	-	-	-	-	-
11	3	-	-	-	-	23	22	21	20	18	17	15	14	12	11	10	9	8	7	7	6	6	5	4	4
	4	4	4	3	3	2	1	1	1	-	-	-	-	-	-	-	-	-	-	-	-	-	-	-	-
12	3	-	-	-	-	24	23	22	21	19	18	16	15	13	12	11	10	9	8	8	7	7	6	6	5
	4	5	4	4	3	3	2	2	1	-	-	-	-	-	-	-	-	-	-	-	-	-	-	-	-
13	3	-	-	-	-	25	24	23	22	20	19	17	16	14	13	12	11	10	9	8	8	7	6	6	5
	4	5	4	4	3	3	2	2	1	-	-	-	-	-	-	-	-	-	-	-	-	-	-	-	-
14	3	-	-	-	-	26	25	24	23	21	20	18	17	15	14	13	12	11	10	9	9	8	7	7	6
	4	6	5	5	4	4	3	3	2	1	-	-	-	-	-	-	-	-	-	-	-	-	-	-	-
15	3	-	-	-	-	28	27	26	25	23	21	19	18	16	15	14	13	12	11	10	9	9	8	7	6
	4	6	5	5	4	4	3	3	2	2	1	-	-	-	-	-	-	-	-	-	-	-	-	-	-
16	3	-	-	-	-	29	28	27	26	24	22	20	19	17	16	15	14	13	12	11	10	10	9	8	7
	4	7	7	6	6	5	5	4	4	3	2	2	1	-	-	-	-	-	-	-	-	-	-	-	-
18	3	-	-	-	-	31	30	29	28	26	24	22	21	19	18	17	16	15	14	13	12	11	10	9	8
	4	8	8	7	7	6	6	5	5	4	3	2	1	-	-	-	-	-	-	-	-	-	-	-	-
20	3	-	-	-	-	33	32	31	30	28	26	24	22	20	19	18	17	16	15	14	13	12	11	10	9
	4	9	9	8	8	7	7	6	6	5	4	3	2	1	-	-	-	-	-	-	-	-	-	-	-

Jumping

The hurdles scale shows the number of pounds three-year-olds should receive from four-year-olds, and four-year-olds from older horses. The steeplechase scale shows the number of pounds four-year-olds should receive from five-year-olds, and five-year-olds from older horses.

Hurdle Races

	Age	JAN	FEB	MAR	APR	MAY	JUNE	JULY	AUG	SEPT	OCT	NOV	DEC
2 miles	3							20	20	18	17	16	14
	4	12	10	8	6	5	5	3	3	2	1	-	-
2½ miles	3							21	21	19	18	17	15
	4	13	11	9	7	6	6	3	3	2	1	-	-
3 miles	3							23	23	21	19	18	16
	4	14	12	10	8	7	7	4	4	3	2	1	-

Steeplechases

	Age	JAN	FEB	MAR	APR	MAY	JUNE	JULY	AUG	SEPT	OCT	NOV	DEC
2 miles	3							15	15	14	13	12	11
	4	10	9	8	7	6	6	3	3	2	1	-	-
2½ miles	3							16	16	15	14	13	12
	4	11	10	9	8	7	7	4	4	3	2	1	-
3 miles	3							17	17	16	15	14	13
	4	12	11	10	9	8	8	5	5	4	3	2	1

Betting

O f all the interlocking elements which make up the wonderful world of horse racing, none is more baffling to outsiders or beginners than the activity at the very root of the game – betting. The mysteries of punting on a horse were neatly satirized by W. C. Sellar and R. J. Yeatman, authors of the classic history spoof *1066 and All That*, in their book *Horse Nonsense*:

It hardly matters really which horse you back. An enormous majority of them will lose the race anyway, so if you want to boast of your losses afterwards you have a pretty large choice. But make up your mind beforehand which way *you want to bet – whether to* win *or to* lose. *Some people (especially when backing the favourite) back it both ways, i.e., to win and to lose: which is pretty safe because the odds are usually on* the favourite instead of against it, *so that you stand to lose more if the horse loses than you stand to win if it wins, and thus, if it wins, you win less than you would have lost if it had been the other way round and had run backwards, or both-ways, while if the horse loses, then you lose too because you betted the bookie you would (unless the horse won). You do follow that, don't you?*

The reality is rather easier to follow, but it helps to remember the basics.

In Britain the punter has the choice of placing a bet at the odds offered by a bookmaker on or the Tote, the key difference being that a bookmaker will provide odds based on his assessment of the chances of the horses in the race, while the Tote (in full, the Horserace Totalisator Board) operates on a pool system where the backers all put their money in and the winners share the payout. The bookmaker's odds will lengthen (offering a higher return) or shorten (offering a lower one) according to how money is being wagered, but the odds at which you strike your bet remain valid for that transaction whatever happens subsequently, unless you bet at starting price; whereas on the Tote, you will not know the exact return on your stake until after the race.

BETTING WITH THE BOOKIES

To many people the principles and mathematics of betting with a bookmaker – to say nothing of the jargon and frantic arm-waving which accompany it – are completely impenetrable, and even its most basic features escape some of the uninitiated: one of the commonest misconceptions among those unused to betting is that you do not receive your stake back along with your winnings in the event of a successful bet (but if this were so why would anyone ever bet at odds on?).

Informed or not, the majority of the population have a bet with a bookie at least once a year, even if it is just a one-off on the Grand National, on which some £75 million was supposedly staked in 1995. The principle of betting with a bookmaker is simple: he offers odds at which you may pitch your money against his. The practice and the maths, however, can be less clear.

For betting to be effective, its practice should be accompanied by an appreciation of the mathematical factors governing the betting market: you may not think that this matters, but the bookmaker certainly will, and every punter should be aware of how a book works and what factors affect the prices so that he or she can take advantage of market moves and identify that most sought-after of betting commodities – value.

ODDS

Odds are a way of expressing the perceived probability of a horse winning. So evens (1–1) means that there is an equal (50 per cent) chance of the horse winning and losing. At 2–1 against there is a 33.33 per cent chance of its winning and a 66.67 per cent chance of its losing (that is, two out of every three chances – 2 plus 1 equals 3 – are against its winning). At 2–1 on (the *on* indicating that the odds are reversed, '2–1 on' being the common way of expressing 1–2) there is a 66.67 per cent chance of its winning and a 33.33 per cent chance of its losing. So any horse at 'odds on' is deemed by the bookmakers to be more likely to win than lose. (A useful way of thinking about odds is that with odds against the first number expressed is the multiple of your stake that you will win, the second number the amount that the bookie will keep if you lose – or, if you like, your stake unit. Thus at 6–1 against you put down one to win six.)

The key to intelligent betting is to compare your own opinion of the probability of the horse's winning with the bookmaker's and to back your fancy if the bookies are offering odds longer than you think properly reflect the chance of that horse: such a bet represents 'value', the 'bargain' which every regular punter seeks. (Value usually becomes apparent *after* the race, of course.)

HOW A BOOK WORKS

If betting is often characterized as a mugs' game, this is because in the long run the intelligent and efficient bookmaker is bound to win over the average punter, for the bookmaker is controlling the maths and constructs the odds (or the 'book') for each race in such a way that, in the long term, he will make a profit. He does this by dictating that the total of the percentage probability chances for each race exceeds 100 per cent. (Mathematically the chances must come to exactly 100 per cent if all the true probabilities are added up.)

To illustrate this we can examine the returned (official) starting prices for the 1995 Tote Cheltenham Gold Cup:

After the 1993 false start fiasco, the Grand National reasserted itself as the biggest betting race of the year in 1994, with 16–1 chance Miinnehoma (Richard Dunwoody) biding his time behind heavily backed 5–1 favourite Moorcroft Boy (Adrian Maguire) at the last. The loose horse is Young Hustler.

Horse	SP	%
Master Oats	100–30	23.08
Jodami	7–2	22.22
Barton Bank	8–1	11.11
Miinnehoma	9–1	10.00
Merry Gale	10–1	9.09
Monsieur Le Cure	10–1	9.09
Val d'Alene	10–1	9.09
Deep Bramble	14–1	6.67
Algan	16–1	5.88
Dubacilla	20–1	4.76
Flashing Steel	25–1	3.85
Young Hustler	33–1	2.94
Nuaffe	50–1	1.96
Beech Road	100–1	0.99
Commercial Artist	100–1	0.99
TOTAL		**121.72**

ODDS PERCENTAGES

Odds on	Price	Odds against
50.00	Even	50.00
52.38	11–10	47.62
54.55	6–5	45.45
55.56	5–4	44.44
57.89	11–8	42.11
60.00	6–4	40.00
61.90	13–8	38.10
63.64	7–4	36.36
65.22	15–8	34.78
66.67	2–1	33.33
68.00	85–40	32.00
69.23	9–4	30.77
71.43	5–2	28.57
73.33	11–4	26.67
75.00	3–1	25.00
76.92	10–3	23.08
77.78	7–2	22.22
80.00	4–1	20.00
81.82	9–2	18.18
83.33	5–1	16.67
84.62	11–2	15.38
85.71	6–1	14.29
86.67	13–2	13.33
87.50	7–1	12.50
88.24	15–2	11.76
88.89	8–1	11.11
89.47	17–2	10.53
90.00	9–1	10.00
90.91	10–1	9.09
91.67	11–1	8.33
92.31	12–1	7.69
92.86	13–1	7.14
93.33	14–1	6.67
93.75	15–1	6.25
94.12	16–1	5.88
95.24	20–1	4.76
95.65	22–1	4.35
96.15	25–1	3.85
97.06	33–1	2.94
97.56	40–1	2.44
98.04	50–1	1.96
98.51	66–1	1.49
98.77	80–1	1.23
99.01	100–1	0.99
99.60	250–1	0.40
99.80	500–1	0.20

A book in which the probability chances add up to over 100 per cent is described as 'over-round', and in this case the book is over-round by 21.72 per cent, which means that the bookmaker expects to have to pay out £100 for every £121.72 that he takes in bets, leaving him £21.72 profit. When a book is over-round the punter cannot back every runner and be guaranteed a return, and as every efficient bookmaker will be betting over-round the notion that you can back every horse in a race and win is clearly nonsense. (Very occasionally the punter can beat the bookies by choosing the best price for each horse from a variety of bookmakers whose prices vary considerably, but this takes great alertness and remarkable powers of mental arithmetic.) Bookmakers do not of course win on every race, but by maintaining the over-roundness of the book they are ensuring that in the long term they will come out on top, for favourites win only around two out of every five races, and in each race the bookmaker will try to contrive the odds so that he has to pay out less than he takes in. (A set of odds in which the aggregate percentages total under 100 is described as 'overbroke'.)

So how does a book work? For big races the betting will begin weeks or even months in advance; for other key races the major bookmakers will advertise prices on the morning of the race and punters may back at these prices – subject to fluctuations dictated by weight of money – until the proper book is formed before the race itself. (A 'steamer' is a horse which has been heavily backed off course before the actual pre-race market has been formed.) A form expert in the bookmakers' employ constructs the 'tissue', a forecast of how the betting on the race will open on the course, and initially the course bookmakers (whose activities dictate the officially returned starting price) will probably bet to these prices. Thereafter each course bookmaker will adjust his prices according to public demand and to how he sees the probable outcome of the race: if he takes a large amount of money for one horse he will shorten its price in order to dissuade other punters from backing it, which would increase his liability in the event of its winning; if (for whatever reason) he thinks that a horse will not win he will lengthen its price in order to encourage punters to back it and swell his coffers. But throughout all these transactions he will be aware of his own liabilities, and if his potential payout on one horse is more than he can comfortably cover from losing bets on the other horses he may decide to 'lay off' by passing all or some of the money he has taken on that horse on to other bookmakers – that is, by himself betting on that horse.

Course bookies communicate such bets among themselves by means of the sign language of 'tic tac', now so familiar to Channel Four viewers through the prestidigitations of John McCririck (see page 150).

As the on-course betting market determines the returned starting prices, it is important that money wagered off course in betting shops and through credit accounts with the large bookmakers can be transferred to the course in order for that weight of money to be reflected in the betting market, and representatives of the off-course bookmakers will bet on the course to put their off-course money into the market. The 'magic sign' is the tic-tac signal (somewhat like drawing a halo over the head) which indicates Ladbrokes money being brought into the market.

THE TOTE

The principle of Tote betting is simple. All the money bet on all the horses in a race forms a pool which following the race is shared out among those who have won, after a deduction has been made from the pool for running costs, which include contributions to racecourses and to the Betting Levy.

There are separate pools for the different sorts of bet – explained on page 148 – and each pool is subjected to a different level of deduction: in the 1994–95 financial year the deductions were 16 per cent from the Win pool, 24 per cent from the Place, 29 per cent from the Dual Forecast, 26 per cent each from the Placepot and Quadpot, and 29 per cent each from the Jackpot and Trio.

The working of the Tote can be seen in a simple example. Say the Win pool for a race consists of £10,000, of which one thousand £1 bets have been staked on the horse which wins:

pool	£10,000
deduction	£1,600
payout	£8,400
dividend	£8.40 per £1 ticket

The dividend (or the 'Tote return') is declared to a £1 unit and includes the stake, so the actual winnings in the above example are £7.40.

Tote counters at Newbury.

ODDS

Some people are baffled by what odds actually mean: 2–1 may be obvious enough, but what is 13–8? Here are a few of the most common odds quoted for horse racing expressed in more familiar fractions:

evens	1 to 1
11–10	$1\frac{1}{10}$ to 1
6–5	$1\frac{1}{5}$ to 1
5–4	$1\frac{1}{4}$ to 1
11–8	$1\frac{3}{8}$ to 1
6–4	$1\frac{1}{2}$ to 1
13–8	$1\frac{5}{8}$ to 1
7–4	$1\frac{3}{4}$ to 1
15–8	$1\frac{7}{8}$ to 1
85–40	$2\frac{1}{8}$ to 1
9–4	$2\frac{1}{4}$ to 1
5–2	$2\frac{1}{2}$ to 1
11–4	$2\frac{3}{4}$ to 1
100–30	$3\frac{1}{3}$ to 1
7–2	$3\frac{1}{2}$ to 1
9–2	$4\frac{1}{2}$ to 1
11–2	$5\frac{1}{2}$ to 1
13–2	$6\frac{1}{2}$ to 1
15–2	$7\frac{1}{2}$ to 1
17–2	$8\frac{1}{2}$ to 1

TOTE BETTING

Win

You bet on one horse to come first. (The record win dividend was £341 2s 6d to a two-shilling stake on Coole at Haydock Park on 30 November 1929: the Tote odds of over 3,410–1 compared with a starting price of 100–8: just over 12–1.)

Place

You bet on a horse to be placed: first or second in races of five, six or seven runners; first, second or third in races of eight runners or more; first, second, third or fourth in handicaps of sixteen runners or more. The record place dividend was £67.32 to 10 pence on Strip Fast (started 66–1), second in an apprentice race at Nottingham on 31 October 1978.

Dual Forecast

In races of three or more runners, you pick two horses: you win if they finish first and second (in either order). Record dividend: £4,609.40 to £1 in the opening race on Cesarewitch day at Newmarket, 15 October 1994 (starting prices 33–1 Chinour and 25–1 Royal Hill).

Trio

You pick three horses to finish first, second and third in any order in designated races. Record dividend £13,430 to £1 in the 1993 Ever Ready Derby (Commander In Chief, Blue Judge, Blues Traveller), Epsom Downs, 3 June.

Jackpot

You pick the winners of the first six races at the designated Jackpot meeting. If there is no winner the pool is carried forward to the next Jackpot meeting. On 22 March 1995 the pool, swollen by the previous week's National Hunt Festival at Cheltenham, reached £2,050,651.59, before finally paying a dividend of £11,933.10 to £1. The record dividend was £273,365.80 to £1 at Newmarket on 2 October 1993.

Placepot

You pick horses to be placed in the first six races (or to win any race with fewer than five runners). The Placepot operates at all meetings. (The record Placepot dividend was declared at Cheltenham on 14 March 1990: £22,203.20 to a £1 stake.)

Quadpot

You pick horses to be placed in the final four legs of the Placepot. Record dividend £2,119.30 to £1 at Ascot on 15 June 1994.

Although on a racecourse you will see displayed approximate Tote odds as the betting takes place before a race, you cannot know exactly what the dividend will be until after the race, and this is the crucial difference between betting with the Tote and with a bookmaker: with a bookmaker you bet either at starting price or at the price which he quotes you or has displayed, and your bet remains at that price; with the Tote you will not know when you make the bet precisely what the return will be.

Because they operate on different principles Tote odds and bookmakers' odds will usually differ, with the difference favouring both sides roughly equally. Occasionally Tote odds about a winning outsider will dwarf the starting price – for example, Super Heights, 33–1 winner of an amateur riders' claiming race at Wolverhampton in February 1994, returned a Tote dividend of £283.70 to a £1 stake – odds of nearly 283–1. The 1995 Martell Grand National winner Royal Athlete returned a starting price of 40–1 and a win Tote dividend of £83.70 – odds of 82.7–1, over double the SP. On the other hand, backers of Klairon Davis, winner of the Guinness Arkle Trophy at the 1995 Cheltenham Festival, would have been better off taking the starting price – 7–2 as against a Tote return of £3.80 or 2.8–1. In the following race Smurfit Champion Hurdle hero Alderbrook paid exactly the same on the Tote as his SP: Tote return £6.50, SP 11–2.

All the other pools operate in the same way, but it is not possible for the television viewer to know how the Tote odds are looking just before the race, and some off-course betting shops do not bet at Tote odds.

The Tote is an important feature of British racing, with a total betting turnover of around £240 million in the financial year 1994–95 and a major programme of race sponsorship – notably of the Cheltenham Gold Cup, the Ebor Handicap, the Cesarewitch, and the Tote Gold Trophy (formerly the Schweppes).

Shouting the odds: leading rails bookmaker Stephen Little.

JOHN MCCRIRICK'S TIC-TAC MASTERCLASS

BETTING SLANG

The language in which book-makers conduct their business adds to the mystery of betting. Slang terms are used to describe odds, amounts of money, horses and other aspects of the betting operation: for some words and phrases the derivation is reasonably obvious, but others are more obscure. Among the commonly used terms, some of which are explained in the main part of this chapter, are:

Bar: if a betting show is concluded '20–1 bar' it means that the horses not listed stand at 20–1 or longer
Bottle: 2–1
Burlington Bertie: 100–30 (rhyming slang)
Carpet: 3–1
Century: £100
Double carpet: 33–1
Ear 'ole: 6–4 (from the tic-tac signal)
Grand: £1,000
Jolly: the favourite (the 'jolly old favourite')
Levels: evens
Monkey: £500
Nap: a newspaper tipster's best bet of the day
On the shoulders: 9–2 (tic-tac)
Pony: £25
Rag: an outsider – a horse with apparently no chance
Rouf ('rofe'): 4–1 ('four' backwards)
Steamer: a horse gambled on significantly on the morning of the race
Tips: 11–10 (tic tac)
Tissue: the course bookmakers' forecast of how the betting will open
Top of the head: 9–4 (tic-tac)
Up the arm: 11–8 (tic-tac)
With the thumb: the price is being taken and won't last long (tic-tac)
Wrist: 5–4 (tic-tac)

5–4 ('wrist')

6–4 ('ear 'ole')

5–2 ('face')

9–2 ('on the shoulder')

10–1 ('net')

33–1 ('double carpet')

THE BETTING BUSINESS

THE COURSE BOOKMAKER

The principal betting ring at most racecourses is in the Tattersalls enclosure, named after the company which in 1866 drew up the first rules on betting transactions. (The Tattersalls Committee is still the authority recognized by the Jockey Club for settling all matters of dispute relating to bets, and has the power to 'warn off' – that is, ban from racecourses – an individual for non-payment.)

Betting is not allowed in the Members' Enclosure, so the larger companies have representatives who take up a position by the rail dividing Members from Tatts, and take bets – some in cash, many in credit – from the members. (These are known as 'rails bookmakers'.) In the main betting ring bookmakers are allotted pitches according to seniority, and they set up shop with a clerk (who records the bets on a large ledger – one column per runner so that the liability on any horse can be rapidly assessed if need be) and other assistants and tic-tac men. The bookmaker himself will handle the money, shovelling it into (and occasionally out of) a large bag suspended from his stand. In order to avoid disputes over bets, some course layers position a small tape recorder beneath their board to provide aural confirmation of bets recorded in writing in the ledger, and in March 1995 a further technological advance was made when one Chepstow bookmaker – taking the hint from common

On-course backers who think betting on photo-finishes is easy money had a shock at Wolverhampton in October 1994 when a photo between Dakota Brave and Ikhtiraa was decided in favour of the former – even though the bookmakers had been offering 8–1 against the winner in betting on the photo!

Course bookmaker Joe Bates at Sandown Park. (Note the tape recorder, and his advertised place odds.) Quickly now: how over-round is his book?

THE YEAR'S BIG BETTING RACES

The major bookmaking firms publish lists of the races which provide the greatest amount of betting turnover. For Ladbrokes, the largest bookmaker in Britain, the top twenty turnover races in 1994 were:

1 Martell Grand National (Aintree)
2 Ever Ready Derby (Epsom Downs) CH4
3 Stakis Scottish National (Ayr) CH4
4 Tote Cheltenham Gold Cup (Cheltenham)
5 Madagans Two Thousand Guineas (Newmarket) CH4
6 King George VI Tripleprint Chase (Kempton Park) CH4
7 King George VI and Queen Elizabeth Diamond Stakes (Ascot)
8 Ladbroke Hurdle (Leopardstown) CH4

9 William Hill Lincoln Handicap (Doncaster) CH4
10 Whitbread Gold Cup (Sandown Park) CH4
11 Energizer Oaks (Epsom Downs) CH4
12 William Hill Cambridgeshire (Newmarket) CH4
13 Smurfit Champion Hurdle (Cheltenham)
14 Racing Post Chase (Kempton Park) CH4
15 Mackeson Gold Cup (Cheltenham)
16 Vodac Stewards' Cup (Goodwood)
17 Ladbrokes Ayr Gold Cup (Ayr) CH4
18 Tote Cesarewitch (Newmarket) CH4
19 Hennessy Cognac Gold Cup (Newbury)
20 Greenalls Gold Cup (Kempton Park) CH4

Of these top twenty, thirteen were shown live on Channel Four – here marked 'CH4'.

There is no such thing in racing as a certainty. In the Chepstow Stakes at Chepstow on 28 June 1947 Glendower, ridden by Gordon Richards, started at 20–1 on to beat his solitary opponent, Markwell. This was, of course, in the days before starting stalls, and as the tapes of the old-style starting gate went up Glendower whipped round and unseated the great jockey, leaving Markwell to win unopposed. Gordon Richards recalled this embarrassing incident in his autobiography, adding: 'I heard afterwards that a certain gentleman was in the habit of picking out my best ride of the day, and then ringing up his bookmaker and backing it to win one thousand pounds. On that day he selected Glendower, but he did not anticipate that I would start at twenty to one on. That race cost him twenty thousand pounds.'

Yet Glendower was not the shortest-priced loser that Gordon Richards ever rode. In the Clarence House Stakes at Ascot on 23 September 1948 he partnered Royal Forest, who started at 25–1 on to beat three opponents (all 33–1 against) – one of whom, named Burpham, beat the favourite half a length.

practice in Australia – pioneered the use of a laptop computer which would provide on-course punters with a written record of the bet struck.

Dozens of bookmakers all shouting the odds provide a British racecourse with its unique sound. When a bookmaker shouts 'five to four the field' (which usually sounds like 'fidah vaudeville') he is indicating that 5–4 is the shortest price he has on offer; 'I'll take six to four' means he is offering 6–4 on, while 'I'll lay six to four' means 6–4 against; 'sixes bar one' means that he is is offering all the runners in the race except one at 6–1 or longer. All the while he will be on the look out for 'faces' – people with inside information whose bets will be highly significant.

Having started betting from the 'tissue', the course bookmaker adjusts the odds according to the flow of money until the race is started, at which point a reporter from the *Sporting Life* and another from the Press Association agree on what is to be the officially returned starting price. They note the prices available all round the ring to arrive at the SP for each horse, and if there are significant differences will often split the difference. So if half the bookmakers have the favourite at 11–10 at the off, and the other half are betting even money the same horse, the officially returned starting price is likely to be 21–20 (which explains other weird SPs like 85–40).

In 1949 a book entitled *How the Other Man Lives*, describing the nature of various occupations, wrote of course bookmakers: 'Only men of strong constitution and iron nerve can stand the tenseness and excitement of bookmaking for any length of time.' And that was before the representative of Channel Four Racing was skulking around watching their every move . . .

BETTING SHOPS

The first betting shops in Great Britain were opened on 1 May 1961. Before then betting on horses could legally take place only on a racecourse or through a credit account; illegal betting, though, was rife, with 'bookies' runners' operating in pubs and clubs and on street corners, and it was in an attempt to end this rash of illicit activity that Home Secretary R. A. Butler brought in legislation – the Betting and Gaming Act – which made betting shops possible. Butler noted in his memoirs that 'the House of Commons was so intent on making "betting shops" as sad as possible, in order not to deprave the young, that they ended up more like undertakers' premises.'

Indeed, the general ambience of betting shops was deliberately kept seedy and inhospitable for decades (they were not allowed to show races live on television or offer light refreshments to their patrons), but in 1986 new legislation allowed a general brightening up and, most significantly, the transmission of races live on television to shops which took the service from SIS (see page 154). Even coffee machines appeared, and the notion of a betting shop as an establishment into which no respectable person should ever stray unless he absolutely had to, in which case the experience should be as shaming and uncomfortable as possible, had at last disappeared. Now, with evening opening and Sunday opening, betting shops are almost becoming respectable outposts of the leisure industry, a move accelerated early in 1995 when they were at last allowed to show their interiors to high-street passers-by, rather than skulking guiltily behind solid display boards in the shop windows.

There are around 9,500 betting shops in Britain, responsible for a large proportion of the £7,500 million bet off-course every year. Since to many people betting shops still have the magnetic but forbidden aura of the bordello, it may help would-be clients overcome their shyness about entering such a place by explaining how you have a bet.

It is very simple. Around the walls are displayed a large array of newspapers and television screens giving all sorts of information on the day's sport. When you have decided what you want to back, you take a carbon-backed slip from the dispenser – different sorts of bet require different slips – and write on the details of your bet. It is essential that you fill in this slip accurately: if you got confused and had a fiver on Master Gale for the 1995 Cheltenham Gold Cup you would have no right to feel aggrieved if the bookmaker called the bet void, and all sorts of disputes arise from wrongly or ambiguously filled-in slips, or slips placing some highly elaborate combination bet when the amount staked does not cover the bets involved.

The slip itself is not very difficult. For a win bet you would just need to enter the name of the horse, the time and venue of the race, and the amount you wish to stake. (You also have the option to have the bet 'tax paid', which means that you pay the betting tax on the stake, rather than have the tax – usually 10 per cent – taken off your returns.) You give the slip and your money to the assistant behind the counter, who will time-stamp the slip in a machine and return the bottom copy to you. You then hang around affecting nonchalance as your horse sweeps to victory, and when the 'weighed-in' signal is given saunter to the payout end of the counter to collect your winnings.

Remember that if you have not bet 'tax paid' 10 per cent will be taken off your returns – that is, your winnings and your returned stake. The imposition of betting tax has made a great difference to betting, as it means that at shorter odds the actual winnings are very much reduced. Say you wanted to have £10 on a horse which starts at even money. When it wins your actual profit on the bet will be only £8, as your return will be £20 (£10 winnings plus £10 stake) less 10 per cent tax (£2) taken off the returns. Betting tax does not now apply to bets struck with a bookmaker on the racecourse.

ACCOUNTS

To use the wisdom of the Channel Four Racing team to the full for betting purposes you would do well to have an account with a bookmaker so that you can bet by telephone at the very last minute, rather than having to keep scuttling down to the betting shop during the adverts or placing all your bets in advance of the afternoon's transmission. It is easy to open an account: all the major credit firms advertise in the *Sporting Life* and the *Racing Post* and give details of how to apply.

You should appreciate the difference between a deposit account – whereby you deposit a sum of money with the bookmaker (probably not less than £100 with the big firms) and can bet until that amount is used up – and a credit account – where you are allowed credit up to an agreed limit. The introduction of accounts using Switch cards makes the debit of money – when you lose – immediate, so you won't be building up huge debts.

You will be sent a statement regularly, and very occasionally this will be accompanied by a cheque. (You can of course use your credit account with these firms' representatives at race meetings: Tote Credit, with 50,000

SYSTEMS

There is an infinite variety of systems with which you can try to beat the bookies, but none is guaranteed to bring you success, and most will confine your betting within so tight a strait-jacket as to remove much of the fun. Systems can involve deliberations and calculations of enormous complexity, or can be very simple.

To back the favourite in every race might seem a sound system, but only around two out of every five favourites win, and in the long term you will lose. Another popular habit is to back the outsider in a field of three.

You might come out on top if you follow the selection of a particular newspaper pundit throughout a season, though few of them consistently show a profit on their nap choices. To follow a jockey or a trainer through a season might work, but not necessarily: if you had placed a £1 win bet on each of Frankie Dettori's 1,318 rides in Britain in 1994 you would have backed 233 winners but ended up £186.90 down. Much wiser would have been to have had £1 on each of Jason Weaver's 1,068 rides that year: his 200 winners brought a level-stakes profit of £158.12.

Bookmakers like backers to follow systems. Enough said.

Opposite page:
The betting ring at Newmarket's July Course.

SATELLITE INFORMATION SERVICES

Satellite Information Services (SIS) made its first live transmission of racing in May 1987 to a few hundred betting shops, and has now grown to supply a network of over 11,000 subscribers around the globe.

SIS provides live coverage of the action from most race meetings and of greyhound racing, as well as betting information, previews, interviews and other sporting news. Coverage of at least two horserace meetings a day is fed to the headquarters in central London, from where the images are integrated with commentaries and announcements and beamed via various 'geostationary' satellites parked some 23,000 miles above the equator to be picked up by customers with the necassary dishes and decoders.

Scheduling the constant flow of pictures and information from several venues is a complex operation, and SIS has the facility to delay the start of a greyhound race by two or three minutes if a horse race is late off and a clash seems likely.

Apart from the services to betting shops, SIS also supplies a number of private subscribers, among them top British and international owners, trainers, jockeys and journalists.

SPREAD BETTING

If you think fixed-odds betting complicated, just try getting your brain around spread betting, the novel form of punting, pioneered by companies such as Sporting Index and City Index, which has grown rapidly in the 1990s.

The essence of spread betting is wagering on a range – a 'spread' – of possibilities. Most sporting events are decided by numbers – runs in cricket, goals in soccer, points in rugby, etc. – and the spread better backs his or her view on what those numbers will be. So if the company is of the opinion that the total number of points scored in a rugby international will be 29, it will quote '28–30'. If you think the match will produce more points than 29, you 'buy' at 30; if fewer than 29, you 'sell' at 28. The punter makes the decision to buy (the higher figure) or sell (the lower) and stipulates the stake, but here comes the key factor: your profit or loss on the bet is calculated by measuring the difference between the price at which you bought or sold, and multiplying your stake by that figure. If you buy the spread at £1 and the total of points is 25, you lose £5 (30 minus 25). So unlike in fixed-odds betting, your losses are not confined to the amount you have staked.

Applications of spread betting in racing have included such matters as how many runners will complete the course in the Grand National; the total winning distances at an individual race meeting; performances of favourites at a meeting, with market leaders scoring points on an advertised scale; and the distance by which one named horse will beat another, wherever they actually finish in the race.

The attraction of spread betting is that the more right you are, the more money you will win; the danger, that the more wrong you are, the more you will lose (though in bets such as those relating to distance a ceiling is usually imposed).

Two other points to remember. You cannot have a spread bet in a betting shop or on the racecourse – only through an account with one of the spread bookmakers. And if you get it so comprehensively wrong that you cannot afford to pay up, beware: unlike with orthodox betting, you can be sued for the debt by your bookmaker. (And he, should it come to it, can be sued by you.)

clients, has a special office on all courses.) Apart from the big companies there are many independents and small local credit bookmakers, who often provide a more homely service than the large firms.

ANTE-POST BETTING

Ante-post betting is betting on an event well in advance of its taking place. For several very big races – the first four Classics, the Grand National, the Cheltenham Gold Cup, the Champion Hurdle and the Triumph Hurdle – bets are struck months before, while most of the big handicaps (such as the Lincoln, the Cambridgeshire and the Cesarewitch) attract lively markets for several weeks before.

You can even bet years before, if the bookmaker will take the bet. In 1966 the famous bookmaker William Hill laid owner Raymond Guest £50,000 to £500 (100–1) against an as yet unnamed yearling winning the Derby in 1968 (and, for good measure, £12,500 to £500 the place): the horse was Sir Ivor, who won the Derby easily in 1968 at 5–4 on. And in 1961 advertising man Bill Gollings took such a fancy to the big horse he had bought as a potential chaser that he backed him to win the 1963 Cheltenham Gold Cup: £50 each way at 200–1 with commission agent Ralph Freeman, and £50 each way at 100–1 with Ladbrokes. (He also backed him to repeat the feat in 1964.) His horse – Mill House – duly won the 1963 Gold Cup, and was second to Arkle in the famous 1964 race.

FURTHER COMPLICATIONS

Rule 4

Rule 4 (of the rules on betting laid down by the Tattersalls Committee) takes account of the distortions in a betting book which occur if one (or more) of the runners is withdrawn shortly before the race: betting will have started in earnest on that race and there may be no time to make a new book. (A common instance is when a horse refuses to enter the starting stalls.) Money staked on the withdrawn horse is returnable to the punters. The shorter the price of that horse the greater the distortion of the market, so a scale is stipulated under Rule 4 whereby a deduction is made from all winning bets in that race, the size of the deduction depending on the price of the withdrawn horse at the time of withdrawal.

Dead heat

In the case of a dead heat the punter receives the full odds to half the stake. So £5 to win on a horse which started at 10–1 and dead-heated for first place would return (forgetting tax) £27.50 – winnings of £25 plus the return of half the stake (£2.50).

No starting price

Occasionally a horse is such a certainty that there is no on-course betting on the race, and no starting prices are returned. Bets struck in betting shops are void.

The British race with the most open betting ever was the 1964 Grand National, when Flying Wild, Laffy, Pappageno's Cottage and Time were co-favourites at 100–7.

The great advantage of ante-post betting is of course that you can get very much better odds than the horse will start at – though this is not guaranteed: the horse's odds may lengthen. But the great disadvantage is that you lose your money if the horse is withdrawn before the race. (If your horse is withdrawn but the race is abandoned you get your money back, for you cannot lose on an event which does not happen.)

Sometimes bookmakers will offer ante-post odds 'with a run' – that is, if the horse does not take part your money is returned. Some clever observers of the ante-post market for the 1989 Cheltenham Gold Cup placed bets on Desert Orchid 'with a run' at 4–1 and 7–2 two months before the race: there was doubt about his participation, but these punters reasoned that at such odds he was a marvellous bet, for if he ran he would certainly start at a shorter price, and the 'with a run' proviso protected them from losing out should he not be in the line-up. They were proved right: he won at 5–2.

Less satisfactory is when you back a horse at long odds well in advance of a big race and it thanks you for your support by turning in a couple of preliminary performances so wretched that its odds for the big race drift: when the race comes a little bit of you is hoping that it will lose so that you are spared the anguish of seeing it come in at a much bigger price than that at which you backed it.

Frustrating, irritating and depressing – but also fascinating, stimulating and, above all, exciting, betting is an emotional activity. Why else would an apparently sane person in a betting shop shout advice at a horse 100 miles away, or a television viewer scream instructions to a jockey riding his fancy on another continent? It is a commonplace of the philosophy of betting that if punters were as worried about backing losers as they are about missing winners, they would have a much more profitable time.

The regular punter gets used to backing losers, and takes it in his stride, for the next bet will surely win: but the hurt of deciding to back a horse, then deciding not to back it, and then seeing it scoot home without your support, takes an age to get over. Yes, the successful professional backers will wait and wait for the right bet, and yes, it's the mug punter who wants to bet on every race who fills the bookie's satchel, and yes, the bookies are bound to win in the long term for they control the odds. The backer is always at a disadvantage, but so what? For the racing enthusiast, life can offer very few better sensations than that moment when you *know* your horse is going to win, and as the nineteenth-century author George Moore wrote in the great racing novel *Esther Waters*, 'A bet on a race brings hope into lives which otherwise would be hopeless.'

In any case, we can hardly disagree with Damon Runyon's character Sam the Gonoph, who so memorably affirmed: 'I long ago come to the conclusion that all life is six to five against.'

TYPES OF BET

There are many different types of bet, some of them involving procedures and combinations of baffling complexity. Combination bets are attractive to small punters as they offer the promise of big returns for modest outlay – and naturally they are difficult to pull off. The most usual types of bet are listed here, with sample calculations which exclude any allowance for tax.

WIN

Betting on the horse to come first. The return on a £5 win bet at 10–1 is £55: £5 stake plus £50 winnings.

EACH WAY

Betting on the horse both to win and to be placed (that is, to finish in the first two in races of five, six or seven runners, the first three in races of eight or more runners, or the first four in handicaps with sixteen or more runners: these stipulations can alter from one bookmaker to another). The odds for a place are normally one-quarter or one-fifth the odds for a win, depending on the nature of the race and the number of runners: the bookmaker will advertise the fraction. An each-way bet is in fact two bets – one for the win and one for the place – and consequently the stake will be twice the unit of the bet: thus a bet of £5 each way costs £10. A bet of £5 each way (with the place odds one-quarter the win odds) on a horse which wins at 10–1 returns winnings of £62.50 (£50 win plus £12.50 place, as the winning horse is also placed) plus your stake of £10 – total return £72.50. If the horse is second you win £12.50 and have your stake on the place bet returned, but lose your £5 win bet: so your return on the £10 invested is £17.50. Obviously it is not worth backing a horse each way if its odds are much less than 5–1, as the amount you will make on the place bet if it is placed but does not win will not cover your loss on the win bet: the niceties of such calculations for off-course bets are distorted by the need to allow for tax, but it should be clear that an on-course each-way bet at 4–1 one-quarter the odds a place will yield no gain and no loss if the horse is placed but does not win – but if you tried to bet each way with a course bookmaker at 4–1 you might hear some unusual language . . .

PLACE

Few bookmakers will bet for place only, though the Tote runs a Place pool on every race with five or more runners.

COMBINATION BETS

These are individual bets which combine two or more horses in a single wager: if one horse loses the whole bet is lost. They can be win or each way, and include:

Double

Combining two horses in different races. If the first wins, the winnings and stake go on to the second. A simple way of calculating the winnings on a double is to add one to each of the odds, multiply them, and subtract one from the total. A £5 double on horses which both win at 2–1 yields a return of £45 – £40 winnings plus £5 stake – as the first win gives a return of £15, which then goes on the second horse at 2–1 and brings £30 winnings plus £15 stake: £45. (A bookmaker will not accept a double bet calculated in this

When Serious Trouble won the two-runner Ruddles Best Bitter Stakes at Brighton on 15 May 1990 his starting price of 33–1 on was the shortest returned since the abolition of on-course betting tax in April 1987.

way on two events where the first result has a direct bearing on the second. For instance, had you wanted to back Celtic Swing to win the Two Thousand Guineas and the Derby in 1995, the odds quoted would have been shorter than a simple multiple of the single odds for both eventualities, as success in the first would significantly alter the chances of success in the second.)

Treble

Combining three horses in different races. Again, add one to each of the winning odds, multiply them, and subtract one from the total to find the winnings. So a £5 treble on three horses which each win at 2–1 yields a return of £135: winnings of £130 plus the £5 stake.

Accumulator

Combining any number of horses to win different races, calculating the winnings in the same way as for a double or a treble. The old ITV Seven was a seven-horse accumulator: had your seven choices in a £5 accumulator all obliged at 2–1 you would have relieved your bookmaker of £10,930 in winnings.

MULTIPLE BETS

These are ways of combining several horses in different sorts of bet. The names under which such bets go are simply a shorthand for a recognized menu of individual bets, so success does not depend on each horse winning. Multiple bets can be win or each way.

Patent

A wager combining three different horses in different races in seven separate bets – three singles, three doubles, and one treble. Thus if the horses are A, B and C, the Patent consists of:

singles	A
	B
	C
doubles:	A with B
	A with C
	B with C
treble:	A with B with C

A £1 win Patent will cost you £7; a £1 each-way Patent costs £14. Say you have a £1 win Patent on A, B and C and they all win at 2–1: your winnings are £6 (three £1 singles each winning at 2–1) plus £24 (three £1 doubles with each horse winning at 2–1) plus £26 (a £1 treble with each horse winning at 2–1: total winnings of £56. But if two of the horses win at 2–1 while the third horse loses, you would still make a profit. You win £4 (two £1 singles each winning at 2–1) plus £8 (one £1 double with each horse winning at 2–1: total winnings £12. But of your seven bets four (one single, two doubles, one treble) have lost, so your profit is £12 less £4: £8.

Yankee

A bet combining four different horses in different races in eleven bets (so a £1 win Yankee costs £11). The horses are connected in six doubles, four trebles and one four-horse accumulator. (A Lucky 15 is a fifteen-bet wager adding four singles to the eleven bets of the Yankee. If one selection wins

On 2 May 1995 a lady pensioner in Nottingham won over £208,000 from Ladbrokes. She had a five pence accumulator on winners Christian Flight (20–1), Don't Forget Ruby (12–1), Romany Creek (20–1), Groomsman (66–1) and How's It Goin (7–1), which netted her £153,644.40, and topped this up with a five pence each way Super Flag bet which took her total winnings to £208,098.79 for an outlay of just over £5. Ladbrokes calculated that the accumulated odds of the five winners – 3,072,887-1 – was a world record.

but the other four lose, many bookmakers will benevolently double the odds for your single winning bet.)

Super Yankee

A bet combining five selections in ten doubles, ten trebles, five fourfolds and one five-horse accumulator – twenty-six bets. (Also known as a Canadian.)

Heinz

A bet combining six selections in fifty-seven bets: fifteen doubles, twenty trebles, fifteen fourfolds, six fivefolds and one six-horse accumulator.

SPECIALITY BETS

These apply to just one race and include:

Forecast

The Tote Dual Forecast involves giving the first and second horses in either order. (A 'combination forecast' involves choosing more than two horses in the hope that any two of them will come first and second. Thus a combination forecast with three horses costs three times the unit stake (AB, AC, BC), with four horses six times (AB, AC, AD, BC, BD, CD), five horses ten times, and so on.) The Computer Straight Forecast is a betting shop wager which involves predicting the first two in correct order (so called because the dividend is calculated by computer, using a formula too complex for mortal man to comprehend).

Tricast

In handicaps of eight or more declared runners and no fewer than six actual runners, the punter must select the first three in correct order. Again, a computer calculates the dividend.

BETTING COUPS

Coups are very carefully contrived bets which involve a great deal of planning by the connections of the horse and others in the know, and can be divided broadly into two categories – the successful and the unsuccessful. The unsuccessful divide again into two further categories – legal and fraudulent. For it is rarely the case that a successful coup will turn out to have been brought about by illegal means: the success of a coup occurs when its perpetrators are paid out by the bookies, and at any sniff of illegality most bookmakers will withhold payment.

Usually a coup will be brought about by the horse being carefully prepared for a race in such a way that the bookmakers have a less accurate idea of its chance than those who are betting on it, and will consequently let it be backed at an over-generous price. The history of the Turf is peppered with occasions when a massive amount of money invested has caused a dramatic reduction in the odds of a horse. Perhaps the most spectacular in recent memory was the case of Father Hayes, who won the Hanover Square Handicap at Sandown Park in June 1992 having been backed from 16–1 down to 5–2 before easing to his SP of 4–1. As the Jockey Club announced an enquiry, the case had a tragic sting in the tail: the gelding's trainer Will Pearce committed suicide two days after the Sandown coup had been landed.

BETTING ON OVERSEAS RACES

With the increasing internationalization of racing, and fixtures such as the Breeders' Cup forming an integral part of the racing year, there is an increasing interest in betting on races abroad, especially when British-trained horses are competing.

Bookmakers will usually advertise prices – and in some cases, such as the Prix de l'Arc de Triomphe, there will be a lively ante-post market – about the major overseas races, and the punter has a choice between taking those prices or betting at the locally returned prices, which are usually (as in the case of France or the USA) Pari-Mutuel prices.

The longest ever starting price returned about a winner in Britain was 250–1 about Equinoctial, winner of the Grants Whisky Novices Hurdle at Kelso on 21 November 1990.

Successful gambles in the Classics include those on Talma II, who was backed down from 100–6 to 7–1 on the day of the 1951 St Leger, which he won by ten lengths, and on Tulyar, backed on the day of the 1952 Derby from 100–6 to 11–2 favourite: ridden by Charlie Smirke, he won by three-quarters of a length from Gay Time. Two spectacular losing gambles in the Derby since the war involved Tudor Minstrel, backed as if defeat were out of the question to 7–4 on in 1947 (he finished fourth, as described on page 120), and Dancing Brave, who just failed to get to Shahrastani in 1986 (see pages 176–7). But big bets are sometimes easier to land in smaller races: the famed professional punter Alex Bird landed one of the biggest bets of his career with Signification in a small race at Liverpool on Grand National Day, 1952: the horse won at 7–2, having opened in the betting at 100–6.

Certainly the coup which pushes against – and sometimes through – the bounds of legality is easier to pull off in a small race which will attract little attention, and the most sensational frauds of the post-war era have taken place in minor events. A horse named Francasal won a selling race at Bath on 16 July 1953 at 10–1, but investigations revealed that he had been switched for a 'ringer' – a horse of very similar appearance but markedly different ability, in this case a much faster animal named Santa Amaro. The main perpetrators of the affair were convicted and jailed.

When Flockton Grey won a two-year-old maiden race at Leicester in March 1982 at 10–1 suspicions were aroused, not least because of the ease of his twenty-length victory: the horse turned out to be the three-year-old Good Hand. Again, those who had masterminded the coup ended up in court, and Flockton Grey himself spent years in police custody: he was subsequently co-owned by Michael Aspel.

But perhaps the most ingenious coup attempted in recent years was the affair of Gay Future, who won the Ulverston Novices' Hurdle at Cartmel on 26 August 1974, Bank Holiday Monday.

The essence of this intricate story is that an unnamed horse had been sent by the planners of the coup, based in Ireland, to the stables of trainer Anthony Collins at Troon in Scotland. Collins had entered a horse called Gay Future and another horse, Racionzer, in the race at Cartmel, and two

Far from the madding crowd of the Tattersalls betting ring at Goodwood's July Meeting, bookmakers ply their trade on Trundle Hill.

other horses – Opera Cloak and Ankerwyke – in races at other courses on the same day and both starting within half an hour of the Cartmel race. On that Bank Holiday morning members of the syndicate who were staging the coup placed bets in a variety of betting shops in London on doubles connecting Gay Future with Opera Cloak or with Ankerwyke: doubles are deemed by bookmakers to be 'mugs' bets', and betting in small amounts in this manner would not have aroused suspicion.

Meanwhile the 'real' Gay Future, who had been prepared for his race in Ireland, had been brought over the Irish Sea, swapped for the horse in Collins's charge, and sent off to Cartmel for the race. Neither Ankerwyke nor Opera Cloak reached the courses where they were supposed to be running (it transpired that they had never left their trainer's stable). When one leg of a double is a non-runner the bet becomes a single on the remaining horse, so a large amount of money was then running on Gay Future; but the 'blower' system transmitting off-course money to the course betting market was not operating to Cartmel that very busy Bank Holiday Monday (as the planners of the coup had cleverly been aware), and by the time the bookmakers realized what was afoot they could get his price down only by dispatching a representative to the course to bet on him there.

The bookies' man did not arrive in time.

Before he had entered the paddock at Cartmel, Gay Future's flanks had had soap flakes rubbed into them to give the impression that he was sweating freely and so put off on-course punters. The horse played his own part in the coup by strolling home fifteen lengths in front of his rivals at 10–1. Most of the betting shops who had taken the bets withheld payment, though some later regarded the matter as a legitimate coup and paid out. (The conspirators stood to win around £300,000.)

The police launched a prosecution, and Collins and Tony Murphy, the Irish building contractor who was the main brain behind the coup, were convicted of conspiracy to defraud the bookmakers, and fined. Conflicting views were aired about whether the matter should have been brought to court; whatever the legality or illegality of the episode, the Gay Future affair was a coup of remarkable cunning and ingenuity.

The Race

THE VALET

The jockey's valet is one of the most important backroom boys of racing. He transports from meeting to meeting most of the equipment belonging to the jockeys who hire him (and who will pay him around 10 per cent of their riding fees for that meeting): boots, breeches, saddles, weight-cloths and so on. He prepares this equipment (supplemented by the owner's colours, which are brought to the racecourse by the trainer) in the changing room before each race, bearing in mind what equipment each jockey will require for each race (what size saddle, for instance) and how much weight will need to be put into the weight-cloth. He will assist the jockeys in dressing, making running repairs, supplying extra equipment which a young or forgetful jockey might not have, and generally ensuring that events in the jockeys' changing room – a scene of sometimes manic activity into which even trainers may not venture – run smoothly. Most top jockeys leave all their equipment with their valet, keeping with them only their own helmets and back protectors; at the end of the day's racing the valet is responsible for cleaning it. The next day, whether at the same course or at some other venue, it will be all ready and waiting for them when they arrive in the changing room.

Bertie Wooster (the P. G. Wodehouse character, not the good old chestnut whose white blaze was such a familiar sight in sprint handicaps over the last few years) observed ruefully of a race in which the horse he'd backed had been beaten, that 'in the case of this particular dashed animal, one had come to look on the running of the race as a pure formality, a sort of quaint, old-world ceremony to be gone through before one sauntered up to the bookie and collected.'

The reality of racing life, sadly for punters, is never like that, but there is a degree of procedure and sequence of events around each race which hardly changes.

BEFORE THE RACE

On arrival at the course the runners are taken into the racecourse stables. Each horse has a passport which identifies it very precisely by its markings (in order to avoid substitution of a 'ringer' – a horse of similar appearance but dissimilar ability) and certifies that it has received all the required vaccinations: without this passport the horse may not enter the course, and even with it may be subjected to examination by a vet to check that it is who the passport says it is. After its morning feed the horse will not eat again until after the race, and will not be allowed to drink from about four hours before the off.

The stable lad settles the horse in its box and gives it a final grooming – often with an eye to the award for the best turned-out horse which is judged on appearance in the parade ring for some races. About half an hour before the race it is taken into the pre-parade ring, where it will be led round to await being saddled by the trainer.

Meanwhile the jockey has arrived in the changing room, where he will change into the colours of the owner (which are kept by the trainer). The jockey's valet will have brought along the saddle (or saddles) which he will be using for that afternoon's racing, and to ensure that the jockey and saddle are at the correct weight for the race will, if necessary, put lead weights into the pockets of the weight-cloth which the horse will carry underneath the saddle. The jockey will check on the changing-room scales that he is at the required weight, and then, when given the signal by a weighing-room official, reports to the Clerk of the Scales to be weighed out for the race, by sitting with his equipment on the scales for confirmation by the Clerk that he is at the correct weight. Included in the rider's weight when weighing out are everything that the horse is to carry except the jockey's skull cap (which is exempt from the weighing in order to remove the temptation to wear a dangerously light helmet), his whip, the bridle, blinkers (or equivalent), breast-plate or breast-girth, martingale, neck-strap or muzzle, and anything worn on the horse's legs: so what is weighed out is the jockey, his clothing (though an allowance of one pound is made for the back protector — hence a jockey weighing out at 9 stone will actually register 9 stone 1 pound on the scales), saddle and weight-cloth.

If the correct weight is registered, the saddle with its related equipment is then passed to the trainer (or his representative) who will go off to saddle the horse in a box by the pre-parade ring, finishing off with a sponge round its eyes and in its mouth. Then the lad leads it off to the parade ring proper.

IN THE PADDOCK, AND GOING DOWN

The parade ring, or paddock, is where the horse is formally displayed to the spectators before the race. In contrast to practice in many other countries – notably the USA – horses spend a good deal of time in the parade ring at British courses, and paddock inspection is one of the key ways of assessing the condition of a runner.

Although to an extent equine beauty, as with human, is in the eye of the beholder, it helps to be aware of the paddock characteristics of some horses,

Previous spread:
The start of the 1994 Martell Grand National.

lest their demeanour before the race prove off-putting. That superb hurdler and chaser Night Nurse, for instance, often seemed half asleep as he walked round the paddock, though he would wake up soon enough in the race; with the 1990 Grand National and Whitbread hero Mr Frisk, well known to be a nervous individual, punters would worry were he not in a lather of sweat. Generally jumpers become much more familiar to racegoers and television viewers than Flat horses, and paddock observers will know what to expect from the appearance of these old campaigners. With less well-known horses it is useful to know what to look for.

What takes the fancy in a horse will always contain an element of the indefinable, and its fitness and well-being in the paddock must be judged on an overall impression. There are several key elements to a good conformation in a horse. Look for an intelligent and alert demeanour, with a bold eye, big ears pointing slightly inwards (though 'lop ears' that flop forwards are often a sign of stamina and genuineness); the carriage of the head should be high, and the neck in good proportion to body size and length. The shoulder should be well sloped back to drive the forelegs to maximum effect and the chest and girth area deep and wide to provide plenty of room for a big heart and good lungs. The back should be short and strong, and the quarters, which drive the hind legs and provide the real power, well-muscled and rounded. It can pay, too, to look for a few more specific signs.

Sweating up

Sweating up before a race is not necessarily a bad sign; it depends on the nature of the sweat. (It also depends, of course, on the nature of the weather, as a horse is much more likely to sweat when it is hot.) Sweating around the ears or eyes is not a good sign, as it suggests agitated nervousness. Nor is 'frothy' sweating. But sweating on the neck can augur well, often indicating keen anticipation.

The walk

A horse which walks well will gallop well, and the horse striding out round the paddock will probably stride out well in the race. A sign of a good walker is 'tracking up': when the hind foot overlaps or falls in front of the hoofprint left by the front foot. Such niceties are not easy to spot on television, but it is simple enough to see whether a horse moves easily and loosely at the walk, rather than taking short, mincing strides. Many horses in the paddock bob up and down as they are led round: this is usually a sign of general keenness. The horse that will not be led quietly round is showing signs of irritation. Horses in the paddock tend to be silent, but unraced or inexperienced two-year-olds may well whinny to each other in alarm at their strange surroundings.

Condition

A fit horse will give off the same air of muscularity and power as a human athlete. A shiny, well-groomed coat advertises its general health, and it is in the horse's quarters that fitness is most apparent. A useful check is to watch a horse from behind: if it is well muscled up around the tail it will display 'hard marks' – grooves either side of the muscle. An unfit horse will appear much flabbier. Irregular twitching of the ears and swishing of the tail tend to be signs of an over-tense horse, while dull eyes, listless carriage of the neck and tired ears suggest that it is not tense enough. A tubby horse will not be fit, and a horse which appears 'tucked up' or 'run up light' (lean and ribby) behind the saddle may have 'gone over the top'.

'Over the top' is where a horse is deemed to have gone when it has had too much racing for the season, and although this can sometimes be diagnosed before a race through paddock symptoms of edginess or

SAFETY LIMITS

All racecourses impose limits on the number of horses which can safely be accommodated on that course for races over each distance. (On the Flat these are often dictated by the width of the course at the start: obviously a narrow course can accommodate fewer runners in starting stalls than a wide one.) If the number of declared runners exceeds the safety limit there are three possible courses of action:

Eliminations: in handicaps, horses are eliminated from the lowest weight up until the maximum number of runners is left; in Pattern races, elimination starts with the horse lowest in the official ratings.

Ballots: for a wide range of races the field is thinned by balloting out the required number of runners, though exemptions are usually allowed for certain horses (such as previous winners).

Division: the race is divided into two (or more) races.

THE DRAW

The draw is the numbered position in the starting stalls which a horse must take up in relation to the other horses at the start of a Flat race. Facing from the start towards the finish, draw number 1 is always on the left-hand side. The draw is made the day before the race and on some courses and over some distances has an extreme effect on a horse's chance; the contours or shape of a course can mean that certain draws are much more advantageous than others.

A draw is not made for National Hunt races as the minimum distance for jumping races is two miles and difference in starting position would have no effect over these longer distances.

listlessness, more often it only becomes apparent after the horse has failed to show its true form in the race. How to interpret paddock appearance depends a great deal on the time of the year and the stage of the season. A horse grows a winter coat, so cannot be expected to be a picture of shiny health on a cold day in February. The condition of early runners on the Flat in the spring will depend on the nature of the previous winter, as most horses (especially fillies and mares) will not thrive until they have felt the sun on their backs. Towards the end of the summer certain horses will obviously be starting to 'train off' – they lose their form and are in need of a break. During the closing weeks of the Flat season on turf a horse will start to 'go in its coat' – grow its winter coat – and although fillies tend to lose form as their coats change it rarely makes a difference to colts.

GOING DOWN

The prologue to most big races is the parade, when the field is led past the stands to give those who are not able to get to the paddock the opportunity to study the horses. Whether there is a parade or not, the horses will canter past the stands to the start, and this is the chance to supplement paddock inspection with a close-up of the horse in action. Much can be learned from the way the horse goes down. If it strides out well on the way to post – 'pokes its toe' – it is at ease on the ground. But a horse who moves scratchily ('goes down short') is clearly not enjoying the going – and is going to enjoy it much less when galloping at racing speed.

It is folly, though, to assume that any horse moving slowly to the start is feeling the ground: another explanation might be that the animal is a hard puller, and the jockey is taking him down gently to avoid his running away. Sometimes a horse is so highly strung that the Stewards of the meeting give permission for it to be taken down all by itself in advance of the other runners, and after Lochsong boiled over during the preliminaries for the Nunthorpe Stakes at York in 1994 it was decided to dispense with parades before sprint races.

The parade for a race such as the Derby puts a great strain on the young and inexperienced horses who take part, but adds immeasurably to the sense of occasion for the racegoers and viewers.

'What do we do now?' After the second false start in the 1993 Martell Grand National, the nine riders who obeyed the recall flag await further enlightenment. In the centre of the picture, the starting tape still wound around his neck, is Richard Dunwoody on Wont Be Gone Long. The other thirty runners set off to race, though several pulled up after one circuit in response to frantic signals from connections. Seven horses – headed by Esha Ness – completed the course, but the race was declared void.

AT THE START

Once arrived at the start, the runners come under the jurisdiction of the Starter, who checks them against the list of runners and riders which he has obtained from the Clerk of the Scales, and calls the roll to remind each rider (in a Flat race) of his draw. The horses will then walk round for a few minutes to settle after the canter to the start and to have their girths adjusted: a horse will usually blow itself out when its saddle is being put on, and by the time it has reached the start the jockey will need to see that the girths are tightened.

All Flat races must start from stalls or, if for some reason stalls are not possible or not practical, by the Starter dropping a flag. (Flag starts are often used for long-distance races, where the importance of all the runners starting evenly is less acute than in shorter races.) National Hunt races are started by a starting gate – normally the type in which an elastic tape is drawn across the course and released upwards by a lever controlled by the Starter – or flag. For a Flat race the horses are loaded into the stalls, odd numbers in the draw first, then even; horses which are known to dislike a prolonged wait in the stalls may be put in last, at the discretion of the Starter, but once a horse has been loaded it cannot be released until the front gates are opened by the Starter.

No horse may be started from outside the stalls, but it is now allowed for a horse of exceptional length not to have the rear gate of the stall shut behind him but to make use instead of a specially designed strap which clips round the open rear gates, thus allowing the horse to stand comfortably in the stalls. Outsize horses owe this modification to the protests of a very big and long three-year-old named Scallywag, who could not be persuaded to enter the stalls for the 1976 King Edward VII Stakes at Royal Ascot; his trainer Bruce Hobbs devised the strap to replace the rear doors, and Scallywag ran third to Crow in the St Leger.

The teams of stalls handlers are supplied by RaceTech and undertake their uniquely awkward job with skill and sympathy. If a horse is reluctant to enter its stall they will try various ways of persuading it – including enticing it with a handful of fresh sweet grass – before resorting to the strong-arm tactics of getting a strap round the horse's backside and heaving it in. If the horse will still not co-operate they will try blindfolding it and walking it round to disorientate it so that it will not realize when it is being led up to the stalls. A horse which simply will not enter is left, and does not come under Starter's orders. It will be reported to the Stewards, and will have to take a stalls test before being allowed to race again.

The condition of 'under Starter's orders' takes effect as soon as the Starter is satisfied that the field is ready to go, so that in the case of a stalls start the horses are normally under orders for no more than a couple of seconds before – the riders' attention having been grabbed by the Starter's strident exclamation 'Jockeys!' – they are released. In a flag- or gate-started race a horse may become unruly after the field is under orders and cause a delay – a nerve-wracking time for punters, as all bets stand as soon as the field is under orders, whereas backers of a horse which is withdrawn before coming under orders have their money returned.

Some 100 yards down the course from the start stands a man with a flag. His role is to wave the runners down should the Starter signal to him that the start was false – say because a fault in the stalls mechanism caused some of the stalls not to open.

It is not easy to pull up a racehorse in full flight and false starts can cause confusion and pandemonium. At the start of the 1986 Portland Handicap at Doncaster the stalls were damaged and the race had to be started by flag. It is one thing to start a field of sedate jumpers or stayers by flag, quite another to dispatch by this method twenty-three sprinters all keyed up to hurtle five and a half furlongs up the Doncaster straight. Two false starts ensued, after the first of which five runners completed the entire course

THE STARTER

In the days before starting stalls, the Starter was able to ruin a race by letting the field go before all the horses were in a line, or allowing an enterprising jockey to steal a flying start. That can still happen in jump racing (the starts of which are often accompanied by a vociferous debate between jockeys and Starter about whether the field is ready to go), but the use of stalls for flat races should ensure a level start for all.

The Starter makes sure that all the horses are at the start, that they start (if appropriate) from the correct draw, and that the starting process goes as smoothly as possible. He can order the exclusion from the race of an unruly horse, and can report any rider guilty of misconduct at the start to the Stewards of the meeting. In between races he will return to the weighing room to witness the weighing out.

WALKOVER

A walkover is a race with only one runner. The jockey must weigh out and weigh in, following the standard procedures, but does not have to cover the entire distance of the race: the horse simply has to be ridden past the Judge's box. (The point-to-pointer Rossa Prince has the unusual distinction of failing to win a walkover: at Tweseldown in May 1990 he bolted while being saddled for his solitary effort and could not be retrieved by the time he was due in the parade ring, so was disqualified. This feat was matched in April 1994 by another point-to-pointer, Mister Chippendale, disqualified after a walkover when his rider failed to weigh in.)

The Judge must occupy the Judge's box (situated in a raised position well back from the winning line) at the time the horses pass the winning post. (The winner is determined according to which horse gets any part of its head – excluding the ears – past the post first.) The Judge must announce his decision immediately – or after consulting the evidence of the photo-finish camera – and his decision is final unless an objection is lodged or a Stewards' Enquiry called and the placings are subsequently altered.

If a mistake does occur, it can be corrected by the Judge up to five days after the race, or by the Stewards of the Jockey Club within fourteen days. (A recent example of a racecourse judge admitting a mistake came after the Captain Quist Hurdle at Kempton Park in October 1994. Judge Jane Stickels originally called a dead heat between Large Action and Absalom's Lady, then after the end of the racing programme – by which time of course the jockeys had weighed in and bets had been settled – she changed her mind following approaches by the connections of Absalom's Lady and declared her the winner, a decision ratified by the Jockey Club the following week – too late for the mare's backers to collect their full whack, though!)

The Judge's other main responsibility is to declare the distances between the horses who finish the race. He bases these on the evidence of the photo-finish strip, the shortest distances being short head, head, neck and half a length; anything over thirty lengths is a 'distance'.

Between races the Judge will familiarize him- or herself with the jockeys' colours in the next race by watching the weighing out and by studying the runners in the paddock.

and had to be withdrawn. The Starter's anguished cry as the field swept off was well picked up by the Channel Four microphones: 'Come back, you buggers!'

But the most famous and calamitous false start in racing history was of course that of the 1993 Martell Grand National, when the tape broke twice and two false starts ensued, leading to chaotic scenes which brought racing a great deal of not wholly undeserved ridicule – and, on a more positive note, caused significant changes in the procedure for starting the most high-profile race of the year.

READING THE RACE

There are three main ways of watching a race. One is simply to enjoy the spectacle, with its colour, noise and excitement. The second is to concentrate all your attention on the horse you've backed, which is fine if your choice is involved in the finish and even finer if it wins, but can distract you from the great events taking shape elsewhere in the field. The third is to try to 'read' the race, to interpret what happens during the race in order to use the information gained on some future occasion.

Race-reading is a difficult art, and the level of difficulty varies according to the nature of the race, the number of runners, the course, the pace, and various other factors, but it is a skill which can be very profitably – and very enjoyably – deployed.

The most obvious way of turning race-reading to good use is in spotting one of the beaten horses running a particularly encouraging race, thus suggesting that its performance will improve (this would be 'one for the notebook'). So a horse in a race over one mile might appear to have difficulty in keeping up with the leaders in the early stages and fail to get into a challenging position, but sustain his pace in the closing stages ('run on'). This suggests that a longer distance will be to his liking, and he may be worth supporting next time out if the race is over one and a quarter miles or further. The point is that not everybody might have noticed his performance in the earlier race, and you may be able to back the horse at good odds.

There are several factors to take into account in forming your analysis of the action:

Pace

A 'truly run' race is one in which the runners maintain a good speed from the start, depending on the distance of the race and the going. Sprint races are almost invariably truly run, for what is the point of dawdling in a sprint? But even big races can be run at a false pace, which often becomes the excuse for a beaten horse. Whatever the distance, a race which starts off at a crawl can develop into a sprint, and thus the form may be suspect. Similarly, a race can be run at a suicidally fast pace: the 1987 King George VI Rank Chase at Kempton Park saw Desert Orchid and Beau Ranger set off at a scorching gallop: it may have been exciting to watch, but they both ran out of puff long before the straight, leaving Nupsala to come through and take the race.

Distances

It is generally felt that a race where all the runners finish very close to one another is unlikely to be a very good race in terms of the quality of its contestants – they can't all be brilliant, so they're probably all mediocre. (This does not, of course, apply to handicaps, which are specifically aimed at bringing about a bunched finish.) But a false pace naturally can distort the meaning of the finishing distances, as a race run at a dawdle gives less opportunity for the field to get strung out.

Style of running

Horses run races in different ways, and have preferences for certain sorts of going, for left-handed or right-handed tracks, for front-running or being held up. A knowledge of the preferences of the horses in a race will help you deduce whether that race is being run to suit a particular horse. And you can tell if a horse is unhappy on the going most obviously when the ground is too firm, when it will seem unwilling to stride out properly (and is said to be 'feeling the ground'), and may be hanging its head to one side or keeping it high. Such a horse may 'change its legs' – that is, adjust its galloping action. A horse will 'lead' with one of its forelegs, the last of its legs to strike the ground during the cycle of the stride. On a left-hand track the horse should lead with its near foreleg (that is, its left front leg), and if it is uneasy on the ground it will change to leading with the other leg, especially when under pressure towards the end of the race.

A horse with a 'round' action lifts its knees high during the stride and is usually better suited by soft ground. Desert Orchid notwithstanding, most horses are happier running left-handed: from early days they are led on the left, saddled from the left, lunged to the left, and so build up an inclination to go to the left. (Significantly, almost all racetracks in the USA are left-handed.)

A horse which is 'green' shows signs of inexperience. Horses race on the Flat very early in their lives – well before they are mature – and it is not surprising that some of them, however well trained, do not immediately realize what is required of them on the racecourse.

The most common form of greenness is an inability to run straight and true to the line: the green horse may be distracted by the crowd and generally bewildered by what is happening around him, and wander off a straight course. This is why a jockey will often keep an inexperienced horse at full throttle even though he is winning his race easily, for the race is an education for the horse and he will benefit from being shown how to stretch out and gallop home.

A word about the whip. The use of the whip has become a controversial issue, and the Jockey Club lays down guidelines for jockeys and Stewards to prevent its excessive use. In the hands of a good jockey the whip is an essential tool, necessary for keeping the horse running straight, and for driving it to an extra effort in a tight finish. Most horses will veer away from the whip, so if in a finish the horse is drifting to the left the jockey will use it on his left side to correct the wandering: the ability to pull the whip through from one hand to the other in a split second is a vital component of jockeyship. Usually the jockey will give the horse a couple of smacks with the whip to get it to its maximum pace and will then wave the whip – without hitting the horse – to keep encouraging it to the line. Some horses resent its application and will not run on (swishing the tail is a common sign of disagreement with the rider's method), and many horses simply give their best without the rider having any recourse to it at all: Bustino's heroic effort in the 1975 King George VI and Queen Elizabeth Diamond Stakes finish against Grundy was a fine example of a horse running as fast as he possibly could under a wise jockey (Joe Mercer) who knew that the whip would not make the slightest difference. To use the whip during such an effort could distract and unbalance the horse: better to stick with 'hands and heels' to keep the horse going.

Taking the jumps

A jump race adds an extra dimension to race-reading, as the decisions which jockeys have to make when putting their horses at the obstacles will affect the outcome dramatically. If two horses are going together into the final fence a good jump can win the race, but an inexperienced jumper may not be able to take off well before the fence in order to gain the advantage, and

Michael Hancock, Senior Judge, studies the photo-finish print.

FALLS

Most falls in jump racing are caused by the horse misjudging when to take off: too soon and it may not be able to clear the jump cleanly, too late and it will not have time to get enough spring into its leap. Either way it will clout the obstacle. Another common cause of falls is over-jumping: the horse jumps too extravagantly and slithers on to its belly on landing. (A horse whose nose touches the ground as it attempts to balance itself on clearing a jump is often said to have 'pecked on landing'.)

Should a jockey part company with his horse he may remount (and be assisted in so doing) as long as he gets on again at the place where contact was severed: the last remounted horse to have been placed in the Grand National was Loving Words, third in 1982 (jockey Richard Hoare had been dislodged at the fourth last).

Falls on the flat – under both codes – are frequently caused by a horse clipping the heels of one in front of it, and by bunching and squeezing.

THE RACE

his jockey may allow him to 'fiddle' it and then ride a finish once the fence has been safely negotiated. But if he is well in the lead at the last the jockey may just ask the horse to 'pop' the fence in order to ensure his safe arrival on the other side. The key to clean jumping is for the jockey to be able to 'see a stride' well before the fence and adjust his horse at the approach so that he will jump it efficiently.

No two races are alike, and often arguments can be made that had the race been run differently the outcome would have been different. But however the race is run, the moment of truth is always the winning post – or rather, the invisible line stretching across the course from the winning post.

AFTER THE RACE

The runners pull up and are reunited with their stable lads. The placed horses are led into the unsaddling enclosure, while the others are unsaddled away from the main ring, and the post-mortem starts. The former jockey Paul Barton has told how he informed a trainer on whose horse he had just finished tailed off in a novices' chase that the horse would be fine when he matured; he needed more time. 'How much time does he need?' asked the trainer: 'he's already eleven.'

The reasons for defeat which jockeys give owners and trainers are legion, and some of them are accurate. But the essence of racing is that hope springs eternal, and this hope must be kept alive.

The jockeys dismount and return to the Clerk of the Scales to weigh in. All jockeys who have ridden in a race may be required to weigh in (unless prevented by injury), at the discretion of the Clerk, and the jockeys of all placed horses must do so: a placed horse whose jockey, for whatever reason, fails to weigh in will be disqualified. So will a jockey whose weight at weighing in is different from that at weighing out, though a jockey is allowed to fall one pound below the weighed-out weight to take into account the possible slimming effects of his exertions. A jockey who weighs in at two pounds or more over the weighed-out weight is reported to the Stewards.

The weight carried by a horse in a race is of crucial importance, and discrepancies between weighing out and weighing in are very serious. In order to prevent any switching of weighable items, the Jockey Club Rules stipulate that 'if a rider touches, except accidentally, any person or thing other than his own equipment before weighing in his horse may, on an objection under Rule 170(iv), be disqualified, unless he can satisfy the Stewards that he was justified by the circumstances.' For some connections, winning a race is justification enough.

If a jockey wishes to lodge an objection over an incident in the race, he does so to the Clerk of the Scales on returning to the weighing room. If all the placed riders weigh in correctly and there is no objection by a jockey nor any Stewards' Enquiry, the announcement 'weighed in' is made, and the result stands – at least, it stands as far as the immediate settlement of bets is concerned: if any prohibited substance is found in the horse's specimen that runner will be disqualified subsequently.

The horses are led away. The winner will usually have to offer a urine specimen (or, if it can't produce one, a blood specimen) for sending off to the Horserace Forensic Laboratory in Newmarket; other runners may be subjected to a routine sampling on the direction of the Stewards. They are then washed down and returned to their horseboxes for the journey home.

Meanwhile the human element takes in any prize-giving ceremony and moves off, either to prepare for the next race or to slip into the bar for celebration or commiseration. A few, of course, will be subjected to the attentions of Brough Scott or Derek Thompson . . .

THE CLERK OF THE SCALES

The primary duty of the Clerk of the Scales is to weigh out the jockeys before the race – when each jockey presents himself to the Clerk with his equipment, sits on the scales (having declared any overweight) and has confirmed that his horse will be carrying the correct allotted weight – and weigh him back in after the race. Should a rider fail to weigh in or weigh in illegally lighter than he weighed out, it is the duty of the Clerk of the Scales to lodge an objection. But the Clerk's responsibilities go much further. He is in overall charge of the racecourse number board, on which will be displayed the rider of each horse in the race, the draw (in a Flat race), allowances claimed, overweight, the wearing of blinkers or a visor, any change of colours, and other relevant official information regarding that race. At the end of each day's racing he makes a return to the *Racing Calendar* Office giving details of the weights carried in every race, of which horses failed to complete the course, and why, of complaints to and decisions of the Stewards, of all fines inflicted, and of all horses sold or claimed.

The greatest ever number of runners in a Flat race was fifty-eight, in the Lincolnshire Handicap at Lincoln on 13 March 1948. They had to start in two lines, as did the largest ever National Hunt field – sixty-six, in the Grand National at Liverpool on 22 March 1929.

GREAT RACES

What makes a race linger on in the memory, sending you searching for the video or compelling you to describe it to friends in the bar after a day on the course years after the event? A bravely fought finish, a particularly brilliant or courageous performance by horse or jockey, a controversial result, the exhilaration of landing a gamble or of witnessing a group of really top-class horses battle it out – all or any of these can do it. The Channel Four Racing team have between them witnessed many thousands of races, but each of the eleven described here was something special.

GRAND STEEPLECHASE DE PARIS

Auteuil, 17 June 1962

By the time the eleven-year-old Mandarin got to Auteuil in June 1962 he was approaching the end of a career which had marked him out as one of the best and toughest chasers of the post-war era. He had won both the Hennessy Gold Cup and the King George VI Chase twice, and in March 1962 had taken the Cheltenham Gold Cup, beating Fortria by a length. But nothing he had achieved matched what was to follow that steamy afternoon in the Bois de Boulogne.

Ridden by Fred Winter (who was severely debilitated by a stomach upset), Mandarin was 2–1 favourite for the Grand Steeplechase de Paris, in which he had finished second three years earlier. The race was unlike anything seen in Britain, being run over 6,500 metres of a track of extraordinary complexity – two separate figures-of-eight in different directions, then once round the outside – and negotiating a varied assortment of obstacles a far cry from the jumps at Sandown or Cheltenham, including such curiosities as 'Le Bullfinch', a white post and rails topping a little bank. At the third fence the rubber bit in Mandarin's mouth snapped, leaving Fred Winter to face the remaining three and a half miles of twists and turns without any means of guiding the horse except pressure from his knees and the swing of his body: he had no contact with Mandarin's mouth, as the bit was dangling uselessly under the horse's neck. Showing the sportsmanship which characterizes steeplechase jockeys whatever their nationality, the French riders, aware of what was going on, helped Mandarin stay in the race by driving up on to his outside going round the bends. Just before the final turn Fred Winter had to wrench the horse away from running out, and at that point the tendons in Mandarin's old forelegs gave: he had broken down.

But still he crashed through the last fence in front and set off for the line, relentlessly pursued by the French horse Lumino. They flashed past the post together, but Mandarin had held on, by a head.

I was lucky enough to be at Auteuil the day Fred Winter won the Grand Steeplechase de Paris on Mandarin. The bit broke in Mandarin's mouth after four fences so Fred had neither brakes nor steering for this unfamiliar twisting four-mile marathon, and then Mandarin broke down three fences from home – but, riding as only he could ride, Fred kept him in front to the end. Both horse and rider richly deserved the accolade Napoleon gave to Marshal Ney – the bravest of the brave.

JOHN OAKSEY

GRAND NATIONAL CHASE

Liverpool, 31 March 1973

The record books supply the facts: Red Rum won by three quarters of a length from Crisp, with L'Escargot twenty-five lengths back in third place and Spanish Steps fourth. And yet, over twenty years later, the result of the 1973 Grand National still seems wrong.

When we watch a recording of this famous race, we can hardly believe, at second Becher's or at the last fence or at the Elbow, that Crisp can possibly fail to win. But every time the recording tells the same story: Crisp, after a display of jumping and galloping the like of which had never been seen at Liverpool, was caught two strides from the post by a horse carrying twenty-three pounds less than he. Crisp was not, in a sense, unlucky; but never has a beaten horse so deserved to win.

Australian-bred Crisp was thought to be best at two and a half miles (the Grand National is nearly four and a half), and had won the Two Mile

'All around me people were jumping up and down with wild excitement, but I sat there like a sphinx, unable to move, trying to take in what was happening': Noel Le Mare's reaction to owning a Grand National winner sums up for me what was the most incredible race I've ever seen.

DEREK THOMPSON

The 1973 Grand National: Crisp (Richard Pitman) soars over second Becher's.

Champion Chase at Cheltenham in 1971 in scorching style. Although there were understandable doubts about his stamina, he was a high-class horse and his jumping was superb, and for the 1973 Grand National (in which he carried top weight) he started 9–1 joint favourite with Red Rum, a scrapper of a horse who had been through several trainers and was now in the charge of the genial Ginger McCain, who mixed training with selling second-hand cars in Southport, not far from Aintree.

Crisp, ridden by Richard Pitman, was towards the head of affairs in the race practically from the start, and by Becher's Brook (the sixth fence) had swung into the lead. Already it was an exhilarating sight, and as he increased his advantage going to the Canal Turn his performance was already something very special: Liverpool clearly held no terrors for Crisp, and by the Chair fence in front of the stands at the end of the first circuit he was a good twenty lengths in front of his pursuers.

He strode out into the country for the second circuit, jumped brilliantly over the five fences before Becher's, then swept over Becher's itself and after the Canal Turn made towards the grandstand still apparently going well within himself. It was an exhibition round, but one of his rivals was not prepared to keep a respectful distance, and as Crisp crossed the Melling Road before lining up the approach to the second last fence it became apparent that Brian Fletcher on Red Rum was slowly closing the gap.

At the second last Crisp still had a very long lead, but his stride was shortening and he was quickly reaching the end of his tether – and all the while Red Rum was scampering closer, full of running. Crisp sent the gorse flying at the last fence and by now it was simply a matter of whether he could last home, for Red Rum was gaining inexorably with every stride. Approaching the Elbow, where the runners veer off the main Grand National course towards the winning post, Crisp appeared to stagger with fatigue. He completely lost his action and had slowed to little more than a trot, but still it seemed he might hang on. Out on his feet, he could not manage it, and Red Rum caught him just before the post.

Red Rum went on to win another two Grand Nationals and become the greatest Liverpool horse of all, but for most people the 1973 race will always be the Crisp Grand National. When the horses next met Crisp enjoyed an easy victory, but that was beside the point. He had put up the most heroic performance ever seen in the National, and had lost. As Peter Bromley said in his radio commentary, 'We will never see another race like that in a hundred years.'

CORAL GOLDEN HURDLE FINAL

Cheltenham, 18 March 1981

Willie Wumpkins shares with Arkle the distinction of having won four times at the Cheltenham National Hunt Meeting since the war. His first victory at what we today know as the Festival came in 1973 in the Aldsworth Hurdle – now the Sun Alliance Hurdle – when he was trained in Ireland by Adrian Maxwell, but the race which he really made his own was the three-mile Coral Golden Hurdle Final.

As an eleven-year-old in 1979 – by which time he was back being trained near Stow-on-the-Wold, not far from Cheltenham, by his owner Jane Pilkington – he was ridden by amateur jockey Jim Wilson and started a 25–1 outsider in a hot field for the race, but beat the favourite Little Owl and Jonjo O'Neill by five lengths. (Two years later Jim Wilson was on board Little Owl when that horse won the Gold Cup.) In 1980, again ridden by Jim Wilson, Willie Wumpkins started at 10–1 and beat King Neptune by four lengths.

Cheltenham crowds love a local winner and Willie Wumpkins had become a great favourite at the course, but it was expecting something for him to return to the winner's enclosure there in March 1981 at the age of thirteen. In the early part of the season he had had a quiet time, then in his pre-Cheltenham race at Newbury had finished an encouraging third, and the bookmakers were taking no chances in the Coral Golden Hurdle Final, sending him off at 13–2 second favourite behind 3–1 chance Fauloon. There were twenty-four runners and the going was heavy: three miles around Cheltenham that day was no task for faint hearts.

Ridden as usual by Jim Wilson, Willie Wumpkins was in the leading group for most of the way. He took up the running halfway round the second circuit, and by the top of the hill only New Top and Wait And See were still in with a chance of denying him a third successive victory. But he shrugged off the challenge of his younger rivals, went well clear going to the last, and stayed on resolutely up the hill to win by twelve lengths from Wait And See, with New Top third. It was his final race.

Willie Wumpkins may not have been Dawn Run or Desert Orchid, but the reception he received that day would have been familiar to them. In any roll-call of post-war Cheltenham heroes, he has an honoured place.

WHITBREAD GOLD CUP

Sandown Park, 28 April 1984

The 1984 Whitbread Gold Cup produced what was probably the finest – and certainly the closest – finish to any major steeplechase in the history of the sport. Even before the race started it promised to be something special, for on its outcome rested several possibilities: should Ashley House or Lettoch win, Michael Dickinson would be champion trainer for the 1983–84 season, while victory by Plundering would give Fred Winter the title; Diamond Edge, a fine chaser who had won the race in 1979 and 1981, was aiming to score a unique treble and consolidate a remarkable comeback from injury at the age of thirteen, and moreover was giving Fulke Walwyn's

Trust me to pick a handicap hurdle! When Willie Wumpkins won his third consecutive Coral Golden Hurdle Final at the astonishing age of thirteen – his fourth Festival win, and eight years after his first – it seemed to me to represent much of what is best about jumping and Cheltenham. A small trainer, an amateur jockey, and some serious planning (!) was described that year by Fulke Walwyn as one of the training performances of the post-war era. Who am I to disagree?

ALASTAIR DOWN

When I kick the bucket, the 1984 Whitbread is the one race I want to be remembered for having called.

GRAHAM GOODE

The 1984 Whitbread Gold Cup: Special Cargo (Kevin Mooney, left) comes into focus to tackle Plundering and Diamond Edge.

jockey Bill Smith his last ride; Special Cargo, who had also returned from a long period of leg injury, was looking to provide the Queen Mother with her most valuable and prestigious triumph; and a win for either Diamond Edge or Special Cargo would give trainer Fulke Walwyn a seventh victory in the race.

Diamond Edge jumping at Sandown Park was always an uplifting sight, and he made much of the running. But three fences out Lettoch and Plundering joined him to dispute the lead; Kevin Mooney on Special Cargo was back in sixth and apparently beaten. Approaching the last fence Lettoch and Plundering were fighting it out, with Diamond Edge hanging on grimly a little behind and, almost unnoticed, Special Cargo beginning to rally.

This is how Graham Goode called the remarkable closing stages for television viewers:

They've got one to jump in the Whitbread! And there's nothing to choose between Plundering and Lettoch – very little to choose between the two, Plundering on the near side, Lettoch on the far side. At the last – they took it together, landed together – with Diamond Edge racing in between these horses again! It's Plundering, Lettoch, Diamond Edge rallying, Special Cargo coming with a run – and Diamond Edge is coming through – Diamond Edge just coming through to shade Lettoch – Special Cargo finishing well – a three-way photo in the Whitbread!! What a fantastic finish – Diamond Edge, Special Cargo and Lettoch, these three in a photo. And Kevin Mooney thinks that he's won on Special Cargo, giving a victory salute . . . You'd have to travel a million miles to see a better race . . .

Kevin Mooney was right. Special Cargo had got up on the line to pip Lettoch by a short head, with Diamond Edge another short head away in third and Plundering a length and a half back in fourth.

John Oaksey, commenting on the television replay, gave the verdict of everyone who saw this wonderful contest: 'I honestly have never seen a finish as exciting as this.'

The 1986 Tote Cheltenham Gold Cup: Dawn Run (right) comes to challenge Forgive N' Forget (left) and Wayward Lad, with Run And Skip back in fourth.

TOTE CHELTENHAM GOLD CUP

Cheltenham, 13 March 1986

Few occasions in racing history have matched the day when Dawn Run became the first horse to add triumph in the Cheltenham Gold Cup to victory in the Champion Hurdle. This grand Irish mare had taken the hurdling crown at 5–4 on in 1984, but she had not found the transition to the larger obstacles easy, and the Gold Cup was only her fifth race over steeplechase fences. Her last outing before the race had been a disaster: she unshipped Tony Mullins at the final open ditch of a chase at Cheltenham in January. Jonjo O'Neill (who had won the Champion Hurdle on her) replaced Mullins in the Gold Cup, for which she started 15–8 favourite. Her main rivals were the 1985 winner Forgive N' Forget, Combs Ditch, the front-running Run And Skip, and Wayward Lad, who had won the King George VI Chase at Kempton Park three times and was the third of Michael Dickinson's first five home in the 1983 Gold Cup.

Of the five principals only Combs Ditch was not in contention as they

Dawn Run, Wayward Lad, Forgive N' Forget and Run And Skip. What a race! I can still recall its finish vividly and I still remember trembling in its glorious aftermath.

JIM McGRATH

The 1986 Prix de l'Arc de Triomphe: a happier moment for Dancing Brave, as Pat Eddery brings him home from Bering (no. 14) and Triptych (no. 9).

Eddery on Dancing Brave was in no hurry. At the turn into the straight he was four from the back, and two furlongs out Shardari took the lead, only to be challenged by a rapidly accelerating Bering. Then Dancing Brave appeared on the outside, surging past his rivals with an electrifying burst of speed to win going away from Bering, with Triptych running on to take third, a short head in front of Shahrastani.

The official verdict of one and a half lengths seriously undervalued the distance by which Dancing Brave beat Bering, but measurement apart it was an extraordinary effort at the end of such a testing race, and will linger in the memory long after the horse's subsequent disappointment in the Breeders' Cup Turf at Santa Anita has been forgiven and forgotten.

Two very good, very tough horses battling out the finish of the top two-year-old race of the season and proving inseparable: neither deserved to lose and neither did – a very good result.

JOHN FRANCOME

THREE CHIMNEYS DEWHURST STAKES
Newmarket, 14 October 1988

The Dewhurst Stakes, run over seven furlongs on the Friday of the big Newmarket meeting which features the Cesarewitch and the Champion Stakes on the Saturday, has long been the most significant two-year-old race of the Flat season. It rarely attracts a large field, and in 1988 only six runners went to post. Favourite at 6–4 was Prince Of Dance, trained by Major Dick Hern and ridden by Willie Carson. The first offspring of the 1983 Oaks winner Sun Princess, he had been an impressive winner of his previous three races (though he had had one victory removed from him when he was found not to have met the qualifications for entry). The outsider of the six was Scenic, trained by Barry Hills for Sheikh Mohammed and ridden by Hills's son Michael. Scenic had won two of his previous three races but started rank outsider in the Dewhurst at 33–1 (he had even touched 50–1).

Samoan led until the final two furlongs, when Scenic took up the running as Prince Of Dance began to challenge. As they entered the final furlong Prince Of Dance took a narrow lead, but Scenic would not be denied, and though he drifted to his left under extreme pressure and seemed to push Prince Of Dance out of his rhythm, he battled on resolutely and refused to give best to his rival. But Prince Of Dance fought back and at the line they could not be separated. Saratogan ran on to be third, half a length behind the dead-heaters. Although the immediate reaction from some quarters was that the form of the race could not be too hot, and Scenic's drifting on to Prince Of Dance had made the latter seem unlucky not to have won outright, it was a superb race: two brave colts battling it out to the line, and neither having to be declared the loser.

But the race had a sad postscript: Prince Of Dance was put down in June 1989 after he was found to have cancer of the spine. Scenic now stands as a stallion at the Coolmore Stud in Ireland.

TOTE CHELTENHAM GOLD CUP

Cheltenham, 16 March 1989

By the time Desert Orchid lined up with twelve opponents for the Tote Cheltenham Gold Cup in 1989 he had already established himself as the most popular steeplechaser in Britain since triple Grand National winner Red Rum. Predictably known to his adoring public as 'Dessie', and to others as 'The Grey Horse' – much as *Macbeth* is traditionally referred to as 'The Scottish Play' – Desert Orchid had by that snowy, sodden day in March won seven races over hurdles and nineteen over fences – notably the King George VI Chase in 1986 (at 16–1) and 1988, and the 1988 Whitbread Gold Cup – and, in the first two months of 1989, scored battling victories against Panto Prince at Ascot and Pegwell Bay at Sandown Park.

But it was not only a dozen of the best chasers around that were pitted against him and jockey Simon Sherwood (who had ridden Desert Orchid eight times previously and never been beaten on him) in the Gold Cup. Additional adverse factors were the course – he was never seen at his best around Cheltenham, and was popularly thought to prefer a right-handed circuit rather than the left-handed Gold Cup course – and the weather: overnight snow and early-morning rain had soaked the ground so severely that there was even a doubt about whether racing would take place at all, and whether Desert Orchid would run if it did.

But all was resolved to the satisfaction of the vast Cheltenham crowd, who sent Dessie off the 5–2 favourite, with Irish challenger Carvill's Hill at 5–1 and Fulke Walwyn's imposing but inexperienced chaser Ten Plus third choice at 11–2.

In the early part of the race Desert Orchid took the lead – as was his wont – pressed by Ten Plus and 1988 Gold Cup winner Charter Party, but the exceptionally wet conditions were taking their toll, and by the top of the hill on the second circuit only seven were left in the race with any chance: Ten Plus from Desert Orchid, Yahoo, Charter Party, Bonanza Boy, Ballyhane and Slalom. Desert Orchid hit the fourth last hard as Ten Plus turned on the heat, but at the next fence tragedy struck as Ten Plus took a fatal fall.

That left the race between Desert Orchid and the 25–1 outsider Yahoo, a dour stayer in his element in this bog of a race, and at the second last all the sentiment in the world could not disguise the fact that the unconsidered Yahoo, ridden by Tom Morgan, was going the better. If a surge of sheer communal will could ever affect the outcome of a race it did now. Desert Orchid, clearly beaten between the last two fences, started to rally, and although Yahoo touched down over the last slightly in front, Dessie, on the stands side, now had the momentum. Halfway up the run-in he got to Yahoo, then veered sharply left towards him before Sherwood yanked him back on to a straight line and booted him into the lead to win by a length and a half as the crowd went berserk. They could not have wetted

Calling a race can get very emotional, and acting as course commentator for the 1989 Gold Cup – when 63,000 people had crowded into Cheltenham to will Desert Orchid home – was one such occasion. The grey looked out on his feet at the last, but his courage got him back up to beat Yahoo. I readily admit to two tearful eyes and a lump in my throat.

RALEIGH GILBERT

The 1989 Tote Cheltenham Gold Cup: owner Richard Burridge and stable lass Janice Coyle seem more drained than the hero of the hour.

themselves with excitement – they were saturated already – but the reaction to Desert Orchid's Gold Cup victory put the occasion right up with Dawn Run's (pages 175–6) in the list of Great Cheltenham Moments.

Desert Orchid ran twice more in the Gold Cup, finishing third on both occasions (to Norton's Coin in 1990 and to Garrison Savannah the following year). In a way it was fitting that he never won the race again, for on that wet, wet, wet day in March 1989 Cheltenham emotion and Dessiemania came together in a unique and unrepeatable way.

TWO THOUSAND GUINEAS
Newmarket, 1 May 1993

By the end of 1992 the outcome of the following spring's Two Thousand Guineas, first English Classic of the season open to colts, had become a simple issue: either Zafonic would win it, or he wouldn't. The evidence in favour of his winning was considerable. Owned by Khalid Abdullah and trained in France by André Fabre, he had blazed unbeaten through a two-year-old season consisting of four races, winning three events in France including the prestigious Prix Morny and Prix de la Salamandre before travelling to Newmarket to demolish his rivals in England's most important two-year-old race, the Dewhurst Stakes. 'I've not had a two-year-old as good as this,' ventured André Fabre, with the tongue-in-cheek rider, 'but I am still a very young man' – and ante-post punters backed Zafonic down to the

Polarization of opinion beforehand gave the 1993 Two Thousand Guineas a special feel: the atmosphere on the racecourse was like a war zone. Afterwards everybody was proclaiming what a great horse Zafonic was, but beforehand there were as many doubters as supporters. He proved his supporters triumphantly right - and I even had a few shillings on for myself!

JOHN McCRIRICK

The 1993 Two Thousand Guineas: Pat Eddery looks around for dangers as Zafonic powers home from Barathea . . .

. . . and one grateful punter pays homage to owner Khalid Abdullah.

shortest-priced winter favouritism for the Two Thousand Guineas since Tudor Minstrel in 1947.

There was a slight hiccough on Zafonic's debut as a three-year-old – he was narrowly beaten by Kingmambo in the Prix Djebel at Maisons-Laffitte on soft ground that did not suit him and under an extremely understanding ride from Pat Eddery – but only temporarily did his Guineas credentials seem dented, and on the day he started a warm favourite at 6–5 on. Of his thirteen rivals, just Craven Stakes runner-up Wharf and Chaddleworth (sixth in the Craven) started at under 10–1, with Barathea (fourth in the Craven) 10–1.

Ridden as usual by Pat Eddery, Zafonic turned in an explosive performance. The pace was fierce as the other runners tried from the start to blunt the favourite's speed, but not for a moment did they look like succeeding. With a quarter of a mile to go, Eddery produced Zafonic on the outside and the colt found a powerhouse burst of acceleration to leave the others toiling in a matter of moments, his jockey peering round for any sign of danger. Barathea – who was to go on and win the Irish Two Thousand Guineas later that April and the Breeders' Cup Mile in 1994 – came second, a respectful three and a half lengths in arrears, with 66–1 outsider Bin Ajwaad another three lengths back in fourth.

Zafonic now appeared locked on course for equine greatness, but he raced only once more, well beaten on unfavourable going in the Sussex Stakes at Goodwood, after which he was found to be bleeding internally. But the downbeat conclusion of his career does nothing to diminish the memory of him in the Guineas, for which there is only one appropriate word: *magnifique*!

MUMM MELLING CHASE
Aintree, 7 April 1995

Although in the public mind the Grand National naturally enough dominates the great three-day festival meeting at Aintree, for most racing purists the race of the meeting in April 1995 was always going to be the Mumm Melling Chase, run over two and a half miles on the Friday, the eve of the National.

Just six went to post. Viking Flagship had won the last two runnings of Queen Mother Champion Chase at the Cheltenham National Hunt Festival, and now the David Nicholson-trained gelding would be reunited with his regular jockey Adrian Maguire, who had missed Cheltenham in 1995 following the sudden death of his mother. Viking Flagship, described by Nicholson as the toughest horse he had ever trained, had established himself as one of the most popular chasers in training – a brilliant jumper and a true battler.

But despite his Cheltenham heroics the month before – he had beaten Deep Sensation by five lengths – Viking Flagship was not favourite for the Melling Chase. That honour went to Martha's Son, the revelation of the 1994–95 jumps season. Unbeaten in his five races that term and winner of his last nine successive runs, Martha's Son had been deliberately kept clear of the Cheltenham Festival in order to wait for this seasonal two-and-a-half-mile championship at Aintree. His last two outings – both in top-class events at Ascot – had proved him an exceptional horse, and the racing world started to drool over his clash with Viking Flagship as soon as the lights had gone out at Prestbury Park.

Deep Sensation, second to Viking Flagship at Cheltenham, was a regular fixture in the top two- and two-and-a-half mile chases, and had won the Queen Mother in 1993. The other runners were Nakir, winner of the Arkle Chase at Cheltenham in 1994 and a high-class chaser, and 33–1 shots Southolt and Second Schedual. But all eyes were on Martha's Son and Viking Flagship: as the *Racing Post* headlined the race that morning – 'All systems go for the clash of the titans'.

The following day George Ennor in the same newspaper described the Melling Chase as 'one of the most wonderful races it can have been anyone's privilege to see', and no one who witnessed it would dissent from that.

Southolt led out of the back straight of Aintree's tight Mildmay course, and approaching the fourth fence from home Adrian Maguire brought Viking Flagship, who had never been far off the pace, into contention just as Rodney Farrant on 11–10 market leader Martha's Son did the same. Martha's Son, who had been jumping sketchily, hit the fourth last without severely curtailing his momentum, and as the big two locked horns for the battle of the season they were joined by a surprise package in the shape of Deep Sensation, brought by Norman Williamson to challenge between the last two. In the straight Martha's Son took a slight lead and looked likely to go on to a hard-fought victory, but at the last there was hardly an inch between the three of them. Viking Flagship looked if anything to be going

A cracking chase, run at breakneck speed, flying every fence. Four jumped the last together; three kicked for home as if their lives depended on it; at the death, two seemed (and deserved) to be inseparable. But one won on the day, with that extra ounce of courage and commitment from horse and jockey that make Adrian Maguire and Viking Flagship what they are. A racegoers' dream.

LESLEY GRAHAM

The 1995 Mumm Melling Chase: all to play for at the last fence between **Martha's Son (Rodney Farrant, left), Viking Flagship (Adrian Maguire) and Deep Sensation (Norman Williamson).**

the least well of the trio when Deep Sensation battled his way into a narrow lead as Martha's Son's effort began to falter. But within twenty yards of the winning post Adrian Maguire conjured one final effort from his mount, and Viking Flagship rallied to join Deep Sensation on the line.

It was so close that neither set of connections dared think they had won, but eventually the result of the photo-finish came through: Viking Flagship by a short head from Deep Sensation, with Martha's Son a length behind in third.

No one needed telling that this was one of the great steeplechases, not only of the season but of recent memory. Alastair Down described it in the *Sporting Life* as one of those races 'that transcend the everyday and make you proud to say simply: "I was there."'

And Adrian Maguire paid tribute to his partner: 'When I die, if I could come back as someone else, I would come back as Viking Flagship. He just doesn't know how to stop.'

DOPING

With techniques for the detection of proscribed drugs in a racehorse's system becoming ever more sophisticated, the likelihood of a horse being deliberately doped – either to win or to lose – is becoming increasingly remote: in 1994 just twenty tests carried out on horses in Britain proved positive. Most horses (but not all) that win a race in Britain are subjected to routine tests (usually of urine) in the course sampling unit, and the specimens are sent to the Horseracing Forensic Laboratory in Newmarket for analysis: not until a horse's specimen has been cleared will the prize money for the race be released to the connections. In addition, the course Stewards may order a dope test to be carried out on any other horse in a race, often one which has run inexplicably badly. A notable example was Playschool, who ran dismally when favourite for the 1988 Cheltenham Gold Cup: many people suspected that he had been 'got at' (or 'nobbled'), but the dope test proved negative.

Normally in such cases suspicion will fall not on those closely connected with the horse (after all, the trainer or lad can ensure that it does not win by much simpler methods than drugs – a bucket of water shortly before the race would stop it quite well). Doping to lose – as in the case of Bravefoot, got at before the Champagne Stakes at Doncaster in 1990 – is far more likely to come from someone involved in the betting on a race: if a bookmaker, for instance, knows that a horse will not win, he can take money for that horse without fear of having to pay out on it.

Doping to win, or to improve the horse's performance, is a different matter. Highly elaborate monitoring of the specimens ensures that a trainer who allows his charge to be given that little extra something is likely to be found out, though chemistry can be one step ahead of analysis. The Jockey Club Rules state unambiguously that the trainer is responsible for whatever is administered to his horses, and if the proscribed substance finds its way into the horse through a contaminated foodstuff the trainer is nevertheless responsible.

Some drugs may be used while a horse is in training – as controlled medication to preserve race fitness – but must not be present in the horse's system when it is racing. Such drugs include antibiotics and anabolic steroids, and it was the steroid 19 Nortestosterone that was detected in samples taken from the chaser Cavvies Clown after three races which he won in January 1988. Trainer David Elsworth revealed that he had administered the drug – of great therapeutic use on account of its body-building effects – the previous November on veterinary advice. That is allowable, but it is not allowable for the horse to race when such drugs are present in its system, so Cavvies Clown was disqualified from the three races, and Elsworth was saddled with a hefty fine of £17,500. The horse will almost always be disqualified if a prohibited substance – a list of them is under constant review and is published in the *Racing Calendar* – is found in its system.

There have been many famous cases over the last few years: French-trained Trepan lost the Prince of Wales Stakes at Royal Ascot and the Eclipse Stakes at Sandown Park in 1976 after traces of a stimulant were found, and Tied Cottage lost the 1980 Cheltenham Gold Cup after theobromine (one of the stimulants in Trepan) was discovered in his urine; his trainer was exonerated but none the less the horse had to forfeit the race. More recently, the specimen taken from Aliysa after she had won the 1989 Gold Seal Oaks was tested positive: trainer Michael Stoute revealed that the substance detected had been a derivative of camphor, commonly used in the treatment of respiratory infections, sprains and strains, but a prohibited substance nevertheless. The ensuing row over testing procedures led to Aliysa's owner the Aga Khan removing his horses from Britain until he was satisfied that the system had been amended to what he considered fair.

The Aga Khan also owned Vayrann, whose specimen after he had won the Champion Stakes in 1981 contained traces of a banned steroid. But the Jockey Club was unable to prove that the substance had been administered to the horse, and veterinary experts concluded that entires are capable of producing an amount of their own steroids naturally. Vayrann kept the race, and in 1986 the Jockey Club introduced the notion of 'threshold levels', whereby some substances are allowed up to a specified level.

Rules on drugs differ from country to country, and discrepancies are particularly keenly felt when British horses go to race in the USA, where some states allow the use of drugs which are banned in Britain: Butazolidin ('bute'), for instance, which reduces the pain of lameness or arthritis, and Furosemide (Lasix), an anticoagulant drug used to combat the bursting of blood vessels.

Bravefoot, subsequently found to have been doped, canters to the start of the Laurent Perrier Champagne Stakes at Doncaster, September 1990.

EQUIPMENT

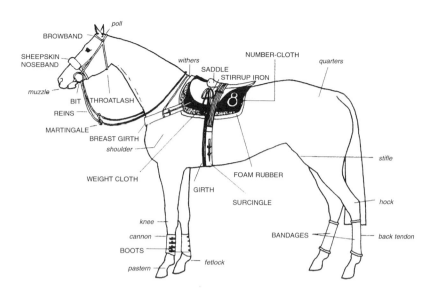

Blinkers are fitted to a horse to help it concentrate during a race, as they reduce its range of vision from 180 degrees to around 30 degrees and thus demand that it look straight ahead. They are sometimes known as the 'rogue's badge' on account of the untrustworthiness which their use implies, but plenty of perfectly genuine horses have run regularly in blinkers. By helping the horse to keep its mind on the job they can bring about a remarkable transformation in performance, and it is often worth taking notice of any horse running in blinkers for the first time.

A **visor** is a pair of blinkers with a slit cut in each of the shields: this allows for a small amount of lateral vision, so that the horse can see other horses alongside.

A **hood** leaves the eyes clear but covers the ears: some horses are affected by noise. (A horse with no or very defective vision in one eye may wear an **eyeshield**, similar to a pair of blinkers but with one eye completely covered over. Some very good racehorses have had only one eye, among them The Dancer, third to Bireme in the 1980 Oaks.)

The equipment which a horse carries in a race varies according to a number of factors, including the preferences of its trainer, the physique and temperament of the horse and the weight it is set to carry. The drawing above (on which a few of the most commonly mentioned points of the horse are given in italic type) illustrates the basic equipment. The **bridle** is normally made of leather, though the part of the **reins** which the jockey will hold is usually coated in rubber to improve grip. In theory the **sheepskin noseband** will encourage a horse to look further ahead, stretch out its feet and keep its head down, but in practice it is often used primarily on account of stable custom. (Another common variation on the standard bridle is the fitting of the **Australian cheeker**, the rubber strip which runs down the horse's nose and is attached to the bit to keep it high in the mouth.) The racing **martingale** consists of two metal rings connected by a leather strap: it keeps the reins in place and prevents them from going over the horse's head. On the horse's back will be placed: a sheet of **foam rubber** (or sometimes a piece of chamois leather); the **weight-cloth** (if needed), a pad incorporating

pockets into which are inserted metal strips which bring the weight of the jockey and equipment up to the required level; the **number-cloth**; and the **saddle** itself. Most jockeys have several saddles, choosing for each ride one appropriate to the weight to be carried: a modern racing saddle can weigh as little as one pound, though a jockey with no weight problem will probably ride on one weighing four or six pounds. (Saddles are usually made of leather – sometimes with a sheepskin-covered seat – but very light saddles may be made of felt.) The saddle is secured in place on the horse's back by the **girth**, which is buckled under the flaps each side of the saddle, and by the **surcingle**, the extra strap which goes right round the horse's belly and over the top of the saddle. Further security is afforded by a **breast-girth** (illustrated in the drawing) or a **breast-plate** (straps attached to each side of the saddle which are joined to the girth by another strap passing between the forelegs). Leather **boots** are common with jumpers, as they afford protection from knocks and cuts when taking the obstacles. Bandages offer some protection but are mainly used as support (like the strapping on an athlete's knee).

Cheltenham with Channel Four

**Previous spread:
Channel Four Racing's Cheltenham encampment.**

Golden Miller pricks up his ears at Big Mac's betting intelligence during The Morning Line.

At 8.45 on the bright but bitterly cold morning of the middle day of the Cheltenham National Hunt Festival, the racecourse is already abuzz with activity.

Many of that afternoon's runners have already been out in the centre of the track to stretch their legs, while back in the stands tables are being set up in the hospitality boxes, bars are being restocked after the hammering which supplies took on the opening day, and an army of cleaners toting mops and pails are clearing away the debris left by the record Champion Hurdle Day crowd. And up by the Golden Miller statue, on the edge of the grandstand, the *Morning Line* team is preparing to swing into action.

Rings glinting in the sun, John McCririck sits at his table in the corner, while the other three presenters – Derek Thompson and Jim McGrath, along with Ted Walsh, seconded for the week to give a highly illuminating Irish perspective on the sport in prospect – jiggle around to keep warm. The team are connected to associate producer Mark Jackson and director Jane Garrod in the comparative warmth of the scanner van – the control centre of the whole operation – by discreetly hidden earpieces, and as transmission time approaches they are asked to make sure they keep still once on air. Jim McGrath promises: 'I'll be still by then 'cos rigor mortis will have set in!'

Clustered around the presenters are a gaggle of cameramen and sound engineers, and floor manager Mark Hinchcliffe alerts them to the approach of nine o'clock: 'Two minutes to on air . . . Thirty seconds to on air . . . Stand by!'

The banter which the presenters have been lobbing at each other subsides, and silence descends. Cue opening music . . .

To the viewer at home the programme seems to go smoothly enough, but live television has occupational hazards – including, this morning, noises off in the form of a resounding crash from down below as a binliner full of empty champagne bottles is mis-lobbed against the side of a dustcart. But it

```
·15.20.00      COMMERCIAL BREAK 3.40
 (approx)

               RACE PRELIMS (Contd) - J.O. & J.F.

               EYECATCHERS

               BETTING CRAWL

 15.30.00      3.30 RACE (2m 5f hurdle) - G.G. & Simon
               POST RACE COVERAGE AS PER YESTERDAY EXCEPT LEAVE TROPHY PRESENTATION AFTER
               WINNING OWNER HAS RECEIVED TROPHY

               B.S./D.T. intros and v/o's
               CAPGEN 1 ONLY tote cheltenham gold cup r ¢ r inc. COLOURS + BETTING

               MAC + GOLD CUP BETTING NEWS

               B.S. intros 4.05 RACE IDENT + R & R + BETTING
               RACE PRELIMS - J.O. & J.F.

               NO VT CLIPS

               WINDOW REQUIRED

               EYECATCHERS

               BETTING CRAWL

 16.05.00      4.05 RACE (3m 1f chase) - G.G. & Simon
               B.S. + poss. INTERVIEW

               B.S. intros
               VT (SOT) TODAY'S WINNERS ANIMATION
               edited to
        VT B.S. v/o 2.50 WINNER (+ CAPGEN)
               edited to
               VT (SOT) 2.15 RACE FINISH
               mixed to
               2.15 S.P. - Simon
               mixed to
               VT ( SOT) 3.30 RACE FINISH
               mixexd to
               3.30 S.P. - Simon
```

Viewing figures for the first Cheltenham National Hunt Festival covered by Channel Four were:

Tuesday: 1.7 million
Wednesday: 1.9 million
Thursday: 2.4 million

A domestic audience of 4 million watched Lammtara win the 1995 Vodafone Derby.

The race which attracts the largest television audience each year is the Grand National: around 11 million people saw Royal Athlete's 1995 triumph.

A page of the Channel Four Racing running order for the Wednesday of the Cheltenham Festival. The 'betting crawl' is when the odds for the coming race are rolled along the foot of the screen; 'v/o's' are voice-overs; 'VT' is a recording on videotape; a 'window' indicates when an interview appears in the corner of the screen while the main pictures continue to be transmitted; 'SOT' refers to 'sound on tape' – that is, not needing a voice-over.

takes more than that to put Tommo off his stride, as he steers the form experts through analysis of the big races of the day – the Queen Mother Champion Chase (Derek, clever lad, asserts that Viking Flagship will win that) and the clash between Banjo and the giant Irish chaser Harcon in the Sun Alliance. As Thompson, Walsh and McGrath discuss the niceties of the form, McCririck phones the bookmakers for the latest moves: anyone who has seen Big Mac screaming 'Hark on! Hark on!' in recent weeks has no doubt where his own sympathies lie.

On the approach to the commercial break, it's time for Turf Trivia: 'Which horse ran twice at the same Cheltenham Festival Meeting, winning the Queen Mother Champion Chase before finishing third in the Champion Hurdle?' Leaving viewers to ruminate on that, the presenters use the couple of minutes' break to resume efforts to keep the circulation going, then the second half opens with the answer to the Turf Trivia – Flyingbolt in 1966 – before going on to consider the other races on the afternoon's card. Before you know it Mark Hinchcliffe is counting down with his fingers: five, four, three, two, one – off air.

Each day of the Festival is a triple-header for Channel Four Racing – *Morning Line*, the afternoon's racing, and late-evening highlights. With Wednesday's first leg out of the way, the team go off for breakfast.

The magic eye of the gyrostabilized tracking camera.

The announcement in summer 1994 that as from 1995 Channel Four Racing would be taking over television coverage of Cheltenham from the BBC did not meet with universal approval. The BBC had transmitted racing from Prestbury Park for forty years, and its coverage of the National Hunt Festival stood with the Grand National and Royal Ascot as triple peaks of its racing output. Nervous correspondents to the racing press suggested that Channel Four would not be sufficiently reverential to the great traditions of Cheltenham, while others looked forward to a change of style, a more direct reflection of the seething excitement of Prestbury Park in mid-March.

Whatever your point of view, Channel Four had a new tradition to establish, so it was with more than the usual rush of adrenalin that the team approached its first Cheltenham year – which got off to the worst possible start when the meeting which should have been the channel's first coverage, on 2 January, was abandoned on account of frost.

In the event the first day of Channel Four Racing at Cheltenham – and a first full rehearsal for Festival coverage – came with the meeting on 14 January, followed by a dress rehearsal in the shape of the fixture at the end of the month when Master Oats further advertised his Gold Cup potential. Next stop the Festival.

The weekend before the world, his wife and his cousin the parish priest from County Wicklow descended on the magical arena at the foot of Cleeve Hill, a wagon train of control vans started lumbering into an area behind the parade ring to set up Channel Four Racing's base camp. The line-up consisted of:

It's not all hard work: the Noble Lord at dalliance with Lesley Graham.

- the **scanner van**, the mobile control vehicle from which the pro- grammes are directed;
- two **VTR vans**, where video recordings are stored and primed for use on ten video machines for transfer to the transmission at the right moment;
- the British Telecom **links van**, full of wondrous fibre-optical technol- ogy by which the programmes are transmitted to Channel Four in London, and thence to domestic receivers;
- the **CapGen** vehicle, the caption tender where the graphics for the transmissions are compiled, results received, betting moves logged;
- other **technical vehicles** and **generators**;
- the '**chuck wagon**' – the mobile canteen.

For the Festival some seventeen cameras are in use, including one in an airship floating high above the course; two hand-held roving cameras; seven radio-linked cameras (that is, connected to the scanner van by radio rather than by cables); and the gyrostabilized 'tracking camera', the giant eye on a pole which provides those spectacular side-on pictures from alongside the runners.

Channel Four Racing is put together by the production company Three On Four (owned one-third each by Yorkshire Television, Anglia Television and Thames Television), and the on-site army consists of around sixty people. The presenters and commentators are the public face of the programme, but behind them this Cheltenham are lined up six production staff, seventeen cameramen, twelve sound crew, six engineers, four videotape editors, assorted drivers and – last but absolutely not least – the cook.

And it is to the cook in his chuck wagon that the freezing presenters and crew of *The Morning Line* repair for coffee and breakfast. Here they are joined by other presenters on duty later in the day – including John Oaksey, for whom the Cheltenham Festival is one step from heaven, John Francome, who rode big Festival winners himself, commentators Graham Goode and Simon Holt, and Brough Scott, who will be fronting the afternoon programmes. Lesley Graham is presenting the evening highlights coverage with Alastair Down. Raleigh Gilbert, who often calls the horses for Channel Four, is this week on duty as Cheltenham's course commentator.

Breakfast over, the team heads off for the regular pre-transmission conference – in a bus!

The conference, which precedes every Channel Four Racing programme, is a forum for discussion and anticipation of the afternoon's coverage, and this week the team's refuge from the maelstrom of Cheltenham Festival activity is an ancient double-decker bus, to the top of which production staff – headed by executive producer Andrew Franklin – and presenters (including McCririck clutching a bacon roll: 'It's only my third!') clamber to prepare for the afternoon.

First, though, reactions to the previous day's coverage – Smurfit Champion Hurdle Day, and Channel Four's first taste of the Festival. Consensus of opinion is that the day went well, and Franklin reports that the powers that be at Channel Four had expressed their approval. More parochially, Graham Goode has to endure teasing about one of the adornments to his commentary on the Guinness Arkle Chase, when he described Jamie Osborne as bringing 'Sparkle to the Arkle', and Derek Thompson relates how he had gone to hold forth to corporate hospitality guests in the grandstand, only to discover on completing his address that he had been in the wrong box!

Among the ideas floated for the afternoon are that Tommo should visit the kitchens of the racecourse caterers – 'Another free lunch!' – for a behind-the-scenes slot, and more ambitious plans are mooted: 'Could we

On the upper deck: something – or someone – takes John Francome's fancy during the morning conference.

TELEVISING RACING

In 1927 the Grand National and Derby were first broadcast on radio, and in 1931 John Logie Baird experimented with televising the Derby, which the following year was broadcast to an audience in the Metropole cinema in Victoria, London.

Live televising of racing to domestic receivers first began in 1946, though regular transmissions were not established until some time later.

When the independent television network was introduced in 1955, coverage of racing increased, culminating in the 'ITV Seven' in which seven races from two courses were shown each Saturday afternoon.

The ITV mid-week coverage shifted to Channel Four in 1984, and all racing on the independent network has been on Channel Four since late 1985. *The Morning Line*, Channel Four's morning preview programme, was first broadcast on Cambridgeshire day 1989.

Sky Television began its coverage of evening racing in 1993.

talk to the man who pours the Queen Mother's tea?' No.

The build-up to each race is choreographed and discussed, and Brough Scott suggests that before the Coral Cup, with a field of thirty runners, the paddock commentators should have the briefest possible say about each horse – which prompts John Francome, famed within the team for the diligence with which he undertakes his homework, to lament: 'That's another four hours pissed up against the wall!' Francome, the one member of the team with recent riding experience at Cheltenham, is deputed to record a piece from the notorious downhill fences, explaining why horses find them so trappy.

The logistics of interviewing owners, trainers and jockeys after each race are analysed, timings are discussed, ideas floated and tested. But with Cheltenham coverage having been planned for months in advance, this is a routine meeting, and the business is soon dispatched.

For the next couple of hours the team disperses – Thompson and Francome to record their inserts for the programme, Oaksey and the race commentators to mug up on the colours, McCririck to his regular table in the heaving press-room to add to the formidable collection of race statistics – 'the stats' – with which he bombards viewers.

Shortly before transmission time they all take up their positions – Graham Goode and Simon Holt in their eyrie high in the grandstand, McCririck in the betting ring, Francome and Oaksey in their glass bubble above the paddock, Scott and Thompson in the parade ring itself. The countdown begins, and on the dot of 1.30 comes the call: cue Brough! 'Hello, and welcome to a tremendous second day of this Cheltenham Festival . . .'

The nerve centre of the transmission is the scanner van, where Andrew Franklin oversees the whole operation and Jane Garrod selects, from a bank of screens, the pictures which viewers see. From there she can talk with each individual cameraman to request a particular shot, and to each presenter with instructions, suggestions and – crucially – cues, the signals to start speaking. On-screen presenters have earpieces. Those who are heard but not seen – such as race-caller GG – have the more comfortable but more bulky headphones, and each presenter, even while on air, receives a constant babble of sound, some – but by no means all – directed towards himself.

The programme follows the running order as far as is practical, but has to reflect the events of the afternoon, and the exact content of the programme is constantly updated. Derek Thompson's visit to the caterers' tent can go out early, and the programme is not very old before we discover him where 120 chefs and forty kitchen assistants are preparing the feeding of the several thousands.

'What have you got there?', Our Man at the Sharp End asks a kitchen assistant.

'Lemons,' she replies: 'Lemons, lemons and more lemons.'

Weaving around the vats of green pea and ham soup, Tommo scrounges a helping of scotch salmon. He tastes, drools, and pronounces it 'Lovely!'

Cue Brough – 'Dear oh dear oh dear!' – and on to the serious business of the day.

The afternoon provides memorable sport, with Viking Flagship's Queen Mother Champion Chase and Brief Gale's Sun Alliance Chase the high points of another great Cheltenham day. The excitement in the stands or the nation's armchairs may reach fever pitch, but with Graham Goode and Simon Holt in their commentary position way up in the grandstand, the atmosphere is one of complete calm. At the climax of a big race it can get *very* noisy up there, but GG does not get distracted.

Graham prepares for every race commentary by drawing up a chart of the colours, together with – as appropriate – a plan of the course and a few basic facts about the runners and the race. He commentates on the race itself both from direct observation through his pair of Zeiss Dialyt 8 x 56 binoculars and from the pictures on the television monitor in his box.

Brough Scott interviews trainer of the week Kim Bailey, whose Alderbrook won the Champion Hurdle on the Tuesday of the Festival, and Master Oats the Gold Cup on the Thursday.

Normally the results and betting shows are read from the CapGen van, but for Cheltenham Simon Holt is sharing commentary, and doubles as results reader from up in the commentary position.

Slip on a pair of spare headphones, and you'd hear a Babel like this:

'Mac on 6 . . . Cue Simon! . . . Stand by, Mac . . . Cue Mac! . . . can't find Tommo . . . voice over, Tommo! . . . cue presentation . . . coming to camera 1 . . . Harcon – talk over it, Brough . . . Cue Brough!'

Then imagine trying to talk coherently to a camera – without the benefit of autocue – while that racket is streaming in your ear, and you begin to get a notion of how being a Channel Four Racing front man is not quite as easy as it may appear.

Punctuated by regular features such as the highly popular Picture Puzzle competition – the cartoon this Cheltenham Wednesday denotes (who else?) Viking Flagship – the programme whizzes by, bringing viewers an afternoon of memorable jump racing and one cameraman an illustration of the occasional hazards of his job: while filming the runners from down in the paddock, he is felled from behind by a horse straying off the paddock path.

But everything else goes smoothly, and at the point denoted on the running order by 'OUT', Channel Four Racing is off the air.

Not that the day's work is done, for presenters or for production crew. Those presenters who are also working the Festival as journalists make smartly for the press room to prepare their copy – John McCririck, for

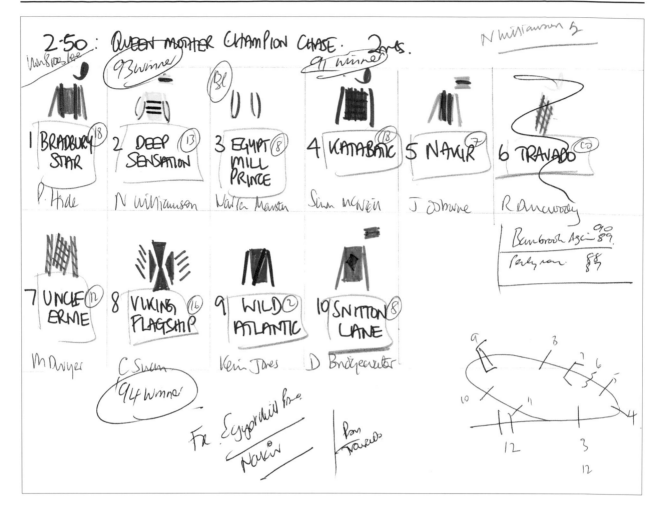

Graham Goode's cribsheet for the Queen Mother Champion Chase. Bradbury Star has won 18 races, Deep Sensation 13. Bradbury Star has won eight times at Cheltenham ('here'). Deep Sensation was the winner in 1993, Katabatic in 1991, Viking Flagship in 1994. Previous dual winners were Barnbrook Again (1989 and 1990) and Pearlyman (1987 and 1988). Egypt Mill Prince and Nakir are both French-bred. Egypt Mill Prince is wearing blinkers ('Bl'). In the lower right-hand corner is a plan of the course, showing the order of the jumps.

example, writes betting-ring reports for the *Racing Post*, Brough Scott has to pen his regular Thursday column for the same paper – and production staff immediately begin to put together the evening highlights programme which, fronted by Lesley Graham, will be transmitted from the course at 11 o'clock.

The Channel Four team did not have it easy for their first Cheltenham, as the three Festival days were followed in 1995 by an extra day's racing at the course on the Friday. No time for a rest even after that, though: on the Saturday the circus moved up to Uttoxeter, and then it would be time to switch attention to the traditional – if not formal – start of the Flat at Doncaster, and a very heavy spring schedule which in early May featured seven consecutive days' live transmission of racing: three (including Sunday) at the Guineas meeting at Newmarket, Bank Holiday Monday at Kempton Park, then three days at Chester.

But fields of bred-in-the-purple Classic hopes scuttling around the Roodee seem a million years away as the lights burn late into the night back at the famous Lygon Arms Hotel in nearby Broadway, where many of the Channel Four team are bivouacked. Homework is being done. Tomorrow is Cheltenham Gold Cup day.

THE CHANNEL FOUR RACING TEAM

Brough Scott rode 100 winners as an amateur and then professional jump jockey between 1963 and 1971, after which he joined what was then ITV Racing. He is also an award-winning journalist, writing a weekly column for the Sunday Telegraph and the Racing Post, of which he is Editorial Director.

Derek Thompson, who had many rides in point-to-points and as an amateur under Rules, worked as assistant trainer to Denys Smith and to Pierre Sanoner before entering broadcasting with the BBC in 1973. He has been presenting racing on television since 1982.

John Francome was champion National Hunt jockey outright six times and shared the 1981–82 title with Peter Scudamore; he won the Cheltenham Gold Cup on Midnight Court in 1978 and the Champion Hurdle on Sea Pigeon in 1981. Since retiring from the saddle in 1985, having ridden 1,138 winners in Britain, he has divided his time between broadcasting and writing novels.

John McCririck worked as a private handicapper and with bookmakers before working for the Sporting Life from 1972 until 1983. He was named Specialist Writer of the Year in 1978, Campaigning Journalist of the Year in 1979, and Sports Presenter of the Year in 1992.

THE CHANNEL FOUR RACING TEAM

Graham Goode gave his first racecourse commentary in 1967, and became senior commentator for ITV in 1981. As an owner he has seen his colours successful in Flat races, hurdles and chases. Graham lists wallpapering among his recreations!

Lesley Graham is married to Newmarket trainer Neil Graham, who held the licence for Dick Hern when the Major was recovering from heart surgery in 1988 and sent out Minster Son to win the St Leger. Lesley was a corporate and bloodstock solicitor until 1993, and combines her Channel Four duties with journalism.

Jim McGrath (here resplendent in his Royal Ascot gear) is a Director of Timeform, famed for its rigorous, dispassionate approach to the study of form.

John Oaksey rode as an amateur from 1955 to 1975, taking the amateur jockeys' title over jumps in the 1957–58 and 1970–71 seasons. He was a narrowly beaten second to Ayala in the 1963 Grand National on Carrickbeg, and won the 1958 Whitbread and Hennessy Gold Cups on Taxidermist. As Audax he wrote for Horse and Hound for nearly three decades and was racing correspondent of the Daily Telegraph from 1957 until his retirement in 1994 (though he has continued writing regularly for that paper since).

THE CHANNEL FOUR RACING TEAM

Simon Holt has worked as a journalist since 1982, and began commentating on racecourses in 1988, joining Channel Four Racing in 1994. He writes a regular column for the Sporting Life.

Alastair Down is Associate Editor of the Sporting Life, and was voted Racing Journalist of the Year in 1994.

Raleigh Gilbert, who began race-calling in 1958, is the first commentator to have operated at ovory Flat and jumping track in Britain. He began commentating for ITV in 1972. Raleigh's racing career includes riding as an amateur in Kenya and serving as manager of the (now defunct) racecourse at Stockton between 1964 and 1965.

Executive producer Andrew Franklin.

Director Jane Garrod.

Associate producer Mark Jackson.

Come Racing!

'Come racing!' When John McCririck issues the exhortation to armchair racegoers to forsake the fireside and get down to the racetrack, he has in mind primarily the betting advantages to be had from being on the course. But there are many other reasons why a trip to the races is such a popular day out. If you have never been racing or go only rarely, these hints might help you plan and enjoy your day.

Racing takes place in Britain on most days of the year, and certain Bank Holidays – Easter Monday, August Bank Holiday Monday and Boxing Day – feature a very large number of meetings. The coming week's fixtures are listed in most Sunday newspapers, and complete fixture lists for the year appear regularly in the *Sporting Life* and the *Racing Post*. Or you can phone the course you want to visit (see panel opposite). All the national daily papers and most of the major regional papers carry programmes for each meeting, except on the very busy days, when they may omit the lesser cards.

It is often a good idea to take advice from a friend in the know about what sort of meeting you might want to attend. Cheltenham on Gold Cup day could put you off the sport altogether if you dislike huge crowds, queueing patiently for a drink, cold, wind, rain, sleet and other climatic extremities, traffic jams, losing money, and the Irish. On the other hand, your spirits might soar at the heroics from horse and rider which the day invariably produces, you might thrill to the experience of being among 50,000 devotees – and you might back a few winners.

Race meetings are different in predictable ways: at Newmarket you will hardly be able to make anything of the race until the runners enter the final quarter mile, as there is no round course, whereas around Fontwell Park's figure-of-eight the horses are never very far away. And they are also different in unpredictable ways: fine weather can make all the difference to your enjoyment, and so can backing winners, but neither can be guaranteed.

Your day will certainly be enriched by attending your first meeting in the company of someone who knows about the sport. He or she will be able to explain what is going on, and to have a winning day while your clued-up friend comes out losing can be exquisitely satisfying. In any case, try to find out what are the attractions of a particular day or particular course, and choose one to suit what you are after – on a scale from being present at a great sporting occasion to having the leisure to witness quietly and at close quarters how a race meeting works.

Each course has its own ambience: at Ascot and at Newmarket you will not make friends by displaying your tattoos in the Members' Enclosure, while at the smaller meetings the clientele is usually more local and easy-going. Remember that great races – and great horses – attract very big crowds and are not always the ideal introduction, however exciting they may be.

Most racecourses are now waking up to the fact that in order to provide a family day out they have to offer some entertainment for children, and several courses have adventure playgrounds and similar distractions. You can usually take small children into the enclosures, but bear in mind that it might be difficult to keep a three-year-old happy for several hours in the open air simply on the prospect of seeing next year's Derby winner.

Facilities for the disabled are being improved, too, with special viewing areas for those confined to wheelchairs now a feature of many enclosures.

WHAT TO WEAR AND WHAT TO TAKE

Nowadays morning dress is compulsory only in the Royal Enclosure at Royal Ascot and the Queen's Stand at Epsom on Derby Day. At several courses a man is required to wear a jacket and tie (or jacket and polo-neck jersey) in Members' – though the rules are not always rigorously enforced – and the wearing of jeans (on either male or female legs) might not be popular with gatemen in such enclosures. If in doubt, or in need of any information which will affect your preparations, do not hesitate to phone the course.

You meet the nicest class of person at the races: an uninhibited punter greets his heroine on Gold Cup Day at Cheltenham, March 1987.

Previous spread:
The parade ring at Cheltenham.

It is very important to dress comfortably and sensibly, as a day's racing can be an energetic affair, and it would be a shame not to watch a steeplechase at Kempton Park from the last fence because you're worried about getting mud – an occupational hazard at most courses – on your best shoes. Contrary to popular opinion, the most important part of the racegoer's apparel is not the hat – brown trilby for a man, some flamboyant Mrs Shilling-style creation for a woman – but the footwear: you will probably be on your feet for several hours and your shoes may suffer a variety of depredations. Galoshes are a good idea for those muddy jumping days in mid-winter.

The key to comfortable dressing for racing is to have enough room in your garb to house the few essentials for a satisfactory day: pencil or pen; racing paper; your official racecard (available at the entrance to the course for a small charge); a notebook; binoculars (which can be hired at the course); cash (a racecourse bookmaker will not expect to be offered a cheque). Bear in mind that at many courses cameras are not permitted in other than the cheap enclosures, and that if you do take a camera on a gloomy day you *must* disarm the flash, as flash photography will upset horses.

You will not normally be able to take alcohol into the course, and you might also wish to leave behind any preconceptions about a day at the races being an excuse for an afternoon's binge *al fresco*, and the equally commonly held error that racing is no fun without betting. Certainly the occasional wager adds spice, but you can have a perfectly enjoyable day without betting at all.

GETTING THERE AND GETTING IN

Aim to arrive at the course at least half an hour before the first race, in order to familiarize yourself with the geography of the enclosures. If you arrive very early, walk round the course – this is usually allowed – to appreciate its contours and features, as well as to gauge the state of the going. To walk the course before a big race can add wonderfully to the build-up of atmosphere and tension.

On very popular days race traffic can be appalling, so allow extra time, and then double the time you've allowed: better to arrive too early and have a leisurely drink while studying the form than seethe in a traffic jam two miles from the course while your fancy in the first race is trotting up. (Parking at many courses is not as plentiful nor as efficient as it might be – especially in soggy conditions – and it can pay to park locally and walk a little extra distance: you will also find it easier to get away after the races.)

Never buy a racecard from a wandering seller in the car park: he will have 'marked your card' and will expect payment for his advice. Buy only from the clearly marked official selling points.

Most racecourses are divided into several enclosures. Top of the range is the Members' Enclosure, for the use of annual members of the course but normally also available to non-members for a daily charge. This charge varies hugely, depending on the course and on the day. To get into the Members' Enclosure at Sandown Park on Whitbread Gold Cup day in 1995 cost £25, while on an ordinary day at Sandown it would cost about half that. (Entrance tickets for the big meetings can usually be booked in advance – the course will supply details on request – and some days, such as Gold Cup at Royal Ascot, sell out early.)

If you go into Members' you will be given a small cardboard badge which you will need to display each time you return to the enclosure having been away from it. (During the ultra-hot summer of 1976 a man was spotted in the Members' Enclosure at Bath racecourse with his badge attached to the sweaty hairs on his bare chest.) The Members' Enclosure will have the best facilities (though no bookmakers – you'll have to leave the enclosure to frequent them, unless you have an account with a 'rails' bookmaker: see page 151) and the best view of the racing, and often will have exclusive use

CALLING THE COURSES

Aintree 0151 523 2600
Ascot 01344 22211
Ayr 01292 264179
Bangor-on-Dee 01948 860438
Bath 01225 424609
Beverley 01482 867488
Brighton 01273 682912
Carlisle 01228 22973
Cartmel 01539 536340
Catterick Bridge 01748 811478
Cheltenham 01242 513014
Chepstow 01291 622260
Chester 01244 323170
Doncaster 01302 320066
Edinburgh 0131 665 2859
Epsom Downs 013727 26311
Exeter 01392 832599
Fakenham 01328 862388
Folkestone 01303 266407
Fontwell Park 01243 543335
Goodwood 01243 774107
Hamilton Park 01698 283806
Haydock Park 01942 725963
Hereford 01432 273560
Hexham 01434 603738
Huntingdon 01480 453373
Kelso 01573 24767
Kempton Park 01932 782292
Leicester 0116 2716515
Lingfield Park 01342 834800
Ludlow 0158 477221
Market Rasen 01673 843434
Newbury 01635 40015
Newcastle 0191 236 2020
Newmarket:
    Rowley Mile 01638 662762
    July Course 01638 662752
Newton Abbot 01626 53235
Nottingham 0115 9580620
Perth 01738 51597
Plumpton 01273 890383
Pontefract 01977 703224
Redcar 01642 484068
Ripon 01765 602156
Salisbury 01722 326461
Sandown Park 01372 463072
Sedgefield 01642 557081
Southwell 01636 814481
Stratford-upon-Avon 01789 267949
Taunton 01823 337172
Thirsk 01845 522276
Towcester 01327 353414
Uttoxeter 01889 562561
Warwick 01926 491553
Wetherby 01937 582035
Wincanton 01963 32344
Windsor 01753 865234
Wolverhampton 01902 24481
Worcester 01905 25364
Yarmouth 01493 842527
York 01904 620911

Contrasts in racegoing: the top-hatted formality of Derby Day 1994, as Willie Carson returns to unsaddle on Erhaab . . .

'A very outstanding feature of the British racecourse is its car-park. This is always a miracle of skill in its arrangement. Every car is fitted in, like a Chinese puzzle, so adroitly that none can be removed until the key car has been found and driven away. The key car is placed with unerring instinct – it is always a large Damliar, the owner of which, upholstered like a musical-comedy duchess, is the relict of an extremely prosperous publican.

'The owner of the key car can never be found. In point of fact, she is always involved after the last race in an argument with a bookie. The trouble is that she had three-and-sevenpence each way on a horse that ran third in the fifth race at 9 to 2. She had instructed the bookmaker to reinvest the proceeds of this on a horse which eventually dead-heated at 11 to 8 in the last. She is now trying to convince the man with the bag that his method of calculating the result is wrong and hers is right. Meanwhile, we are waiting to get home.'

(From *They're Off! or, The Rough's Guide to the Turf* by 'Riff and Raff', published in 1936)

of good vantage points for parade ring and unsaddling enclosure.

The next enclosure down is normally Tattersalls ('Tatts'), which has access to parade ring and unsaddling enclosure but tends to be further from the winning post than Members'. This is where the main betting ring will be situated, and the entrance charge will be between half and two-thirds of that for a day badge to Members'.

Below Tatts comes the Silver Ring (so called because most of the betting in the enclosure used to be in silver rather than in notes), which normally would command no view of parade ring or unsaddling enclosure but which would be correspondingly cheap to get into. There is often also a 'course' enclosure where the facilities are somewhat rudimentary and the view very restricted, though there will be a small number of bookmakers betting there. All enclosures normally have Tote facilities. (Note that different courses have a different combination of enclosures – Sandown Park has no Silver Ring, for example – and some courses combine enclosures, such as Members' and Tatts, on some race days.)

BETTING

Do not feel you have to bet, any more than you have to quaff champagne or bawl 'Come on, my son!' as the runners swing into the straight. But if you do want to bet, bear in mind that there is no betting tax on bets struck with an on-course bookmaker, whereas an off-course bookmaker would have to tax you 9 or (more probably) 10 per cent on stakes ('tax paid') or on returns. (If you used the on-course betting shop a tax of 6 per cent would be levied, however.)

The bookmaker will display the amount of the minimum stake he will accept (usually £2 or more) and, on a board, the odds he currently offers for each horse in the next race. When you strike a bet with him the odds displayed apply to that bet irrespective of whether they subsequently lengthen or shorten, and he will announce the bet to his clerk as it is made with you.

Thus if you wish to have £5 on Master Oats to win and he is displaying Master Oats at 2–1 you should approach him with your fiver and say: '£5 to win, Master Oats'; he will announce '£10 to £5 Master Oats' to his clerk, to whom he will also call the number printed on a coloured card which he will give you. (If he has rubbed off the '2' against Master Oats's name on his board by the time you get to him you will not be able to bet at that price.) The card is your record of the bet, and it is wise to make a note on the card of the transaction (in case you find yourself at the end of the afternoon with several cards and you can't remember which is a winning one). When Master Oats wins you return to the bookmaker (after 'weighed in' has been announced, though most bookmakers will settle sooner if the result is obviously clear-cut), and give him the card; he announces the number to his clerk, who tells him what the bet was. He then gives you £15 (your winnings plus your stake). A racecourse official visits the ring after each race to arbitrate in case of any dispute arising.

Among the boons of being on course among the bookmakers is that you can bet 'in running' – that is, a bookmaker will not stop taking bets once the race has started but will continue to offer odds based on his reading of what is happening in the action. Many course bookmakers will also offer odds on the outcome of a photo finish or a Stewards' Enquiry. But the great joy of betting on course (beyond the absence of tax) is that by watching carefully how the betting market is moving you can 'beat the book' by taking a price longer than that at which the horse will start. (For more details, see the chapter on betting.)

Many first-time racegoers are nervous of encountering the mysteries of wagering with bookmakers and prefer the more anonymous experience of betting with the Tote, 'the Machine' which operates on a pool basis (see pages 147-9). To place a Tote bet you simply go to one of the many counters situated all over the course and state the nature of your bet, your stake and the number (not name) of the horse – or numbers of the horses. You will be given a ticket which, if successful, you take back to any Tote counter to exchange for your winnings (plus stake).

Tote dividends are declared after each race to a £1 unit and include the stake. Remember that the big difference between a Tote bet and a bet with a bookmaker is that with the former you will not know the exact odds of your horse until the dividend is declared, though screens by the counters will give you the approximate odds at any time, and you can thus work out whether you are likely to do better or worse than bookmakers' prices by betting with the Tote. (If you are celebrating so vigorously that you forget to collect by the end of the day, don't throw away your ticket: you can send it in to the Tote and they will forward your winnings by post.)

MAKING THE MOST OF IT

A day at the races can be an absorbing experience, and to get the most out of it you should be prepared to move around a good deal and witness every aspect of the sport at as close quarters as is practical and permissible. (And if too much horseflesh starts to pall, many courses – especially at the big meetings – have trade stands.)

Go to the pre-parade ring, where the horses walk round before being saddled. This is the place for a good long look at individual runners, and at many courses has an atmosphere all of its own: the pre-parade area at Newmarket's July Meeting is set among tall trees, Ascot's is appropriately spacious and magisterial, while Sandown Park's is a haven of peace and quiet in contrast to the press of people crowding around the parade ring proper. Here you can pick up valuable clues about the well-being and temperament of the horses. Watch them being saddled, in boxes by the pre-parade ring, and see how they become keyed up – or not! – as the saddle is put on. Then to the parade ring, to study the runners in more detail and assess whether your fancy looks the part: watch it canter down to the start, nip off to have your bet, and then find a good place in the stand.

After the race you rush off to witness the return of the victorious horse to the unsaddling enclosure. Watch the condition not only of the winner but of the placed horses: have they had an easy or a hard race? And the demeanour of the connections of beaten horses can be instructive: are they annoyed at not winning, or pleased with a performance which promises greater things next time out? (Reach for that notebook.) This is the time to keep your ears open: try to catch what the jockeys of beaten horses – including those being unsaddled outside the enclosure for the placed horses – are telling the owner and trainer, and pick up hints for the future.

Allow yourself leisure later in the afternoon for a little reflection over a drink and a sandwich (but remember that racecourse food is notoriously expensive). Should your reflection lead to the conclusion that you are skint, some courses have banks – or the course Secretary may cash you a cheque.

Getting out of the racecourse can be no less problematic than getting out on your betting, for several thousand years of human development have failed to find a solution to the problem of how to clear racecourse car parks on even a mildly popular day. Often you just have to accept that hundreds of cars all approaching one exit at about the same time are likely to cause a blockage. Time was when you could linger in the bar, watch a re-run of the day's racing on television and indulge in that pleasurably painful activity which ends most days at the races – the exercise of hindsight. By the time you had realized where you'd gone wrong the traffic would have cleared. Nowadays the bars tend to close half an hour after the starting time of the last race.

A day's racing is a busy day, and there is much more to do and to see than many people realize. Even the most ordinary day is a refreshing experience, and occasionally it will turn into one of those very special sporting occasions when you are simply grateful to be able to say, 'I was there.'
Come racing!

. . . and mass deployment of garden chairs on Ebor Handicap Day at York.

Do not watch every race from the same position: try to find different vantage points for different races, and certainly go right down to the rails for at least one race to experience the thrill of the action close up. Watch a race from the main betting ring, and hear how the bookies bet 'in running', altering the odds as the race unfolds. At jump meetings, desert the stands for a race or two and position yourself by a fence or hurdle to get the real flavour of the sport: it is the immediacy of standing by a jump as a field of chasers streams over, birch flying, jockeys urging, whips cracking, hooves pounding, which cannot be properly transmitted by television. The true speed, colour and noise of racing can be appreciated only in the flesh.

THE LANGUAGE OF RACING

The novice racegoer, like any traveller in a strange country, is advised to learn a smattering of the language. Basic betting slang is translated on page 150, and here are explanations of a few of the terms you may hear around the racecourse. Many are explained more fully in the main text of the book; if you need a more advanced course, please consult the index on pages 206–8.

Acceptor an original entry for a race still left in after a forfeit stage

All-weather racing on artificial surfaces, at Lingfield Park, Southwell and Wolverhampton

Apprentice young jockey tied by annually renewed contract to a licensed trainer while he or she is learning the business of race riding; an apprentice's **allowance** is the weight concession the horse is given to compensate for its rider's inexperience

Backward used of a horse which needs time to mature

Bay colour of a horse: brown, with black 'points' (muzzle, mane, tail and extremities of the legs)

Blinkers hood fitted over a horse's head to prevent backward vision and focus its concentration ahead

Break down severely ruptured tendons in the leg

Broodmare mare used for breeding

Bumper National Hunt Flat race

Change legs when galloping a horse extends one foreleg further than the other; 'changing legs' is when the horse shifts its leading leg (that is, the one which strikes the ground last during the cycle of the stride) from one foreleg to the other

Claimer of a race: a claiming race (page 69); of a jockey: an apprentice who can claim an allowance (page 115)

Close-coupled (of a horse) with a compact conformation

Colt male, ungelded horse up to four years old

Condition the muscular formation of a horse: a horse which is said to 'carry plenty of condition' carries an impressive amount of flesh

Conditional jockey the jumping equivalent of the apprentice

Dam mother of a horse

Declaration final notification that a horse is an intended ('declared') runner

Distance, a more than 30 lengths between two finishers in a race

Distance, the an unmarked point 240 yards from the winning post (thus, 'below the distance' means closer home than that point)

Distances the margins between finishers

Draw the positions horses in a Flat race take up in the starting stalls; facing out of the stalls, number 1 is on the left

Entire an ungelded horse

Eye-shield like blinkers, but with one eye of defective vision completely covered

Field all the runners in a race

Filly female horse up to four years old

Foal horse of either sex from the time of its birth until 1 January of the following year

Furlong 220 yards (one-eighth of a mile)

Gelding castrated horse

Genuine game and consistent

Going the state of the ground

Gone in its coat the condition of a horse in the autumn when it has started to grow a winter coat

Green inexperienced

Hand the unit of four inches in which a horse's height is measured, at the shoulder

Handicap race in which each runner is allotted an individual weight in order to give the whole field a theoretically equal chance of winning

Handicapper (1) a horse which usually runs in handicaps

Handicapper (2) the official responsible for adjusting the official ratings of horses and thus constructing handicaps

Hanging the motion of a horse failing to keep a straight line

'Headquarters' Newmarket

Hood like blinkers, but leaves the eyes clear and covers the ears

Judge official responsible for declaring the finishing order of a race and the distances between the runners

Juvenile two-year-old horse

Maiden horse which has not won a race

Mare female horse five years and over

Near side the left-hand side of a horse

'Not off' not trying to win

Novice steeplechaser or hurdler which has not won a chase or hurdle (respectively) prior to the current season

Nursery handicap for two-year-olds

Objection complaint by one jockey against another regarding breach of the rules during a race

Off side the right-hand side of a horse

Off the bit/off the bridle describes a horse being pushed along by its jockey, losing contact with the bit in its mouth

On the bit/on the bridle describes a horse going well within itself, still having a grip on the bit

Open ditch steeplechase fence with an artificial ditch on the take-off side

Overreach cut on the heel of a foreleg caused by a hind leg striking into it during the gallop

Over the top where a horse is said to have gone if it has passed its peak for the season

Pattern the elite races, divided in Flat racing into Groups One, Two, Three and Listed, in jumping into Grades One, Two and Three

Penalty weight added to the allotted handicap weight of a horse which has won since the weights were originally published

Penalty Value total sum of money won by the winner's connections of a race, before mandatory deductions

Permit holder person entitled to train, under National Hunt Rules, only horses which are the property of his or her immediate family

Plate shoe worn by horse for racing

Plater horse which usually runs in selling races (selling 'plates') – thus an indication of a horse of little ability

Retainer contract by which a jockey is retained to ride for a particular owner or trainer

Rig horse which is imperfectly gelded

Ring area where the main on-course bookmakers operate

Ringer one horse substituted for another

Run free describes a horse going too fast, usually early in the race, to allow it to settle and preserve its energy for a finishing effort

Run up light describes a horse which appears too thin to be fully fit

SIS Satellite Information Services, the company which transmits live television coverage of horse and greyhound racing into betting shops

Schooled trained to jump

Scope the potential, judged from a horse's physical condition, for significant development and improvement

Seller selling race, where the winner has to be put up for public auction immediately after the race

Sire father of a horse

Spread a plate lose a horseshoe

Squiggle mark in Timeform denoting an unreliable horse (the double squiggle indicates complete unreliability)

Stallion entire horse used for breeding

Steward unpaid official responsible for seeing that the Rules of Racing are adhered to

Stewards' Enquiry enquiry by the stewards into the running of a race

Stipe common slang for the Stipendiary Steward, or Stewards' Secretary, a paid official responsible for providing professional advice to the stewards regarding interpretation of the rules

Supplement to enter a horse for a big race, entry for which has already closed, by paying a large supplementary entry fee

Syndication the dividing of the ownership of a stallion into shares

Tote body that runs the totalisator system of betting

Tucked up describes a horse which is tightly drawn up around the abdomen, possibly because it has gone over the top

Tubing operation whereby a hole is made in a horse's neck and a metal tube inserted in order to bypass a defective larynx

Unfurnished (of a horse) not well grown

Valet person who takes care of a jockey's equipment during and after racing

Virus varieties of equine flu and other respiratory disorders

Visor pair of blinkers with a slit cut in each of the eye-shields to allow a small amount of lateral vision

Walkover 'race' with only one runner

Weatherbys racing's administrative civil service

Weigh in/weigh out weighing of jockey before and after a race to ensure that the correct weight has been carried

Weight-for-Age scale scale of weights devised to compensate for the immaturity of younger horses when racing against their elders

Yearling Horse of either sex from 1 January to 31 December of the year following its birth

INDEX

Page numbers in bold type refer to definitions or main descriptive entries; page numbers in italic type refer to illustrations.